ALSO BY JUSTICE MALALA

We Have Now Begun Our Descent

Let Them Eat Cake

Before the Rains Come

SIMON & SCHUSTER

New York   London   Toronto   Sydney   New Delhi

JUSTICE MALALA

THE PLOT TO SAVE SOUTH AFRICA

The Week Mandela Averted Civil War
and Forged a New Nation

Simon & Schuster
1230 Avenue of the Americas
New York, NY 10020

First Simon & Schuster hardcover edition April 2023

SIMON & SCHUSTER and colophon are registered trademarks of Simon & Schuster, Inc.

For information about special discounts for bulk purchases, please contact
Simon & Schuster Special Sales at 1-866-506-1949 or business@simonandschuster.com.

The Simon & Schuster Speakers Bureau can bring authors to your live event.
For more information or to book an event, contact the
Simon & Schuster Speakers Bureau at 1-866-248-3049
or visit our website at www.simonspeakers.com.

Interior design by Ruth Lee-Mui

Manufactured in the United States of America

1   3   5   7   9   10   8   6   4   2

Names: Malala, Justice, author.
Title: The plot to save South Africa : the week Mandela averted civil war
and forged a new nation / Justice Malala.
Identifiers: LCCN 2022027751 (print) | LCCN 2022027752 (ebook) | ISBN
9781982149734 (hardcover) | ISBN 9781982149758 (ebook)
Subjects: LCSH: Hani, Chris, 1942-1993—Assassination. | Mandela, Nelson,
1918-2013—Influence. | De Klerk, F. W. (Frederik Willem)—Influence. |
South Africa—Race relations. | South Africa—Politics and
government—1989-1994.
Classification: LCC DT1970 .M338 2023 (print) | LCC DT1970 (ebook) | DDC
968.07/1—dc23/eng/20220616
LC record available at https://lccn.loc.gov/2022027751
LC ebook record available at https://lccn.loc.gov/2022027752

ISBN 978-1-9821-4973-4
ISBN 978-1-9821-4975-8 (ebook)

The murder of Chris Hani was the touch and go moment. This was the darkest night facing our country, but it was also the brightest moment. Every moment in the life of a nation can be seen either as the darkest moment or as the brightest moment. Usually both are present and it is our opportunity, by the way we respond, to determine what we make of it.

—Mac Maharaj, African National Congress leader,
freedom fighter, and democracy negotiator

To make peace with an enemy, one must work with the enemy, and that enemy becomes your partner.

—Nelson Mandela, *Long Walk to Freedom*

CAST OF CHARACTERS

This is the story of the nine days of political upheaval that started with the assassination of the popular ANC leader Chris Hani on April 10, 1993. Biographical details of the characters are as of April 10, 1993. For the latest biographical information, see the "Where Are They Now" section.

ANC LEADERS:

NELSON MANDELA: President of the ANC. Released from prison by F. W. de Klerk in 1990 after twenty-seven years' incarceration

HARRY GWALA: Fiery ANC leader in KwaZulu-Natal, former Robben Island prisoner

BANTU HOLOMISA: Military leader of the Transkei "homeland" and a close confidant of Mandela

GILL MARCUS: ANC spokeswoman

PETER MOKABA: President of the ANC Youth League

CARL NIEHAUS: ANC media manager

CYRIL RAMAPHOSA: ANC secretary-general and lead negotiator in democracy talks

TOKYO SEXWALE: ANC leader in the Pretoria-Johannesburg-Vaal region

MONDLI GUNGUBELE: ANC leader in violence-racked East Rand area, deputy head of ANC "peace desk," Chris Hani protégé

NATIONAL PARTY LEADERS:

F. W. DE KLERK: President of South Africa who became state president in September 1989 after ousting P. W. Botha, "Die Groot Krokodil" (the Big Crocodile), who refused to end apartheid

HERNUS KRIEL: Minister of Law and Order in the final years of apartheid

ROELF MEYER: Minister of Constitutional Affairs and Communication, the government's lead negotiator

GERT MYBURGH: Deputy Minister of Police

ADRIAAN VLOK: Minister of Prisons between 1991 and 1994, Minister of Law and Order between 1986 and 1991

THE CONSERVATIVE CIRCLE:

JANUSZ WALUŚ: Polish immigrant, member of the extremist Afrikaner Weerstandsbeweging (Afrikaner Resistance Movement) and the Conservative Party

CLIVE DERBY-LEWIS: Conservative Party member of Parliament

GAYE DERBY-LEWIS: Propagandist for the Conservative Party and wife of Clive Derby-Lewis

SOUTH AFRICAN POLICE FORCE:

CAPTAIN NICOLAAS "NIC" DEETLEFS: SA Police Security Branch member. Notorious for torture of antiapartheid activists

WARRANT OFFICER MIKE HOLMES: Lead detective assigned to the Hani assassination

CRAIG KOTZE: Police spokesman

GENERAL JOHAN VAN DER MERWE: National Police Commissioner from 1990 to 1995

OTHERS:

MUHAMMAD ALI: Former world heavyweight boxing champion, civil rights campaigner

RETHA HARMSE: Hani's neighbor

PETER HARRIS: Head of the Wits-Vaal Regional Peace Secretariat, regional structure of the National Peace Accord (organization formed in 1991 bringing together political leaders, police, business, civil society organizations, and 15,000 ordinary South Africans who volunteered to monitor and mediate in volatile situations to keep the peace)

ARCHBISHOP DESMOND TUTU: Antiapartheid cleric, Nobel Peace Prize laureate

PHUMELELE CIVILIAN HERMANS: An ANC member in the town of Port St. Johns

RICHARD STENGEL: American writer working with Mandela on his autobiography

ALASTAIR WEAKLEY AND GLEN WEAKLEY: White, politically progressive brothers holidaying in the Port St. Johns area

ORGANIZATIONS

ANC   African National Congress: a South African liberation organization formed in 1912 and led by Nelson Mandela between 1991 and 1997

AWB   Afrikaner Weerstandsbeweging (Afrikaner Resistance Movement): a violent, extreme right-wing whites-only organization

CODESA   Convention for a Democratic South Africa: the negotiating forum of nineteen groups launched on December 20, 1991, almost two years after the unbanning of political parties and Nelson Mandela's release, with the goal of overseeing a peaceful transition to democracy

COSATU   Congress of South African Trade Unions: South Africa's largest trade union federation, a political ally of the ANC

CP   Conservative Party: a far-right political party formed in 1982 by Andries Treurnicht to preserve apartheid. It was the official opposition in the whites-only House of Assembly in the last seven years of minority rule

IFP   Inkatha Freedom Party: a conservative Zulu nationalist cultural movement and political party

MK   the popular nickname of the armed wing of the ANC, shortened from Umkhonto we Sizwe, meaning Spear of the Nation

MPNF   Multi-Party Negotiating Forum: this successor to the CODESA negotiating forum held its first meeting on April 1, 1993, just days before the assassination of Chris Hani

NP   National Party: a white Afrikaner nationalist party that instituted apartheid in SA and was in power from 1948 to 1994

PAC   Pan Africanist Congress of Azania: an ANC splinter organization. Its armed wing was the Azanian People's Liberation Army (APLA)

SACP   South African Communist Party: a long-standing ANC ally with a very small membership but nevertheless huge influence on the ANC

SADF   South African Defence Force: the SA army, navy, and air force

SSC   State Security Council: a government body comprised of security ministers. Established to determine South Africa's national security policy and strategy, it allegedly morphed into the de facto cabinet of the country in the 1980s, operating secretly, violently, and without accountability

TEC   Transitional Executive Council: a multiparty body that oversaw the running of South Africa in the five months before the April 27, 1994, election—set up to ensure fairness and freeness of the poll

TRC   Truth and Reconciliation Commission: a body set up in 1996 to hear, record, and investigate human rights transgressions during apartheid

UDF   United Democratic Front: an organization established in 1983 linking more than five hundred groups (from trade unions to churches) together in the struggle against apartheid

TIME LINE OF KEY EVENTS IN SOUTH AFRICA'S DEMOCRATIC TRANSITION, 1990–1993

FEBRUARY 2, 1990: President F. W. de Klerk unbans all liberation organizations.

FEBRUARY 11, 1990: Nelson Mandela is released from Victor Verster Prison outside Cape Town after twenty-seven years' incarceration.

SEPTEMBER 14, 1991: The apartheid government and eighteen other organizations—including trade unions, political organizations, and churches—sign the National Peace Accord, committing themselves to a peaceful process of negotiation. Political violence intensifies despite this.

DECEMBER 20, 1991: First session of democracy talks, named the Convention for a Democratic South Africa (CODESA), launched after two years of "talks about talks."

JUNE 17, 1992: At least forty-five residents of Boipatong township are killed by two to three hundred mainly Zulu-speaking residents of a male worker hostel affiliated with the Inkatha Freedom Party. The ANC accuses the South African Police of arming the attackers.

JUNE 20, 1992: Angered by the Boipatong Massacre, Nelson Mandela withdraws the ANC from the CODESA talks until the government takes steps to restore peace. He embarks on a program of protest marches, work stayaways, and pickets.

SEPTEMBER 7, 1992: Twenty-eight ANC supporters and one soldier are shot dead by the defense force of the nominally "independent" homeland of Ciskei when the ANC marches on the Ciskei town of Bisho as part of its mass action campaign following the Boipatong Massacre.

APRIL 1, 1993: Democracy talks resume under the banner of the new Multi-Party Negotiating Forum, which includes a wider array of participants, including right-wing parties such as the Conservative Party and the Afrikaner Volksunie.

APRIL 10, 1993: Chris Hani, the most popular Black leader after Nelson Mandela, is murdered.

PROLOGUE

They made us work on Holy Saturday because we were the rookies. I didn't mind. I was twenty-two, a gangly kid from a South African backwater, and all I wanted to do was work.

The newsroom was empty when I walked into our offices on 47 Sauer Street, Johannesburg, at 9 a.m. on Saturday, April 10, 1993. It was my first day as a reporter at one of the most prestigious English-language daily newspapers in South Africa, the *Star*. Over the next nine days I would end up witnessing the greatest story of my life. It was a story that would bring together a man who has been called the world's last great hero, his fierce opponent, and a whole group of characters across the country's political and racial divide to save the emerging new South Africa from collapse and civil war.

I wasn't even a proper rookie. I was in the third month of my six-month training at the journalism program run by the paper, a floor down from the newsroom where my heroes churned out thousands of words daily. Two days before, three of the twelve students had been called upstairs. The head of the journalism school and the editor of the weekend newspaper, the *Sunday Star*, told us to report for duty on the Saturday before Easter. We were to do the "donkey work," as the senior journalists referred to it: hourly calls to the police to check for crime updates, answering the phone for tip-offs about political killings, and checking the wire feed for breaking news.

"You won't really be needed," said Chris van Gass, the gentle head of the journalism school, before heading off for a weekend of bird-watching. He was right. The *Sunday Star* ran big exclusive features, not trivial reports of murder. That was for the daily paper. Making crime calls for the *Sunday Star* was almost useless.

So, just after 10 a.m. on Holy Saturday I was sipping my tea and reading that day's edition of the paper when the news editor rushed up to my desk.

"Get a car! Go out to Dawn Park now!" she said, agitated. She was holding out a transport authorization slip so I could get a vehicle from the carpool. I stared at her, waiting for a briefing.

"Don't just stand there!" she said. "Chris Hani has been assassinated outside his home in Dawn Park!"

I went cold.

Chris Hani, the chief of staff of the military wing of Nelson Mandela's African National Congress (ANC) and general secretary of the South African Communist Party (SACP), was no ordinary man. A recent survey had found he was the most popular Black leader in South Africa after Mandela himself. He was a hero in the townships, where young people would turn out in large numbers to hear him deliver fiery speeches. If my generation, already referred to as "the lost generation" by sociologists because of our disrupted education and alleged hopelessness about the future, had a hero, then it was this man. Charismatic, energetic, articulate, he had built a reputation as a brave guerrilla fighter during his twenty-seven years in exile. He was also loved by the intelligentsia, who were in thrall to his ability to discuss Marxism in one breath and Sophocles in the next.

He was hated by large swathes of white South Africa for his allegiance to communism and his uncompromising stand for racial justice. He helped direct the ANC's armed struggle, infiltrating the country with guerrilla fighters from the organization's exile camps to set off attacks, like the bombing of the air force head office in Pretoria in 1983. Yet Hani was not a warmonger. He saw the possibility for a new South Africa, one within the grasp of freedom- and peace-loving citizens. In the months before that fateful Saturday he had been a key member of Mandela's team negotiating with the government to end apartheid and usher in nonracial democracy. He called for peace everywhere he spoke.

When the news editor told me Hani was dead, one thing was clear as the crisp blue autumn sky that day: the pain and the anger in the Black community would be deep, so deep that it might trigger a new racial war worse than the one Mandela and his comrades were trying to end.

The world was changing, and so was South Africa. In 1991, the Union of Soviet Socialist Republics had collapsed, bringing the Cold War to an end. The year before, after forty-two years of formal apartheid modeled on the US's Jim Crow laws, talks had begun between Nelson Mandela's ANC and the whites-only government led by President F. W. de Klerk to transform the country into a multiracial democracy. It was a time of hope after three decades in which the ANC had been banned, thousands of its leaders incarcerated or exiled, and those antiapartheid activists still inside South Africa detained, tortured, or disappeared. But the now–three-year-old democracy negotiations had been slow, punctuated by bitter sectarian violence. For three years, South Africa had been in limbo, as talks progressed, reached stalemate, or broke down completely. Political prisoners and exiles returned home, and yet the land they returned to was hardly freer than the one they'd left. Freedom was messy. And it was taking too long. In June 1992, as political violence escalated, the democracy talks were called off. Hope in the morning was followed by despair in the evening, with no sense of what the next day would bring.

Yet just nine days before the devastating news of Hani's murder, the talks had been restarted and all sides once again had high hopes for progress. Now, with the assassination of Hani, the talks could very well collapse, with militants on both sides taking up arms again. Throughout that day, as the anger mounted and talk became loose, as right-wingers drove to the Communist Party head office in central Johannesburg and shot up its façade and their friends taunted Black people in the streets, my feeling of dread increased.

Like so many other Black South Africans, politics was my life. I was born at a Johannesburg gold mine where my father had worked himself up from underground laborer to wages clerk. We lived on the mine's compound for Black families, hemmed in between the packed single-sex hostels of the Black laborers and separated from the white families of the mine managers. When I was two, we were kicked out because the apartheid government designated the land on which our home stood for "whites only." Those notorious segregationist signs went up everywhere. We moved to the Blacks-only dormitory suburb of Soweto, the famous sprawl of townships to the south of Johannesburg. Four years later, on June 16, 1976, police shot and killed at least 176 schoolchildren protesting being taught in the language of their oppressor, Afrikaans. We lived a few streets down from Morris Isaacson High School, one of the three schools where the students began protesting. That evening my parents moved us to my aunt's home in a small, impoverished rural village in the far north of South Africa, hoping that the state would leave us alone. Eight years later, my brother was in police detention for protesting against apartheid. All four of my siblings became ANC political activists.

The final three years of my schooling were disrupted by political protests. After a national State of Emergency was declared in 1986 (there was a partial State of Emergency in 1985, covering areas designated as volatile), more than 13,000 people, some as young as eleven, were detained without charge for a month or more in just the first six months. The release of Nelson Mandela and the unbanning of the ANC and other liberation organizations in 1990 gave us hope that apartheid was on the way out. Many young people like me had envisaged a future in which our entire lives would be overshadowed by apartheid. We could either work within its racial constraints, cowed and policed at every turn like our parents, or leave the country as exiles. Now, we believed freedom was coming. We could finally live. I applied for a job at the *Star*, my own small investment in a future people like me could believe in.

On April 10, 1993, the hope that I had for that future seemed naïve. The streets convulsed with rage. That afternoon, I drove to Soweto with a photographer. Burning cars barricaded the road.

By nightfall, as I walked through the city back to the apartment I shared with friends in the fast-changing flatland of Hillbrow—once a white neighborhood, now increasingly Black—accounts of violence were spreading. Police reported that at least one man had been shot at one of the many impromptu gatherings to commemorate Hani. Residents said that three people had been killed. The ANC said another man had died fighting police. In the Strand, near Cape Town, an angry crowd had burned to death two white men who had ventured into the Lwandle township. Similar reports came from across the country. On the radio, white callers were jubilant, saying Hani had lived by the sword and deserved to die by it. Leaders called for calm, yet the anger seemed to increase. So did the violence. Alone at the apartment late that evening, I felt loneliness and dread. My roommates had all gone home to spend the long weekend with their families. One of them, Saul Molobi, had launched the first antiapartheid organization in my rural village. I wondered if it would be safe for him to return to Johannesburg.

Three decades have passed since Hani's death, but every year, around Easter, I have thought about that day and those that followed. Today it may seem as if the defeat of apartheid was inevitable, but it was not. Extremists in De Klerk's cabinet and in Parliament armed hit men and galvanized paramilitary groups. There isn't a point in South Africa's transition to democracy when the country was as much on the edge of a return to all-out war as it was that week. The old forces of racism and segregation were refusing to die. People were prepared to set the country on fire to retain the apartheid system.

Mandela once told Richard Stengel, the American journalist who collaborated with him on his autobiography, that "the book that I would really like to do, after Long Walk [to Freedom], is a book about how close South Africa came to civil war." The closest was in those days after the assassination of Chris Hani.

This is the story of that second week of April 1993. I have re-created the events of those days based on the words of the main actors—through their testimony in court, at the Truth and Reconciliation Commission, in writings, interviews, and through original reporting of my own—as well as in the words of those around them. I wanted to write this story because, at a time when the world seems to be regressing to the divisions of the past and exhibiting selfish forms of leadership, Nelson Mandela and—to a lesser but important extent—F. W. de Klerk offer us lessons in how to listen, learn, collaborate, and lead in a complex and perilous situation. Leadership matters. And ethical leadership—whether in corporate settings or schools or government—can be the difference between going to war and doing something much more difficult: making peace. Mandela and De Klerk, despite provocations, despite their own fears, failures, histories, and doubts, chose the path of peace. I don't know where South Africa would be today if they hadn't.

Nelson Mandela is a hero. He's revered across the globe. But we tend to forget that he was also human. One of his most famous quotes was a denunciation of the pedestal he had been put on: "I am not a saint, unless you think of a saint as a sinner who keeps on trying." In that week Mandela displayed human frailty: he prevaricated, he stalled, he was booed, and he grieved. Yet he kept trying. That's leadership: it's messy, unglamorous, hard.

I also wanted to write about the dangers of hate and extremism. The story of what happened in 1993 reminds us that we dare not forget the danger they posed then, and pose today, to our present and our collective future. They are on the rise now, in South Africa, the United States, Europe, across the globe. Where once they operated in the shadows, the forces of illiberalism now sit in parliaments and in executive positions, pulling us to the extremes on any number of issues from immigration to race, gender, health care, reproductive rights, and so many others. The need for ethical, values-driven leadership such as that displayed by Mandela in that week has never been as urgent as it is today.

I grew up on stories told to me by my parents and my older brother, who introduced me to books that ranged from murder mysteries to political thrillers. The story of that week has always seemed to me like a political thriller unfolding in real life, full of complex heroes and awful villains and unpredictable twists. It's a bloody good yarn. It's worth telling.

EASTER SATURDAY
April 10, 1993

Murder most foul, as in the best it is,
But this most foul, strange and unnatural.
Hamlet, Act 1, Scene 5

9 a.m.
Qunu village, Eastern Cape Province

Nelson Mandela walked faster. The lanky, tall former prisoner was seventy-five, but the younger men with him—four bodyguards and a thirty-eight-year-old American writer and former college basketball player, Richard Stengel, who was collaborating on his autobiography—were struggling with the pace set by the older man. It was always this way on walks with Mandela: slow at first, but by the end of the four hours he would be striding ahead, seemingly getting stronger and more energized, leaving his young companions huffing and puffing behind.

It had been a chilly morning when he'd emerged from his house at 5:05 a.m., but now the sun's rays were strong and warm. The walk had drawn a "long, lazy" circle, Stengel was to write two decades later in his book *Mandela's Way*, through the gently undulating hills and yellowing autumn grass of the area. The six men were trudging along quietly, headed back to Mandela's home now, when he stopped and pointed to the crest of a hill overlooking the village of Qunu, where he had grown up. He was pointing at the crumbling remains of a white brick building.

"That was my first school," he told the men. It had consisted of a single room, with a Western-style roof, small windows on either side, and a smooth mud floor. This was where, at age seven, Mandela had started school, wearing his father's trousers cut off at the knee. The length had been fine, the waist not so. His father had drawn the waist in with a piece of string. "I have never owned a suit I was prouder to wear than my father's cut-off trousers," Mandela would write in later life.

This was the school where, on that first day, his teacher Miss Mdingane gave each of her pupils an English name. As Mandela explained it, whites were either unable or unwilling to pronounce an African name and considered it uncivilized to have one. It was therefore common practice at the time for children to be given a "Christian" name by schoolteachers or priests when they got baptized. A "Christian" name was one of the keys to getting ahead. And so, Mandela wrote, "that day, Miss Mdingane told me that my new name was Nelson. Why she bestowed this particular name upon me I have no idea. Perhaps it had something to do with the great British sea captain Lord Nelson, but that would only be a guess."

The men inspected the old school building, then set off toward Mandela's house, a country dwelling which fulfilled his belief that "a man should have a home within sight of the house where he was born." He hadn't quite followed the maxim. Mandela had been born in the village of Mvezo, on the banks of the Mbashe River, about thirty-two kilometers to the south of Qunu. It was when a magistrate summarily stripped Mandela's father of his chieftaincy following a dispute over an ox that he moved to Qunu with his mother. That was where he was raised, where he played and fought with other boys from the village.

Which is why, soon after being released from prison in February 1990, he started planning to build himself a house in Qunu. Two years later, the house was complete. It was not luxurious, and its genesis was an oddity for many, for it was based on the floor plan of the house Mandela had been incarcerated in in the final two years of his imprisonment, after being moved first from the notorious Robben Island prison, where he spent nearly twenty years of hard labor, to the equally infamous, violent Pollsmoor Prison in 1982. Six years later, Mandela had been moved again, this time to Victor Verster—a converted warden's quarters. Many thought his Qunu house seemed like he had moved from that prison to another. He didn't see it that way. "The Victor Verster house was the first spacious and comfortable home I ever stayed in, and I liked it very much," he would write. There was a certain convenience to it too: "I was familiar with its dimensions, so at Qunu I would not have to wander at night looking for the kitchen."

When the group of men made their way back to the redbrick house around 9 a.m., there were about twenty people already there despite the early hour, half of them milling about outside. They were drop-in visitors, some hoping for food, others to meet the great man. Mandela greeted them amiably, then proceeded to the study with Stengel to work while waiting for their breakfast.

Like Mandela, most South African political leaders wanted to take a break from politics that weekend. The multiparty negotiations to end apartheid and introduce democracy had started with great optimism in March 1990. That was quickly dashed when political violence—starting with a massacre in Sebokeng that July in which twenty-seven people were killed by police—broke out across the country. More than 9,000 people would be killed in political violence in the next three years. The negotiations had been halted by Mandela in June 1992. He was angry that the government was doing nothing to stop the political killings. After nine months of acrimony, the negotiations had restarted on April 1, 1993— and the optimism of 1990 was back.

After the intensity of the previous nine months, the country seemed to have taken a collective break from political news for the weekend. So slim were the pickings that weekend that, in a country as obsessed as South Africa was with its own politics, most of the newspapers were following the events in Waco, Texas, where the leader of the Branch Davidians cult, David Koresh, and his supporters were in a standoff with police and the Federal Bureau of Investigation. The siege in Waco as it entered its forty-second day was covered by the newspapers as though it were a soap opera that the country needed as a respite from its own political news.

Mandela settled his slim frame—he had been a big, brawny boxer when he was first jailed in 1962 and at his conviction at the Rivonia Trial in 1964, but had returned in 1990 a thinner man—in his chair and continued to tell Stengel about his life and thoughts. Twenty minutes later a bodyguard came to the door and announced that the Transkei police rugby team had popped in to greet him. Mandela had promised a colleague that he would see them, and so he unhooked his microphone, excused himself, and walked outside, where he began to shake the hands of the massive rugby players, saying a few words to each one.

As he shook their hands, his housekeeper, Miriam, ran out to him. *"Tata, Tata!"* she said, using the traditional Xhosa term, equivalent to "Father," for an elder or respected man. This is how everyone referred to him in many settings, especially rural ones. Miriam was crying. She told him that there was an urgent phone call he had to take. Mandela excused himself and went back inside.

The person on the line was Barbara Masekela, the chief of staff in Mandela's office. The sister of world-famous jazz musician Hugh Masekela, she had run the ANC's administrative office in exile from Zambia in the early 1980s before becoming the head of the ANC's department of arts and culture, which among other activities organized the global cultural boycott of South Africa that saw many international acts refuse to perform in the country. She joined Mandela's personal team shortly after his release from prison and had been by his side through political turmoil and personal pain, including his divorce from his second wife, Winnie. Masekela was street-smart (raised in the notoriously dangerous Alexandra township of the 1950s in a middle-class family). She was also an academic who had taught literature in the US at Rutgers University and a member of the ANC's National Executive Committee in her own right. She had a tough job—keeping some distance between an adoring world and the globe's most popular politician, who still had freedom and democracy to deliver to his people. She was often so worried about Mandela's heavy schedule that she would not tell anyone except his closest circle about his whereabouts just so he would get some time off, she told me. She would not call on a weekend like this if it was trivial.

The news she was about to give Mandela that morning was possibly the worst she'd ever have to share.

Mandela loved Chris Hani, was fascinated by him. He regarded him as a fellow soldier and a patriot. This was a man Mandela saw at least once a week, a man in whom he saw the same anger and impatience that he himself felt when he was young. Mandela pointedly asked his aides to include Hani on his trips and meetings whenever the younger man was available. He recognized Hani as the great hero of the country's angry and impatient youth. But his desire to keep Hani close went beyond practical considerations: he loved him like a son, Masekela told me.

Despite her own feelings of shock and sorrow, Masekela was in a somber but controlled mood, the way she knew Mandela would want her to be. Theirs was an office run on professionalism—"we were not there for ourselves, we were there for a particular purpose," as Mandela had said to her. So Masekela, whose bright smile can turn into a severe frown, said the words she knew would devastate Mandela: "Chris Hani has been assassinated."

There was a long silence on the other end of the line. Then in a quiet, controlled voice, Mandela came back on.

"Have you told Oliver?"

He was referring to Oliver Tambo, his former partner at their law firm in the 1950s and the man who had steered the ANC through twenty-nine years of exile as president after Mandela was jailed for life. Tambo was frail, having suffered a stroke in 1989, just four months before Mandela's release from prison. Although Mandela had been elected ANC president in 1991 to replace the ailing Tambo, the two men spoke to each other almost every day and Mandela tried to consult him on every major issue.

"No, I called you first," Masekela answered.

Mandela started issuing instructions. He told her to call Tambo and his other partner—Walter Sisulu, the man who recruited and signed him up to the ANC in the 1940s and with whom he had spent twenty-seven years in jail—and inform them. These two men were not just comrades to Mandela. Their associations were so deep they were like brothers.

"Make sure you accompany Oliver to Chris's place," he said.

He put the phone down, went outside, and continued to greet the rugby players with a smile on his face. He had just lost a man he considered a son. He was grieving, but he needed to fulfill this obligation.

It was more than grief that the stoic man who went from one rugby player to the next felt, though. He was also deeply afraid of what the news of the murder of South Africa's most popular antiapartheid fighter—besides himself—might unleash across the land.

10 a.m.
Dawn Park, Boksburg, Johannesburg

The stalking of Chris Hani had started early that Saturday morning, just about the time Mandela had hit his stride as he walked through Qunu's undulating hills.

The athletic-looking killer with the blazing blue eyes and the blue shirt had been warned that the entire Easter weekend was off limits for the mission he had come to believe was his life's purpose: to put a match to the tinderbox that was South Africa in 1993 and ignite a race war that would put a stop to all attempts to end apartheid. Janusz Waluś's mentor, Clive Derby-Lewis, a Conservative Party member of Parliament who had recruited him into the pro-apartheid movement, had drummed the warning into his head. It wasn't that the chaos they would ignite by their deed would be any terrible thing. Chaos is what they desired. By their reckoning, the killing of Mandela's protégé would trigger riots, murder, and general mayhem. Intervention by the apartheid government's hard-line generals would follow. The peace-making process between F. W. de Klerk, the president they viewed as "selling out" whites and Afrikaners, and the "terrorist" Mandela would be stopped. White supremacy would be reinstated in South Africa. It was a simple but perfect plan, thought Waluś. This was, after all, a country whose favorite expression, among the whites he socialized with, was "five minutes to midnight"; a doomsday scenario of the country "falling" into Black hands and racial warfare breaking out was, they believed, fast approaching. Better to start that war now, while whites still had the upper hand.

Hani's murder would set the wheels of that plan in motion. Yet Waluś had been told repeatedly: not Easter weekend. There would be too many people in the neighborhood, too many people at home and not at work in the factories around Boksburg, the industrial city just east of Johannesburg. Hani lived with his family in one of Boksburg's residential suburbs, Dawn Park. Derby-Lewis had warned Waluś against action earlier that week, as he handed him a stolen Z-88 pistol and a silencer he'd had specially made in Cape Town. Waluś could be seen, identified, and arrested during the Easter weekend, he had said. It was not a good time to start their own special war.

On the Tuesday before Easter, the two men had enjoyed breakfast in the Derby-Lewis's dining room before they repaired to the study. Gaye, Derby-Lewis's wife, had gone shopping, leaving Waluś with the man who was a leading light in far-right politics in South Africa. Derby-Lewis was born in the heart of South Africa, and though he had never been in the Royal Air Force, he liked to put on the quaint mannerisms (as depicted in comic books) of its upper-class officers, such as cultivating their favored handlebar mustaches. He had a forced posh English accent, making him sound as if he were being asphyxiated whenever he got excited. In the study, he had showed Waluś the pistol, still in the manufacturer's box. The silencer came with three rounds of subsonic ammunition.

Now, as he drove to the house of target number three on their hit list, that gun was in Waluś's sports bag on the floor behind the passenger seat of his red Ford Laser. The list was fastidiously compiled by Gaye with the help of a journalist friend who shared her extremist beliefs.

Although it had started with nineteen names, the hit list had been whittled down to just nine individuals—enemies of the apartheid system or "sellouts" of the white race. Whether this was a hit list or not was to become a subject of contention in later years, with Gaye claiming the list had only been drawn up as part of research for a newspaper article. But the Truth and Reconciliation Commission settled the matter in 1999 when it found that "the names constituted a hit list compiled for the purpose of planning assassinations." In 2000, the Cape High Court dismissed an application by Derby-Lewis and Waluś to overturn the Truth and Reconciliation Commission's decision. In 2001, the Supreme Court of Appeal in Bloemfontein dismissed with costs their bid to challenge the Cape High Court's dismissal of their earlier application.

At the top of the hit list was Mandela. Alongside his name was a picture of his house in the affluent suburb of Houghton, Johannesburg, and an entire page of descriptions of the property's security details. The second name on the list was that of Joe Slovo, the popular (among Blacks) general secretary of the South African Communist Party. Slovo was a lifelong fighter against apartheid. He had already lost a family member to political assassination; his activist wife, Ruth First, had been murdered in exile in Mozambique by a parcel bomb sent by government agents in 1982. There was no address for Slovo on the hit list. The third person on the list was the man whose house Janusz Waluś was now heading to: Martin Thembisile "Chris" Hani. He had picked his brother's name Chris as a nom de guerre in exile, and the name stuck. Waluś knew everything there was to know about his quarry's home arrangements. He had been there five times before, casing the joint.

Waluś and his associates had already tried to go for the big prize, Mandela. Assassinating one of the world's great icons would have led to the overwhelming chaos they desired. But Waluś had told Derby-Lewis, after one reconnaissance mission of Mandela's house, that "the old goat was not worth it." Security was tight in Houghton. As they couldn't source an address for Slovo, he was out too. It was Hani, then. Waluś and his associates believed there would be no need to continue going down the list once he was dead. The popular Hani's murder would be enough to trigger the mayhem they wanted.

Waluś had not thought that the chance to kill Hani would present itself that morning as he got out of bed at his apartment just below the Union Buildings complex—the seat of the South African government—in Pretoria. It was a beautiful day: clear, bright-blue skies, with a slight chill in the air that signaled the autumn in South Africa. Waluś had left a wife and daughter back home in Radom, Poland. He followed his father and brother, Witold, to South Africa in 1981 as part of the thousands of Polish émigrés who took advantage of a government scheme to attract white anticommunist entrepreneurs and professionals to the country. His wife, Wanda, and their child, Ewa, had visited South Africa twice to try to make a life together, but it had not worked out. He now had a lover, Maria Ras. They had been together for ten years. She had taken Easter week off to spend time with him.

Waluś had told Ras that he was off to the Stan Schmidt School of Karate in Sandton to practice Shotokan karate, as he did every Saturday morning when he was not too hard up to pay the club fees. Things had been tough for Waluś lately. He'd been driving trucks and doing odd jobs, which was never how he'd pictured making a living at the age of forty. He, his father, Tadeusz, and his brother, Witold, had owned a glass-making factory that exploited Black workers and tax breaks available to whites and foreign firms in the Black "homeland" of QwaQwa in the eastern Free State. Homelands were pieces of land designated as "independent countries" by the apartheid government, to which it forcibly removed millions of Blacks from "white" urban centers and fertile agricultural land. The factory had gone bust in 1989 when the generous government credits and incentives that had accrued to the business under apartheid were withdrawn, exposing the factory to global competitive forces.

Waluś drove from Pretoria to Johannesburg's northern suburbs. He had dabbled in rally driving in his native Poland; there are reports he reached the national championships in 1977. Disappointment awaited him in Johannesburg. Most facilities were closed for Easter, including the Stan Schmidt School where he trained.

"Don't do it over the Easter weekend," he had been told again and again. That, he thought defiantly, did not preclude him from doing yet another recce. He had time. He turned his Ford around and pointed it toward nearby Corlett Drive, where there was a gun exchange shop. He bought twenty-five more rounds of the subsonic ammunition, specifically designed to reduce the *crack* sound of an ordinary bullet. If he did not have killing on his mind that Easter weekend, why did he buy extra ammunition that day?

Back in the car, the blond man put on a pair of gloves and loaded the gun. He wasn't going to use the silencer because he knew by then that the specially commissioned piece of hardware didn't work. He had discovered this when testing the gun at Witold's farm in Pretoria. Witold had done well for himself by going into the army surplus business, buying and selling old military vehicles and other material, when the glass factory went belly-up.

So, no silencer. It did not fit properly onto the barrel and dislodged when fired, meaning that he'd have to fix it back on after each shot. He put the useless silencer and the gun in his sports bag on the floor behind the passenger seat. He also had a second gun, his registered, Czech-made CZ-75 9mm pistol. He put that next to him in a case on the passenger seat. He had a hunting knife strapped to his ankle and another knife in his back pocket.

For a man who was to later claim he did not intend to commit murder that day, Waluś was unusually methodical, displaying a carefulness unlike in his previous reconnaissance jaunts to Hani's house, when he'd driven by without any attempts to cover up the stickers on the back bumper of his car. He drove to a hardware store near the Stan Schmidt gym to get masking tape. Again, he was frustrated by the holidays: that store was also closed.

Then there were his registration plates. He couldn't go to Hani's house with the registration plates on the car. The car was registered in his boss's name, the truck owner Peter Jackson. If anyone remembered the plate number, it would be over. One piece of white sticker tape that he had in the car did the trick. His registration number was PBX 231 T. He stuck a crude "7" over the "1," and it held. It wasn't ideal, but it was a change.

That's when he turned the car toward Chris Hani's house: Number 5 Hakea Crescent, Dawn Park, Boksburg, on the corner of Deon Street. Just to look. Just a recce.

Dawn Park wasn't a place one would have expected a leading Black figure of the ANC and the South African Communist Party—the two organizations had an alliance pact that allowed for dual membership—to settle. When the apartheid government stopped enforcing segregatory laws in 1990 (they were formally repealed in June 1991), opening the white suburbs to Black homeowners, the neighborhood had embarked on a mass campaign with the slogan "Keep Dawn Park White." It hadn't worked. The new Black middle class and returning ANC exiles had moved into the area steadily, thanks to real estate agencies that courted prospective Black homeowners prepared to pay handsomely for their new houses. The Hanis were among these pioneers, although not entirely by design. After returning from exile in Zambia, Hani's wife, Limpho, a native of Lesotho, had been confused by the design of sprawling Johannesburg. So instead of ending up in the city proper, the couple and their three daughters had taken out a $50,000 mortgage and bought a rose-brick house in Dawn Park.

Right-wing propaganda replayed itself in Waluś's head as he drove east toward Dawn Park. The words he had heard at political rallies, like the one he had attended with Derby-Lewis back in 1990, where the Conservative Party leader Andries Treurnicht had exhorted his followers that the "third freedom struggle had begun," echoed in his mind.

"We have to do something," Waluś told himself. He'd been saying it for years now.

His uncle—a hunter—had given him shooting lessons when he was a boy of eleven. Even then he'd had an air gun that he used to shoot at target ranges. Over the previous few weeks he'd been practicing with the Z-88 on Witold's farm.

He was as ready as any assassin could be.

Chris Hani had woken up early and alone that day. His wife, Limpho, and their twelve-year-old daughter, Lindiwe, were visiting relatives in Lesotho. Their oldest daughter, Neo, was in Cape Town and he was at home with their fourteen-year-old daughter, Nomakhwezi.

He wasn't big on breakfast, but he enjoyed a cup of tea first thing in the morning. He'd been gaining weight, so he pulled on his tracksuit and went for a jog around the neighborhood. The jogging freedom fighter was a familiar sight in the neighborhood. He told anyone who would listen that he wanted to be trim for the day freedom finally arrived.

When he got home his daughter was already up, early for a typical teenager. He decided to get a newspaper at the nearby Dawn Park shopping center, but Nomakhwezi called him back as he was stepping out of the house.

"You haven't made up your bed," she scolded him. She had looked into his bedroom.

The two had special plans for the day. He'd had a punishing schedule of meetings and rallies over the previous three years, so time with his daughters was precious. He had asked Mondli Gungubele, a leading figure in the regional ANC and one of his protégés who happened to live just four minutes away in Dawn Park, to accompany him into town to send his eldest daughter, Neo, some money. Hani had insisted that his three bodyguards take the weekend off. It was Easter. But he needed Gungubele to pretend to be his bodyguard and keep the crowds away. Hani was usually mobbed when walking in public. Then he and Nomakhwezi intended to go to a hair salon in the nearby Spruitview township. Then, in the afternoon, he planned to drive to Rand Stadium in Rosettenville to watch the South African national soccer team—recently welcomed back after years of exclusion from international competition as part of the ANC-inspired international sports boycott—play against the island nation of Mauritius.

But before all this, Hani had to get his morning fix: newspapers. Like Mandela and many of the ANC's formerly exiled or imprisoned leadership, he read every available newspaper—across the language and political spectrum, even those diametrically opposed to his views (Mandela even read all the Afrikaans newspapers)—voraciously every morning. So, after he dutifully did his bed, he jumped into his car. He headed toward the strip mall, away from a proud billboard elsewhere in the neighborhood that declared: "Dawn Park: Where The Future Is."

. . .

The killer's red Ford Laser turned onto the quiet street just as Hani's gray Toyota Cressida pulled out of the driveway. Waluś knew it was Hani's car and suspected it was Hani himself at the wheel. He'd had a chance to study him a few days before when he had followed Hani to the Johannesburg Sun & Towers, a glitzy hotel in the city center. The Pole had approached Hani but was stopped by bodyguards.

Now he followed as Hani drove, leisurely, to the strip mall a few blocks away. The sedan entered the parking lot, found a parking space, and the man at the wheel stepped out and into a café.

Waluś parked his car. He did not get out, but monitored Hani's progress with his eyes. It was Hani, of that he was now certain. He watched him as he entered the café. Suddenly, Waluś felt thirsty, so he jumped out of his car, went into a nearby market, and bought a can of Fanta Orange.

Waluś's mind was in a whirl. Derby-Lewis's words were whirring around and around in his head: *Not this weekend. Too dangerous.* And yet . . .

That was when Waluś says he made the decision: he, Janusz Waluś, was going to kill Chris Hani that day. Waluś jumped back into his car. After five trips checking out the area, he knew the neighborhood well enough to know a shortcut back to Hakea Crescent. He drove fast, arriving at the Hani home a few minutes before the leader.

Not this weekend . . . The warning leapt, again, into his head. *Too dangerous.* Yet at the same time his justifications for the crime ran through his mind: "They will destroy this wonderful country. They will squander all that was built here by whites with such difficulty . . . everything here will be destroyed in the name of a multiracial utopia that will never work." He *had* to kill Hani. And with no bodyguards around, this was the best chance he'd ever have to do that.

He stopped on the side of the road near Hani's house, pulled his gloves back on, tucked the Z-88 pistol into the back of his trousers, and felt his belt hold it in place comfortably. Then he followed Hani, watched as his gray Toyota eased into the driveway of the rose-brick house, enclosed by a six-foot redbrick wall. The gate was open. The freedom fighter, dressed casually in a tracksuit, got out of the car.

Waluś, too, got out, then threw his can of Fanta Orange away carelessly near the driveway. He walked toward Hani. The leader, oblivious to his stalker, approached his front door.

Hani's daughter, Nomakhwezi, heard her father's car as he turned off the engine. She rushed to the door and opened it. Soon, they would be off for their visit to the salon. She spotted the red car behind her father's and saw the white man walking behind him. She heard the man say something. "He is greeting you," she said to her father, who was walking nonchalantly toward her.

The white man in the blue shirt and the blue eyes wasn't greeting Hani. He'd had an attack of conscience. *I don't want to shoot him in the back,* Waluś thought. So he had called out, "Mr. Hani!"

Clutching two newspapers in his hands, Hani turned around. Waluś calmly walked toward him. He drew the gun from behind his back.

Assassins know that the most effective way to ensure accuracy is to aim for a large target, and this is what Waluś did. From a few meters away, he shot into Hani's body first. The gun was so powerful that the bullet went through Hani's body and through the garage door behind him, hitting the interior wall.

Waluś shot again, this time into the chin. Hani fell over backward, his body turning sideways as it hit the ground. Waluś ran toward his victim and stood over him. He aimed at the back of his head, at the area behind the ear, and pulled the trigger twice. Blood splattered onto his shoes.

He turned and walked slowly back to his car. The gun was smoking in his hand. He opened the door of the red Ford, got in, and drove off toward the town of Boksburg.

Hani lay bleeding on the ground, clutching his newspapers to his chest. Nomakhwezi was screaming. Hani was dead.

Chris Hani's lifeless body lay in front of his house for nearly three hours as word of his assassination spread across the world. Weeping comrades, harried journalists, and curious and frightened neighbors descended on Dawn Park. It is impossible to describe how devastating the sight of a lifeless Hani was to those of us who saw it—this man was a life force of the South African antiapartheid struggle, full of wit and charm and an unswerving and deep commitment. He engaged almost everyone—from men and women at airports and in the streets to cabinet members—in debate on everything from the prospects of the national rugby team to the economy and to literature and philosophy. When he was engaged he spoke fast, his words coming in a *rat-tat-tat* fashion like a machine gun, and he seemed to always have a smile at the ready to take the sting out of his words and those of his opponents and haters. When listening, he would squint his left eye ever so slightly, his attention fully on his inter-locutor, as if the person speaking was the only one who mattered in the world.

Hani's assassins had targeted him because no other leader in South Africa's volatile political environment elicited as much love and hate, as much admiration and scorn, as the ANC's most famous military com-mander. In villages and townships across the country, he was a hero. But to those reading the Afrikaans press (and certain parts of the English press), he was a villain, a Machiavellian plotter who wanted to turn South Af-rica into a mini Soviet Union, nationalize the land, and build what they dreaded most—a place where the races mixed and coexisted as equals.

The real Chris Hani was far from this caricature. He had been born poor in Sabalele, a small, impoverished village close to Cofimvaba in the rural Eastern Cape. Mandela would describe the place as harsh: no run-ning water, no electricity, no decent housing, inadequate health care, and little formal education. And that was in 1993, not when Hani was born in 1942.

Hani was one of six children born to devout Catholics Gilbert and Nomayise Mary. Three of his siblings would die in infancy. Hani's fa-ther was constantly away working on construction sites or as a hawker in Cape Town while his mother raised the children off her subsistence farm-ing. As a boy, Hani walked ten kilometers every morning to the nearest missionary school—and ten kilometers back in the afternoon. He took the same trip every Sunday for Mass. By the age of eight he was an altar boy in the Catholic church. He dreamed of becoming a priest, but his father, Gilbert, forbade it.

The altar boy developed an interest in the law, studying Latin and English at the famous University of Fort Hare. He was suspended after a political protest but managed to complete his degree through Rhodes University, to which Fort Hare had been affiliated, and graduated in 1962. It was perhaps inevitable that a bright, curious young man like Hani would be attracted to politics when he arrived at Fort Hare, a hotbed of political activity and the alma mater of ANC leaders such as Mandela. There, he "became openly involved in the struggle," as he put it, getting "exposed to Marxist ideas and the scope and nature of the racist capitalist system."

After graduation, Hani moved to Cape Town, where he clerked at the law offices of Schaeffer and Schaeffer while living in the Black township of Langa. In his spare time, he involved himself with the trade union movement. He was soon arrested under the Suppression of Communism Act. He skipped bail and escaped into exile. He received military training in the Soviet Union for a year and, on his return to the ANC's exile headquarters in Zambia, was told to establish an ANC military training camp in Tanzania. In 1967, Hani was ordered to lead a contingent of ANC fighters called the Luthuli Detachment to support the Zimbabwe African People's Union (ZAPU), then engaged in guerrilla warfare against the white minority regime of Rhodesia. A free Rhodesia (later Zimbabwe), went the ANC's thinking, would be a frontline base to attack the apartheid government along the 225-kilometer border. It was here that Hani's reputation as a heroic fighter was born. But, although his mission—known as the Wankie Campaign—twice forced the Rhodesian army to retreat and has become legend in ANC lore, it was largely a tragedy: half of the fifty ANC combatants who fought alongside Hani were killed. About ten of the combatants, including Hani, retreated to neighboring Botswana after running out of food and supplies. They were arrested in Botswana and spent about a year in prison before being deported to Zambia.

Hani and his comrades were furious with ANC leaders for sending them into the bush without proper logistics and intelligence support. On his release from prison, he was one of seven Umkhonto we Sizwe (MK) members who penned a blistering critique of the ANC's leaders in exile. They complained about secret trials and executions of ANC members in training camps, favoritism, political ennui, and a plethora of other failings in a document that was to become known as "the Hani Memorandum." All seven were expelled from the party, with some leaders calling for their execution. But their actions forced the ANC to hold its first major meeting in exile, the Morogoro Conference of April 1969, to reflect on what it had become and to chart a way forward. Hani and his coauthors were vindicated by the meeting and they were reinstated.

Hani's star continued to rise. He traveled the world representing the ANC and was appointed to the party's highest structure, the twenty-two-member National Executive Committee (which developed its strategy and tactics and managed its ministate of army, camps, finances, publicity, training, housing, and logistics) in 1974. At thirty-two, he was one of the two youngest members. That year Hani moved to Maseru, the capital of Lesotho—a tiny country surrounded entirely by South Africa—where he established a recruitment network and infiltrated guerrillas into South Africa. He was soon appointed deputy commander and then, in 1987, chief of staff of MK, which brought even greater police attention and danger. There were several attempts to assassinate him in the seven years he was based in Lesotho, including a car bomb that went off in his absence and a plot that ended in the abduction and murder of his driver. In 1982, South African security police launched a cross-border army raid targeting a block of apartments in Maseru. At least thirty ANC members were killed. Hani survived. He was not at home at the time.

The ANC pulled Hani back to Zambia, where he helped quell several mutinies in ANC camps there and in Tanzania and Angola. This was a dark time in the ANC's history—and the biggest stain on Hani himself. About 90 percent of the party's troops in Angola rebelled against the leadership's slowness in infiltrating them back into South Africa to pursue guerrilla

strikes against apartheid, as well as terrible camp conditions, favoritism, orders to fight alongside the ANC's ally, and sponsoring the MPLA
(Movimento Popular de Libertação de Angola, or Popular Movement
for the Liberation of Angola) in Angola's civil war, which was fighting the
apartheid-backed Unita guerrilla movement led by Jonas Savimbi. The
ANC responded by detaining many in prison camps, where conditions
were terrible. Nineteen of the rebellion's leaders—by Hani's account—
were executed. "Torture and deaths," one Amnesty International report
declared, "were routine." Although much of the blame for the torture, detentions, and executions in the camps was the work of his comrades in the
ANC's security and counterintelligence departments, Hani—like many of
the party's senior leaders—knew of the horrors in the camps but did not
do enough to stop violations quickly. The tragic irony is that the ANC
"dissidents'" claims are exactly the same as Hani's in his memorandum
from 1969.

And yet Hani's popularity continued to grow among many new and
old combatants, mainly because of his role in intensifying bombing and
sabotage campaigns against the apartheid government in the 1980s. After
numerous attacks on electrical substations and government buildings—
mainly courts and police stations—MK cadres detonated a car bomb
at the entrance to the South African Air Force headquarters in Pretoria
in 1983, killing 19 people and injuring 217, many of them employees of
the country's notorious military intelligence department, which was located directly opposite. More attacks followed. "The bombs were to tell
the whites: we can creep and crawl next to you. Be careful . . . ," Hani explained, in the ANC's defense. They had another purpose, too, he said:
"demonstrating to our people that we are still around."

By the late 1980s, the apartheid state was under siege: international
sanctions were biting, the economy was limping badly, antiapartheid protests and riots were a daily occurrence, and the country's leaders had lost
all their international allies—including the conservative US president
Ronald Reagan and Britain's Margaret Thatcher. F. W. de Klerk, who had
been elected leader of the National Party, maneuvered his recalcitrant

predecessor, P. W. Botha, out of power in August 1989 after the man suffered a stroke and yet refused to resign as state president, even when his party asked him to. De Klerk came from the conservative wing of the National Party, but even these conservatives (unlike the extreme right) wanted an end to protests, detentions without trial, and endemic violence and fear that gripped the country. In September 1989, the National Party led by De Klerk won the whites-only general elections and immediately began freeing jailed antiapartheid leaders such as Walter Sisulu in October. Mandela was freed and liberation organizations were unbanned in February 1990. Hani returned to South Africa that March, the last of the ANC's leaders to be granted the provisional amnesty that allowed them free movement after decades of being on the police's Most Wanted list. The following year, at the ANC's first free conference since its banning in 1960, Hani received the highest number of votes from delegates—94.7 percent of the total—for a seat on the National Executive Committee. In December 1991, after Joe Slovo was diagnosed with cancer, Hani was elected the new general secretary of the SA Communist Party.

Charismatic, humble, and thoughtful, Hani was far more like the man he was often contrasted with—Nelson Mandela—than most thought. The most striking similarity was that both were masters at studying their enemies before seducing them.

Hani had been caught by surprise when the ANC was unbanned and was not invited to take part in the initial secret conversations between the National Party and the ANC about the country's transition to democracy before 1990. He was considered "public enemy number one" by many whites, said the influential business daily newspaper *Business Day*, not so much because he was a fighter for freedom—which many Afrikaners understood and even respected due to their own folklore about fighting the British during the Anglo-Boer War—but because he was a communist who had overseen an extensive bombing campaign.

But F. W. de Klerk's eyes lit up when I asked him about his impressions of Hani. De Klerk told me about a meeting in February 1991 between leaders of the ANC and the National Party. At this meeting, Hani's first with government leadership after the government had caved in to ANC pressure to allow their nemesis to be part of its delegation, his target for seduction was De Klerk's "principal strategist," Gerrit Viljoen. The then seventy-five-year-old constitutional development minister was a senior, respected member of the party and leading light in the Afrikaner community: he had at one point chaired the Broederbond, the secret, exclusively Afrikaner male organization dedicated to the advancement of Afrikaner interests. Hani knew something else about Viljoen: although an Afrikaner through and through, Greek ran through his family's blood. He studied classics at the University of Cambridge and earned a doctorate in classical philology at Leiden University before becoming a professor of Greek at Pretoria University.

Hani made a beeline for Viljoen during a tea break, and the two men fell into a deep, impassioned conversation about Sophocles's tragedy *Philoctetes*. De Klerk, hearing about the discussion later, was astonished by his own blinkered view of Hani. It is a revealing anecdote about the stories apartheid made many of its adherents tell themselves about their enemies—in one fell swoop their view of Hani as a savage terrorist was turned on its head by his education and erudition. That one conversation changed De Klerk's perception of the man profoundly.

Archbishop Desmond Tutu condemned communism, but he loved Chris Hani, who floored him at their first meeting in 1990 by singing the famous Xhosa hymn "Lizalis' idinga lakho, Thixo Nkosi yenyaniso," composed by Tiyo Soga, the first Black South African to be ordained as a minister of religion. Hani, the altar boy blessed with a beautiful tenor, made the song fly.

By 1993, Hani, for many, wasn't just one of the brightest, most politically astute, and smartest of the ANC's young leaders—he was very possibly the party's next leader, the man to succeed Mandela. Mandela identified him as the young leader most like his younger self. He also recognized that a Hani who was not fully on board with the negotiations could potentially be the greatest threat to the peace talks by walking away in anger—taking a substantial chunk of the ANC's radical wing with him.

Mandela firmly believed in keeping his friends close—and his potential enemies even closer. He was fascinated by Hani, his chief of staff Barbara Masekela told me in an interview in Johannesburg. At the same time, he was aware of the younger man's power and potential to scupper the process, wrote Stengel. Thus, Hani was both a friend and a potential foe.

The conundrum that Hani presented to Mandela was that the young leader did not think a commitment to peace meant relinquishing his militancy. In his view, one had to be "militant for peace." He was quick to call out apartheid's leaders for their complicity in the wave of political violence that had erupted across the country since 1990. He had no qualms with threatening to pull the ANC out of negotiations and resuming the armed struggle if the government did not abolish all repressive laws, such as the Internal Security Act (which gave the state broad powers to ban gatherings and detain people without trial), dismantle state-sponsored right-wing terror groups such as the Wit Wolwe, and dismiss the defense and police ministers who were accused by the ANC of continuing to run anti-ANC underground security structures that provided guns and other weapons to groups such as the Inkatha Freedom Party.

And yet, despite the tough talk, Hani was fully committed to peace negotiations. Two days before he was assassinated, Hani had appeared on television to defend the peace process. "The ANC has suspended military operations and related activities," he insisted. "This means it is not going to bring arms into this country in order to contribute to the momentum of peace."

At a rally on April 7, he criticized the second-largest liberation movement in South Africa, the Pan Africanist Congress of Azania (PAC), for its continued campaign of bombings and attacks on the state and white civilians.

Founded in 1959 by Black activists who opposed the multiracial alliances the ANC was forming with the South African Indian Congress and the white, largely communist Congress of Democrats, the PAC was now experiencing a moment of rejuvenation among radical Blacks. The PAC had refused to match the ANC's renunciation of armed struggle. Its best-known slogan was "One settler, one bullet!" Whenever it communicated with the government, it would flatly refuse to even discuss laying down arms, saying "the bullet cannot be abandoned until the ballot has been attained." Its military wing, the Azanian People's Liberation Army, only intensified its attacks on white civilian targets after the unbanning of all liberation movements in 1990. It declared 1993 "The Year of Great Storms," threatening greater attacks on whites and government institutions alike. Five days before Hani's assassination, the liberation army's chief commander, Sabelo Phama, said he would "aim his guns at children—to hurt whites where it hurts most."

Hani was incensed by this. "The ambushing of ordinary white kids and women along some of the highways is something that is not acceptable," he told his supporters at the rally. "And I am saying to these comrades here that everyone should be a combatant, a fighter, for peace." He spoke of transforming ANC self-defense units into street-based peace units akin to neighborhood watch groups and encouraged listeners to become "ever bolder and more creative" in building momentum for peace.

In the months before he was murdered, Hani had been demonized by the Afrikaans press. Six days before his murder the anticommunist Afrikaans newspaper *Rapport*, the country's second-largest Sunday paper, alleged that Hani and Mandela's former wife, Winnie—a member of the ANC's National Executive Committee and an outspoken, formidable, and militant leader in her own right—were plotting to form a "Black People's Army." Much of the domestic and foreign—particularly British—press coverage of Mandela and the ANC had from 1990 evolved from painting the party as a terrorist group (UK prime minister Margaret Thatcher once described the ANC as "a typical terrorist organization") to a reasonable grouping ready to do business with De Klerk. But the demonization of Hani and a handful of other leaders—primarily Winnie—continued among many conservative outlets. Hani was painted as a violent, racist terrorist—an anti-Mandela hell-bent on race war despite the fact that the two men frequently stood at the same podiums and Hani had been part of the ANC negotiations team since 1991.

That depiction was far from the truth. Hani was committed to a better South Africa for all South Africans. In a *Newsweek* interview he insisted: "Whether we like it or not, whites are South Africans like ourselves. They took power away from us and oppressed us, but we didn't get into the struggle to destroy the white group. We want to convince whites that democracy is better than apartheid, that . . . they will continue having a better life and a more normal life. They won't fear the Blacks they've feared for years."

But Janusz Waluś and his coconspirators wanted to keep white South Africans in fear—and use that fear to trigger a race war. So Waluś shot Hani four times, got into his red car, and drove away from Hakea Crescent, leaving the lifeless body of Chris Hani in a pool of blood.

10:10 a.m.
Dawn Park, Boksburg, Johannesburg

Nothing about Retha Harmse would have marked her out as a hero. With her permed blond bob and her high-pitched voice, she seemed like any ordinary married thirty-year-old white Afrikaner from Dawn Park, the sort who enjoyed sitting down for tea with her mother on a Saturday morning and had a passion for collecting and recycling plastic bags.

She worried about property values. When the Hani family moved into the neighborhood in 1992, she and her husband, unlike most of their neighbors, thought that house prices might actually rise—not fall— because the communist leader had brought guards to protect him. *They can help to protect the neighborhood as well,* she had thought at the time. Not the rest of her neighbors, though. The FOR SALE signs quickly started appearing.

Four years before the Hani family had moved into Boksburg, as the national government moved toward the ending of residential segregation, conservative Boksburg went the other way. The local council had voted to retain apartheid in its classic form, fencing in municipal parks and putting up EUROPEANS ONLY signs at amenities meant for whites. When the first cohort of middle-class Blacks such as Hani moved in they found places such as Boksburg Lake, a popular picnic and tourism spot (tinged with some notoriety after a sensational 1964 murder that had dominated the headlines), designated for whites only.

It was no surprise, then, that when Hani and other Black families started moving in, some white people moved out. In the run-up to the last whites-only referendum, in which De Klerk asked the white population to vote yes to his peace and reform talks with Mandela (he won by 68.73 percent) in 1992, the place was awash with posters depicting a confident Mandela looming over a kneeling, fawning De Klerk above a caption that blared: "*Stem nee vir Mandela en sy Klerk*" (Vote no to Mandela and his Clerk).

Holy Saturday of 1993 was an ordinary day for Harmse. She was set on going to Shoe City, a popular chain where you could buy anything from boots to running shoes for bargain prices, when her mother unexpectedly popped in for morning tea. Her husband, Daan, was standing at the front garden gate that morning when he saw Hani jogging past. Daan knew his famous neighbor—they had first met when Daan was out on a walk. "I'm Chris," Hani had introduced himself, as he always did, always the first to hold out his hand. He had told Daan that he needed to run because he was getting fat, a regular refrain of his that year. He'd told journalists the same thing: he wanted to be fit and ready for freedom. Often Hani would be joined on his runs by another ANC leader, the Pretoria-Witwatersrand-Vereeniging (PWV) regional chairman, Tokyo Sexwale, who lived a few blocks away.

When Hani would bump into Daan on his morning jogs, they would always greet each other good-naturedly. So, early that morning, when Daan saw Hani trotting past, he felt comfortable enough to shout: "Hey, Chris, lift those damn legs so that you run, man. You're getting lazy!" Hani, always ready with a smile, waved and carried on.

An hour or so later, tea with her mother done, Retha Harmse jumped into her car and headed down Hakea Crescent for her shoe shopping. It was just before 10 a.m. As she drove past the Hani home, she wondered where the family might be spending the Easter weekend. *Maybe he is on holiday somewhere by the sea*, she remembered thinking as she drove past, unaware that Daan had seen Hani jog by. It was a common misconception that ANC leaders were wealthy. Most, having been in exile or prison for most of their adult lives, had no savings. Those lucky enough to be in full-time ANC employment received a monthly salary of about R 2,500, the equivalent of a junior reporter. Most depended on handouts from benefactors or relatives. Few could afford a holiday. Hani's wife, Limpho, worked in administration at a Johannesburg firm, supplementing their income. That was how they could afford to live in a middle-class suburb such as Dawn Park.

As she drove on down the road, Harmse suddenly remembered that she had forgotten to take plastic shopping bags with her. She needed to collect milk bottles in them on her way back from the shoe store. She stopped, turned the car around, and headed back home.

As she made her way back to her house, she saw a red car come to a stop in the street in front of Hani's driveway. Inside the gate, in the driveway, was Hani's familiar Cressida. The red car's door opened and a tall, thin blond man got out, slightly bent, with his arms stretched out in front of him. He had a pistol in his hands, and she knew that he was getting ready to shoot.

There was something startling about how Harmse would later tell the story. "I know what a man looks like just before he is about to shoot," she told a famous Afrikaans journalist, Hanlie Retief. "I also have a pistol, I have learnt how to shoot."

It was all in some sort of slow motion. Harmse could hardly believe what she was seeing. "When I came close, he pulled two shots," she recalled. "Clearly. *Doof doof.* It was half dark under the shed. I thought, maybe it is someone who is shooting at a crook, we have the armed response guys [private security] here."

The blond man was not done. She watched in horror as he moved forward, bent over, and shot his victim twice more in the head. *He is really shooting at someone!* Harmse thought.

She drove away, slowly, still in shock. When she looked back, she saw the blond man getting back behind the wheel of the red car. He looked unhurried, relaxed. He reversed out from the Hani home. She wondered again if he was part of the neighborhood's private security firm but dismissed the thought: if he was security and had just shot dead a criminal, he would have stayed there and phoned the police.

I should get his registration number, she thought.

She put her foot on the brakes, stopped, and put her car in reverse, looking at the red car to try to get its registration.

Then she drove toward her house—fast. Daan was at the fence, talking to a neighbor, Daniel Starling, as she drove in. She shouted at both men: "Remember PBX 231!"

Harmse ran straight into the house and called the police.

"Somebody has just been shot at Chris Hani's house!" she said. It was exactly 10:10 a.m. when her call to the Boksburg police came through to Sergeant Dearham. As an emergency call, it was notable for the lack of urgency displayed by the police in responding.

"Listen here," said Harmse, using a colloquial Afrikaans mode to denote urgency. "I've just driven past Chris Hani's and someone has just shot a Black there."

"Just a second . . ."

Harmse held, listening as Dearham spoke to someone in the background.

"Do you know anything coming from Chris Hani's house?" he was saying.

A Constable Van der Merwe answered: "No, if I knew it would be on the air already."

Dearham spoke again, according to the transcript of the call, seemingly into the police radio frequency.

"Has anyone else said anything about Chris Hani? Smal, are you busy with the Chris Hani story? In front of Chris Hani's house a Black has been shot. Do you have Chris Hani's house there?"

A Constable Smal answers: "Yes."

Dearham returned to Harmse's call.

"We already got that," he said to her.

Harmse seemed disconcerted that someone had already called the shooting in. It had, after all, just happened minutes before.

"Is it?" she said, using a South African rhetorical question meaning "Is that so?"

She pressed on: "Because it just happened now."

Dearham: "Yes."

On the police radio, the Constable Smal chipped in: "Dearham, just take a proper address there."

Harmse continued to Dearham: "Oh, okay, I saw the car that was there. What happened there?"

"We don't know, ma'am. Can you tell me what is the correct address, because we don't know what exactly is the address."

Harmse gave him the address, explaining the one-street access to the three streets that made up the immediate area around her house and the Hanises'. Many of the streets, such as Hakea Crescent, had dead ends and Deon was one of the few that proceeded out onto the main road toward the Boksburg city center.

Then, without Dearham's prompting, she started explaining what had actually happened. The news that someone had called the incident in seemed to have disconcerted her, putting an apologetic tone to her delivery.

"I'm sorry . . . uhm . . . I saw a car there, actually I saw this white guy shooting this guy there. And he was in a car, a Ford red, a red Laser, and the reg PBX."

Dearham: "Okay, what is this, what's the registration number?"

"PBX."

"P for Peter, B for Bertie . . ."

"Ja."

"X."

"Two hundred thirty-seven."

"Okay, ma'am, what's your name?"

She gave him her surname. After that Dearham takes the conversation off on a random, inexplicable note. As if there isn't a man shot four times in his jurisdiction, Dearham then asks in Afrikaans: "Are you Afrikaans?"

"Yes," answers Harmse.

"Why are we speaking English, ma'am!?"

"No, I don't know. I just began speaking English. Listen here, I must go. My man will be here."

She gave him her address and then, perhaps because of shock, returns to the shooting again.

"What happened is that I drove past the . . ."

"Yes."

"I turned back to get something from the house. When I drove back, I saw this car stop and this fellow climbs out and shoots twice and then we see there is something on the ground and he shoots the person on the ground too."

"Yes . . ."

"It's all that I . . . and then I rushed home, and I looked very quickly what his car registration is."

"Very good work there, ma'am," says Dearham. "We appreciate it very much. Okay, ma'am. We will send the police so that they can get a statement from you."

"Okay."

The call was three minutes long, ending at 10:13. Harmse got off the call and looked at her husband. The enormity of what had just happened seemed to hit them both.

"If it was Chris Hani that was shot, there will be big trouble," Daan said.

10:45 a.m.
Boksburg

Waluś's assassination of Hani was swift and professional. The shots to the head killed the freedom fighter instantly.

In contrast, Waluś's escape was completely amateurish. After shooting

Hani he got back in his car and drove toward the Boksburg city center at a leisurely speed rather than getting onto one of the nearby motorways—where police generally did not set up roadblocks—and heading toward Pretoria.

As he neared downtown Boksburg twenty minutes later, a white Nissan Sentra with two uniformed policemen sped past him. He held his breath. They did not seem to have noticed him.

He sighed with relief.

As he entered the city there was a traffic jam ahead. The road had two lanes, and as he came to a stop he found himself side by side with the policemen in the Nissan Sentra. One of the policemen looked over and signaled to him to pull to the side of the road.

The two cops, Constables Du Toit and Olivier, were riding patrol in a squad car. They had heard the callout for a red car on the police radio. Waluś's registration was not the same as the one they had heard—PBX 237T. This registration, PBX 231T, was close enough. Waluś pulled over.

One of the police officers walked over to his window.

"Do you have a gun?" the officer asked.

He answered yes. He showed them the gun, his unused second carry. The man looked at it, put his nose to its cold barrel, and seemed satisfied. For the second time since the killing, he was to say later, he felt his fear of arrest receding. It was short-lived.

The policeman said he would like to search the car. The officer looked over at the passenger seat, then at the back seat, and spotted the bag behind the passenger seat. He riffled through it and found the Z-88. Keeping an eye on Waluś, he put the gun to his nose. It was still warm, still smelled of gunpowder.

Waluś gave up all pretense. "Well, guys," he said, when the second policeman came over. "What would you like to know?"

The two cops were confused by the man's equanimity. His actions would remain confusing to those investigating the assassination for years to come: Why had he driven his boss's bright-red car to a murder? A professional would have changed cars soon after leaving the scene of the crime, would have used a car that blended in rather than a highly visible red. And why had he done such a poor job of disguising the license plates? Was he really that inept? Or had he wanted to be found?

The officers took Waluś to Boksburg Police Station. The arrest had happened within half an hour of the murder.

10:30 a.m.
Johannesburg

It was just before 11 a.m. and David O'Sullivan had his feet on his desk. He was nursing a slight hangover. O'Sullivan, twenty-seven, was supplementing his meager salary as a law clerk with weekend shifts compiling and reading the news at one of only two independent radio stations in South Africa: Radio 702, in Johannesburg. It was, he figured, going to be yet another dull day in a long, empty holiday weekend. Then the switchboard phone rang.

A woman told him that her neighbor, Chris Hani, had just been shot and killed. O'Sullivan called the police spokesman, who told him that he knew nothing about it but would check. Then O'Sullivan called the ANC spokesperson, a woman called Gill Marcus. Marcus had left South Africa as a twenty-year-old university student and gone into exile with her parents in 1969. After twenty years of ANC antiapartheid underground work, mainly in the UK, she had returned in 1990 as part of the ANC's Department of Information and Publicity. She had a reputation for being the first in the office and the last to leave: she confesses that "work is all I did."

Sullivan gave her the story, but she was "somewhat unmoved."

"We get hoaxes like this all the time," she told him. But she promised to check it out.

There was no confirmation of the story by the time he went on air with the 11 a.m. bulletin, so good journalistic sense dictated that he not include it in the lineup of stories he read out. Then, just as he finished the bulletin, police spokesman Frans Malherbe called.

O'Sullivan ran back to the recording studio, yelling at the DJ to find the "breaking news" jingle. News of Chris Hani's assassination reverberated like a thunderclap across the country and the world.

As O'Sullivan's breaking news bulletin was going out on air, Hani's neighbor, Noxolo Grootboom, a Xhosa television news anchor, was arranging for Hani's daughter Nomakhwezi to be moved out of the neighborhood. Grootboom had been standing in her bedroom when she heard the gunshots and then the screaming of a child. She had run to her son's bedroom to check on him. Then she ran outside and saw Nomakhwezi screaming, coming toward her.

"They have shot my daddy. I saw it, it was a white man," she cried. Grootboom got the distraught child to call the last person to speak to her father, the activist Mondli Gungubele, who was supposed to accompany Hani to send money to his daughter in Cape Town and then ride with him and Nomakhwezi to the hair salon.

10:30 a.m.
Dawn Park

Mondli Gungubele has the readiest, happiest, and most generous smile of anyone I have ever met. It starts from the corners of his mouth and spreads across his face as he listens to you speak, as he prepares his answer, and when he starts speaking his smile seems to engulf the room. Yet when he recalls that day's telephone call from Nomakhwezi, his face clouds over, wrinkles knot his high forehead, and he looks pained.

When he answered the phone the person and noises on the other end were unintelligible. He put the phone down. It rang again. This time it was intelligible, yet he wished it wasn't. It was the voice of Nomakhwezi on the other end.

"Uncle Mondli, please come, they have shot my dad."

He went into shock, he says now. And he believes he was in shock for the rest of that week, doing what he needed to do like an automaton. That morning he had put on his favorite red polo shirt, a pair of blue jeans, and trainers. He had a double date. Hani, his hero and leader, was going to call—and he needed to be ready. After that he was going on a picnic with his wife, Queendy.

Both Mandela and Hani liked to refer to people by their clan names, which is a sign of respect in many Black South African cultures. For example, Mandela is universally referred to by his clan name, Madiba. Gungubele's clan name is Mthembu, and on the evening of Friday the ninth he had received a call at home from Hani.

"Mthembu," he said. "Tomorrow I am going to send money to Neo. Will you come along with me to the post office?"

There was no question of saying no. From the day they met, Hani had treated the thirty-six-year-old like his protégé—the way Mandela treated the fifty-year-old Hani. Gungubele was the lead ANC activist in the East Rand region, the hub of conservative Afrikaans-speaking industrial towns east of Johannesburg that included Boksburg, Benoni, and the suburbs around them such as Dawn Park. Around these "white areas" were the Black townships of Thokoza, Vosloorus, and Katlehong, all of them racked by the worst political violence in the country outside Natal on the east coast. The violence emanated from the male-only workers' hostels built during apartheid that sat at the edges of townships to house migrant laborers from the rural "homelands." In the 1990s these hostel dwellers were recruited or coerced by the Inkatha Freedom Party to sign up, and attacks on innocent township residents spiked—with evidence that apartheid secret police armed, trained, and even directed these hostel dwellers in their attacks on the townships. Gungubele had risen to prominence by bringing along heavyweights—Hani and others—to the area to talk peace to angry communities.

Gungubele's emotions were a maelstrom on hearing about Hani's killing. First there was disbelief, then shock, then confusion. Then he was "overwhelmed by anger," he told me.

Yet he still managed to operate. He remembers jumping into their first-ever family car, a white Toyota Corolla, and heading to Tokyo Sexwale's house to pick him up. Sexwale was the chairman of the ANC in the

PWV area, the region that encompasses South Africa's powerful economic triangle of Pretoria (administrative capital of SA), the mining-dominated Witwatersrand (that includes Johannesburg), and the industrial complex along the Vaal River. Sexwale, recently released after thirteen years on Robben Island and a Hani friend and jogging mate, had not heard the news. Together they rushed to the Hani home, where they found their comrade dead on the redbrick driveway. Nomakhwezi was taken to Sexwale's home just a few blocks away.

By then the news had spread like wildfire. In South Africa, news of Hani's murder has become a "where were you when . . ." moment. Every year on April 10, people ask each other this question in a manner that places it on a plane of major historical moments such as the release of Mandela from prison in 1990.

"It was like the sky had come down," said Pallo Jordan, a member of the party's National Executive Committee and the political head of the Department of Information and Publicity.

When he received the news, he immediately started making calls, putting together the team that would conduct the ANC's response to the crisis, including party spokeswoman Gill Marcus; a young former political prisoner and Christian activist called Carl Niehaus, who had become the ANC's media manager; a former political prisoner and ANC speechwriter named Saki Macozoma; and a handful of others. One of the first calls he made was to Joel Netshitenzhe, the editor of the party journal *Mayibuye* and one of the party's rising strategists.

Sitting in his apartment in Hillbrow, having recently returned from exile, Netshitenzhe knew that this latest assassination was potentially even more calamitous than the Bisho and Boipatong massacres of the previous year. In Bisho, in September 1992, twenty-eight ANC supporters were killed when soldiers of the Ciskei homeland opened fire on 80,000 unarmed people led by Hani in a protest march. The protesters wanted the "independent" homeland of Ciskei to be reincorporated into South Africa. The Boipatong killings the previous June had been worse. On the night of June 17, 1992, a group of about 300 armed men from a steelworks hostel

had attacked and killed forty-five residents of Boipatong, a township outside Vanderbijlpark, south of Johannesburg. Many residents insisted the
attackers were supporters of the Inkatha Freedom Party (IFP), a Zulu nationalist party that was a rival to the ANC. Worse, witnesses claimed that
the South African Police had escorted the killers into the township and
out again, a charge the government denied.

This latest killing left Netshitenzhe feeling raw. *What next would these
forces try?* he wondered. He assumed the government had to have been
involved.

Within the ANC, there was still fear of a "Dingane Scenario," even
three years into negotiations with the government. The name referred
to an incident when, in 1838, the Zulu king, Dingane, invited Afrikaner
leader Piet Retief to the royal uMgungundlovu household to celebrate
the signing of an agreement between the Zulus and the Afrikaners who
had abandoned the British-controlled Cape Colony to establish their own
settlement in the hinterland. Dingane, however, believed the treaty was a
prelude to his being ousted by the Afrikaners, who had two years earlier
defeated the Ndebele king, Mzilikazi, in order to take over his land in the
interior of the country. At the royal gates Retief and his party were asked
to "observe Zulu protocol" by leaving their weapons at the door. Once
inside, traditional beer was served and dancing commenced. Then, during the entertainment, Dingane ordered his men: *"Bulalani abathakathi!"*
(Kill the sorcerers!) Dingane's men immediately surrounded Retief and
his men. They took the captives up a hill and impaled all one hundred of
them on their spears, ensuring slow and painful deaths. Now the party's
leaders asked themselves: Had the ANC been lured into a similar trap?

For ANC activists who had for decades been pursued across the
globe, kidnapped, tortured, and jailed, the idea that the South African
government suddenly wanted to cooperate with them seemed suspect.
In February 1990, soon after the unbanning of liberation movements,
the government's top spy and one of the men who had started talks with
Mandela in prison, Niël Barnard, traveled to Bern, Switzerland, with a delegation from the National Intelligence Service to meet ANC leaders in

exile, including Thabo Mbeki and Jacob Zuma. At the meeting, Mbeki informed the government delegation that some of his comrades believed the government wanted to use the occasion as a pretext for luring them back to South Africa, only to put them behind bars.

Now, with Chris Hani dead, Netshitenzhe said, "People started asking whether the whole exercise" of trying to negotiate with the government "was worth the cost . . . [I]t dramatically affected confidence in the entire process."

Ronnie Kasrils also had his suspicions. Like Hani, he was a senior member of Umkhonto we Sizwe and of the SA Communist Party central committee. He was playing football when he received the news of Hani's murder. His wife appeared at the side of the field, "waving her arms and calling me," he recalled, recounting the story he had told many times before. "But the ball was passed to me and I ignored her. Suddenly she was on the pitch and I thought she was crazy. 'Chris has been shot,' she cried . . . She didn't know if he was dead. She had come by car and we drove straight across Joburg to the Hani home—me in my football gear— to join the comrades keeping vigil there."

It was not just his comrades. Journalists, residents, the police . . . Suddenly, all roads led to Dawn Park, and fear was in the air.

11:15 a.m.
Krugersdorp

Clive Derby-Lewis and his wife, Gaye, had been enjoying milk tart and tea in the garden of their friends, the Venters, when the phone rang.

The Derby-Lewises were leading members of the extreme, English-speaking white right wing. A third-generation white South African born in Cape Town in 1936, Clive Derby-Lewis grew up in the diamond-rich mining town of Kimberley, where Afrikaans was the main language of communication. He nevertheless cultivated an upper-class English accent, attending the prestigious Christian Brothers College and volunteering with the South African Citizen Force (a whites-only reserve component of the South African Defence Force, essentially an official citizen militia that could be activated at any time) for nineteen years while working as a chartered accountant. He also worked on his political career, joining the powerful National Party—which won the 1974 and 1977 whites-only national elections by 56 percent and 65 percent of the vote respectively, defeating the liberal Progressive Federal Party—and becoming mayor of Bedfordview, a suburb of Johannesburg, in 1974. Derby-Lewis presented himself as the English-speaking face of South African racial conservatism, cultivating an image of himself as an upper-crust Brit, wearing cravats and patterned neckties implying membership in a private club or military regiment. He packed a gun as a matter of routine.

In 1982, Derby-Lewis and other hard-line adherents of apartheid split off from the National Party, which had become "too liberal" because of reforms, spearheaded by P. W. Botha. Botha's reforms, implemented in 1983, ushered in a new constitution that created a tricameral parliament with separate houses for white, Indian, and colored South Africans but not one for Black African people. Derby-Lewis and his comrades formed the Conservative Party. Derby-Lewis ran for the conservative town of Krugersdorp's parliamentary seat in 1987 and lost. He, however, still made it to Parliament after he was directly nominated by the CP on the party list. He was, according to the leader of the antiapartheid Progressive Federal Party, Harry Schwarz, the "biggest racist in parliament" during the late 1980s.

He didn't even try to hide his racism. In 1989, Derby-Lewis remarked in Parliament that "if HIV/AIDS stops Black population growth it will be like Father Christmas." At another time he lamented a report that a plane had had to brake to avoid a Black man on the runway at the Johannesburg airport. "What a pity," he said. Even by the standards of the Conservative Party, Derby-Lewis's racism was sometimes too much. "I think sometimes he became an embarrassment to us," Andries Beyers, a senior Conservative Party official, remembered. He once made his colleagues cringe when he ventured: "There are cultural differences between Blacks and whites and it is a fact that Blacks like to make babies."

Derby-Lewis lost his seat in the 1989 whites-only election but was then directly appointed by the Conservative Party to the President's Council by virtue of the party's 31.5 percent haul of the votes (the National Party, led by De Klerk, won 48 percent and the liberal Democratic Party just 20 percent). The President's Council was a multiparty advisory group to the president that held veto power over any political reforms contemplated by the executive. The President's Council gained a reputation as the forum where attempts at reform went to die.

Derby-Lewis also found favor in international pro-Nazi and anticommunist organizations. He was elected honorary president of the Western Goals Institute, a London-based far-right pressure group, succeeding Salvadoran death squad leader Major Roberto D'Aubuisson, who was alleged to be behind the 1980 murder of Óscar Romero. He befriended David Irving, the Holocaust denier and historian who once called the Auschwitz gas chambers a "fairy tale" and insisted that Adolf Hitler had protected the Jews of Europe. Irving referred to surviving death camp witnesses as "psychiatric cases" and asserted that there were no extermination camps in the Third Reich. Irving visited South Africa, sponsored by the Stallard Foundation, the organization founded by Derby-Lewis for English-speaking conservatives, where he delivered speeches countrywide on "the march of communism." He must have been pleased with his visit, for he told a newspaper that "there are more pro-Hitler people in South Africa" than he expected, but he didn't know why this was so. He returned in 1989 and again in March 1993—coincidentally, just weeks before Hani's murder.

Even Derby-Lewis's religious affiliations were racist. After the largest Afrikaans church, the Dutch Reformed Church, decided to open its doors to all races and to renounce apartheid, a group of right-wingers formed their own church, the Afrikaanse Protestantse Kerk. Derby-Lewis promptly signed up, even though English speakers were also unwelcome. In joining, he was defecting from his position as a lay minister in the Roman Catholic Church in Johannesburg.

The Johannesburg *Sunday Times* wrote that Derby-Lewis was "clearly dominated by, dictated to and frequently put down by his more intelligent and at least as vituperative wife Gaye who . . . complained that her husband was spineless."

Born in Australia into a devoutly Roman Catholic family, Gabriella Maverna "Gaye" Derby-Lewis wanted to be a nun at fifteen, became one at twenty, but soon turned against the church and moved to South Africa, where she married an intelligence officer, Anton Graser. Gaye's radicalization seems to have intensified while she worked in the deeply corrupt Department of Information, apartheid government's propaganda wing. For nearly four years, Gaye worked for the minister of information, Dr. Connie Mulder, a rising star in the apartheid government who was widely regarded as the front-runner to succeed John Vorster as prime minister until Mulder and Vorster were exposed in one of apartheid South Africa's biggest political scandals. Starting in 1973, Mulder had, with the blessing of the prime minister, set up a slush fund, using money from the defense budget, amounting to 64 million rand over the years of its operation, to undertake a series of propaganda projects to improve South Africa's reputation and standing in the Western world. Using secret Swiss bank accounts, the ministry planned bribes of international news agencies and the purchase of the American *Washington Star* newspaper. In South Africa, a millionaire Afrikaner businessman was given money to establish a government-controlled, conservative English newspaper, the *Citizen*. Ultimately, Mulder and Vorster both lost their jobs.

When Clive Derby-Lewis and other hard-line apartheid adherents formed the Conservative Party in 1982, Gaye signed up and was soon elected to the party's executive council in the Transvaal, the economic hub of the country. She was put in charge of day-to-day operations and later elevated to the Head Council, the party's highest decision-making body. She sat on various committees and was particularly active on the information committee. In a curious move for an ultraconservative at that time, the former nun took over the management of Truckers, a gay bar in the liberal Johannesburg suburb of Hillbrow. Until 1994, homosexuality was a crime punishable by up to seven years in prison in South Africa.

In 1986, after divorcing Graser, she married Derby-Lewis and joined the Conservative Party's Afrikaans-English newspaper, the *Patriot*, as executive editor of its English pages. She was a prolific writer of letters to the mainstream press, excoriating liberals and others she saw as enemies of the causes she believed in. She also edited the newsletter of her husband's Stallard Foundation, which was particularly popular among East European émigrés such as Janusz Waluś, who shared its passionate hatred of communism.

For Janusz Waluś, meeting Clive Derby-Lewis opened a new door in his life. He first met the politician in 1985 at an address by the Holocaust denier David Irving. After chatting over several months, Waluś was invited to the Derby-Lewises' house in Johannesburg. Waluś had few friends and was attracted by the Derby-Lewises' confirmation of his passionate hatred of communism. Long lunches and discussions followed. Waluś was introduced to the Stallard Foundation newsletter and became a subscriber. The Waluśes were doing well at that time—they had a massive house in Waterkloof, Pretoria's most expensive and elite suburb, home to top diplomats and millionaires. Their factory in QwaQwa had revenues of US$750,000 a year (the equivalent of $2 million in 2022 terms). He started contributing money to the foundation, regularly giving about R 1,000—equivalent to US$500, a substantial amount at the time.

Waluś joined the Conservative Party and began meeting the who's who of the right wing. He listened to the fiery rhetoric of Afrikaner Resistance Movement (AWB) founder Eugène Terre'Blanche—regularly mocked in the English press—speaking at a Stallard meeting and "realized that what he had to say and what the media had to say about him were completely different things." He was so taken by Terre'Blanche—a man who used the Nazi salute as his greeting, arguing that "I come in peace: how can I help it if Hitler also used it?"—that he accepted an invitation to visit him in Pretoria. He soon signed up for membership in the AWB.

11:15 a.m.
Krugersdorp

The people sipping tea at the Venters' house that morning as the phone made its shrill sound had been in touch several times in the previous two months. At a meeting of the notoriously racist Krugersdorp Town Council in February 1993, Derby-Lewis had walked over to another right-winger, Lionel du Randt, and told him that a man would deliver a weapon, wrapped in a sweater, to his house. That man was Faan Venter, who was sitting opposite the Derby-Lewises just after 11 a.m., also enjoying his tea. He had dropped off the gun with Du Randt, who had then given it to Derby-Lewis.

Now, weeks later, Faan Venter and his wife, Maureen, were sipping tea and eating milk tart with the Derby-Lewises at exactly the time Chris Hani was murdered with that same gun—given to Waluś by Derby-Lewis just four days before. What transpired afterward on this morning is jumbled because the Derby-Lewises and their associates subsequently changed their stories so many times that it becomes impossible to determine where fact lies and fiction takes over.

Maureen Venter says she went into the house and answered the ringing phone. One of her sons was on the line.

"Do you have the radio on?" he asked.

"No, we are having tea," she said. "We were sitting outside and do not have the radio on there."

"Mommy, did you hear that they shot Chris Hani?" he said.

"Are you sure?"

"Yes, Mother," he answered.

It was around 11:15 a.m.

Maureen went outside and told the Derby-Lewises the news. She later told the police that the couple were "extremely surprised," but then changed her story and said the Derby-Lewises' attitude was "normal" and that they "did not display any noticeable reaction." Derby-Lewis himself admitted later that he was shocked by the news because he had expressly said Waluś should not kill Hani during the long weekend. The shooting was "totally out of character" because to him Waluś was "a steady sort of person and he was calm and came across as being competent." He claims his first thought was: *Jeepers, has something come to our rescue? We don't have to do what we planned.*

What everyone present agrees about is that the Derby-Lewises were suddenly in a hurry to leave, as though they had been waiting to hear the news and were now free to go on with their day. They claimed that they had people coming to visit. As they left, Clive Derby-Lewis turned to Maureen Venter and said: "Don't worry, it's not that weapon."

Then, according to Gaye, "We went shopping." No one was coming to visit.

12 p.m.
Dawn Park

Among those who descended on the Hani home that Saturday afternoon was Peter Harris, the head of a unique nine-month-old body in South Africa: the Wits-Vaal Regional Peace Secretariat. Harris shared something with Gungubele, the Hani protégé who was the first to be called by Hani's daughter: he worked daily to bring peace to the violence-torn area, and news of this latest incident left him shocked and deeply afraid. The secretariat was the regional structure of the National Peace Accord, a body bringing together representatives of all political organizations, the police, clergy, nongovernmental organizations, and businesspeople to help monitor and mediate political clashes. At the national level you had the main political party leaders (Mandela, De Klerk, Mangosuthu Buthelezi of the IFP, and twenty-three other signatories to the accord) and the structures cascaded down through provincial branches (in this case the Transvaal), regional branches (the Wits-Vaal region where Harris and Mondli Gungubele operated), and local branches (townships and street levels). In the secretariats sat political leaders, police, business representatives, civil society organizations, and 15,000 ordinary South Africans who volunteered to intervene in volatile situations to keep the peace. They had no guns, little equipment (mainly cars), and two-way radios—and their white bibs with the NPA logo of two white doves signifying peace. In small groups, these volunteers often intervened in volatile situations where groups of thousands were about to enter fights.

Gungubele and Harris had seen violence close-up in the East Rand townships. Once, Harris had witnessed a man being stabbed with a spear and die in broad daylight, blood gurgling out of his punctured throat. He had been in a situation where he and his fellow peacekeepers were surrounded by crowds of 40,000 or more, armed with spears and *knobkieries* (fighting sticks), and expected to keep the peace. He had arrived at township hospitals after reports of massacres to find twenty or more bodies lined up outside.

For both men, the murder of Hani cut at a personal level. Gungubele's world had been opening up when Hani came into his life in the early 1990s. He'd had a hard life. Born in the Eastern Cape in 1957, he grew up with no knowledge of who his father was. One day in 1973, when he was just under sixteen, one of the many patches sewn onto his trousers came off. He remembers that on that day his family—his mother, his four siblings—was on its third straight day with no food. That's the day he decided to tell his mother that he was leaving home to seek work in the mines, in Johannesburg, where the father he had never met apparently was. The mines had a strict rule: no under-eighteens. But the mine recruiter knew his family was destitute so he took him on and sent him to Johannesburg, falsifying his age on the forms. He was scrawny but strong and worked like a demon. Soon, he was promoted to "boss boy"—assistant to the white underground manager.

But he wasn't satisfied with being a mine worker. He went back home, went back to school, and sat in class with kids five years younger than him, excelled, and returned to the mines with an outstanding school certificate. He kept studying by night, qualifying as a nurse (the only profession he could get into without being forced to cease work completely) and

enrolling for a law degree, while working by day. He joined the mine workers' trade union that his older comrade and now ANC secretary-general
Cyril Ramaphosa had founded in the early 1980s.

In 1990, he was fired from his job for taking a day off to give a political
speech. He challenged the mine bosses and his union representative at the
hearing was a woman, Rebecca "Queendy" Madipoane. Gungubele fell in
love the minute they met. They moved in together in Vosloorus, one of
the volatile townships in the East Rand.

The East Rand was one of the most violent parts of South Africa in
the early 1990s. Battles raged daily between the police, ANC youths who
had formed self-defense units, and the Inkatha Freedom Party members
who were being secretly funded by the security forces to foment violence
in the townships. Gungubele called the East Rand a "Little Liberia," a war-
torn country.

"There were corpses all over. Kids in the East Rand were playing with
corpses. I don't know how many times we went to mortuaries and we saw
hundreds of corpses. Death was normal. People in Kombis were mowed
down, people in a bus . . ."

It was so dangerous that in 1992, Queendy unilaterally decided that
it was time to flee the township of Vosloorus. Rumors had swirled that
Gungubele was a target for assassination. Gungubele had arrived home at
midnight one evening to find a note telling him to come to 10 Bushbuck
Street in Dawn Park. Queendy had moved the family. Their new home
was a four-minute drive from the Hani family.

Harris's life was also in transformation. Harris had made a decision
early on in his life and legal career that he would use the law to fight apartheid. In the late 1970s, he had been visiting a friend, Paul Pretorius, an ad-
vocate and former student leader who was banned (meaning he couldn't
leave his house, speak or write publicly, be with more than one person at
a time, and was randomly checked on by the police—or face five years in
prison) at the time. Pretorius had given him a copy of Mandela's famous
three-hour speech from the dock at the Rivonia Trial. Delivered in 1964

before he was sentenced to life imprisonment, Mandela had ended his speech (it was also banned in South Africa at the time—possession led to imprisonment) with the lines:

"I have fought against white domination, and I have fought against Black domination. I have cherished the ideal of a democratic and free society in which all persons live together in harmony and with equal opportunities. It is an ideal which I hope to live for and to achieve. But if needs be, it is an ideal for which I am prepared to die."

It had changed Harris's life. He had gone on to become part of a small group of antiapartheid lawyers challenging the system, representing Black trade unions, and defending activists and ANC fighters through the 1980s. In 1992, he had been seconded by his law firm to head up the Wits-Vaal peace secretariat to help bring peace to the area with the highest number of political killings outside the Natal region.

He believed in a future South Africa. Married to a producer for an international television network, they were raising their four children—a boy of five, a girl of two, and newborn twin boys—with the expectation of a country shorn of the horror of apartheid.

Now Hani was dead. *Nothing had put the transition to democracy in as much jeopardy as this one act*, thought Harris.

Gungubele understood that the right wing saw Hani as a threat to them because of his communism. He also knew that a sense of racial superiority, fostered over centuries and girded by beliefs that they were God's chosen people, made some believe that they had a right to simply murder a Black person. He viewed all this as tragic. He thought: *They killed somebody who guaranteed their future in this country. If there was a man fighting for peace in this country, it was Chris.*

He was also palpably aware of the anger the murder would unleash. "I don't know what we are going to tell these youth now," he told one reporter who approached him at the Hani house. "It's going to be difficult. If they kill somebody who is fighting for peace, who are they not going to kill?"

In his time with the peace secretariat, Harris had noticed a pattern in the violence: after every positive forward move in the negotiation process, there would be a major violent episode, almost timed to frustrate the progress. Hani's murder, he thought, was envisaged as something that would destabilize the situation irrevocably. It was an attempt to stop the peace and democracy project.

For both men, and for millions of South Africans, it would mean the end of the new South Africa they had been working to give birth to.

12 p.m.
Van Rooy family farm, The Karoo, Eastern Cape Province

On the sixth of September 1966, thirty-year-old Frederik Willem "F. W." de Klerk had been in a deep post-lunch holiday nap with his wife, Marike, the tropical heat and the sound of the Indian Ocean's waves having lulled them to sleep, when he was rudely awakened by his friend Du Toit van der Merwe, who told him that Prime Minister Hendrik Frensch Verwoerd was dead.

Disbelief and anguish roiled De Klerk. The young man was an attorney just setting out on his political career, emulating his father—the sitting minister of home affairs—and his uncle, J. G. Strijdom, a former prime minister of South Africa. De Klerk's family had been at the heart of the apartheid project since the National Party won elections in 1948, replacing Jan Smuts of the United Party. De Klerk's father had been a member of Verwoerd's government as it ruthlessly wrote, enacted, and enforced laws that regulated every single aspect of Black life: where Black people could live, where they could sit, where they could work or even walk, whom they could sleep with, where they could drink, whom they could befriend, what shows they could watch, even what doors they could use. Not that there wasn't white supremacy or racial segregation before 1948. In the period between 1910, when the Union of South Africa was formed, and 1948, white supremacy had been effected in three key ways. First, Blacks were stripped of the right to own land and confined to rural or urban "reserves," leaving Blacks with just 13 percent of the land despite making up more than 80 percent of the population. The legacy of that dispossession continues today—a 2017 government land audit revealed that whites own 72 percent of the total farms and agricultural holdings by individual land-owners, followed by colored (meaning mixed race) at 15 percent, Indians at 5 percent, and Black Africans at 4 percent. Second, Blacks were stripped of the vote. Finally, Blacks were severely restricted in their access to the so-called white cities unless they held a permit allowing them to live and work in the urban areas, where residence and amenities were strictly seg-regated. The Verwoerd era had accelerated these divisions.

Today, on this beautiful, clear Easter Saturday nearly thirty years on, in 1993, it wasn't someone that De Klerk revered who had been murdered, but a political opponent. This time, a local policeman drove up to the Van Rooy family farm in Steynsburg, a small farming town in the vast semides-ert in the interior of South Africa called the Karoo, to tell the president of the turbulent Republic of South Africa the news.

De Klerk was at home here, in the Karoo. His ancestors had walked and colonized these lands over a century and a half before. Just forty-five minutes away by car was Burgersdorp, the town where in 1825 his ances-tor Johannes Cornelis de Klerk had bought a beautiful farm called Spioen-kop (Spy Hill). Johannes Cornelis's sons—De Klerk's great-grandfather, Barend, and his brother—had lived and farmed on Spioenkop, their houses just a hundred yards from each other. Then they'd fought over reli-gion, with the one brother going with the hymn-singing Dutch Reformed Church while Barend followed the austere, conservative Reformed Church (the "Doppers"). The feud became so bitter that they had to erect a fence between their two houses. The two men never spoke to each other again. They are buried, silent and bitter, next to each other on Spioenkop.

Through the sparse Karoo veld ran the Van Rooy breed of domestic sheep, the Van Rooy White Persian, first developed in 1906 by De Klerk's great-grandfather on his mother's side, the politician J. C. van Rooy. The Easter gathering was of the Van Rooy family.

On the morning of Saturday, April 10, 1993, De Klerk felt happy with the negotiations process that had started three years before, when he had shocked his fellow countrymen and the world by announcing in

Parliament that the man the white government had feared for decades, Nelson Mandela, would be released from prison after twenty-seven years. De Klerk knew that the journey he had embarked on over the past four years—after he had replaced the uncompromising P. W. Botha as National Party leader and state president—had made him and others within and outside his party some very powerful enemies. He was considered a traitor and an autocrat by conservatives, who believed that De Klerk had betrayed his own constituency by deciding to unban the Communist Party and the ANC. Conservative Party MP Clive Derby-Lewis accused him of doing so to "ensure . . . [his] future positions in a Black-ruled South Africa." It did not matter that in 1992, De Klerk had won 68 percent of votes cast in a whites-only referendum that asked voters to endorse or reject his reforms: he had become many white South Africans' "most hated adversary."

Yet De Klerk had not come from the *verligte* (an Afrikaans expression meaning enlightened or liberal) side of the National Party. He had defeated the more "liberal" candidate, Barend du Plessis, by eight votes to become leader of the National Party in 1989, buoyed by the party's conservative wing. He was not engaged in the peace process because he was a progressive, or because he had awoken to the fact that his fellow Black South Africans deserved full human rights. De Klerk's main motivation for his reforms—abandoning all "petty apartheid" laws of racial segregation, for example, and unbanning all political organizations—was that he still put his own Afrikaner people first and hoped to ensure a white veto power of some sort on a future dispensation. If his people faced a race war, they would, he believed, surely lose. "I was deeply aware of my responsibility for assuring the best possible future for my own people," he was to write in his autobiography in later years, before adding, in a revealing afterthought, "as well as for all the other peoples of our incredibly complex society."

De Klerk had learned at his mother's knee of the history of the Afrikaners. He felt at one with them, his being knotted with theirs. "The dream that they had dreamt of being a free and separate people, with their own right to national self-determination in their own national state in southern

Africa, had been the dream that had motivated the ancestors who stared sternly at me from our old family photographs," he wrote in later life. He believed in the essential goodness of that dream, and of his relatives who'd pursued it. He characterized his father as a "good and a kind man."

Yes, the government they had created had "applied segregation much more methodically and systematically than any of its predecessors," but he believed that the story of human history was a story of oppression and bigotry. The National Party, he was to write, "had not invented racial discrimination." Still, by 1993, the man who had come from one of South Africa's most enduring political dynasties knew that for the Afrikaners to take a journey separate from their Black compatriots would only lead to disaster.

Apartheid had become an albatross for De Klerk and many other Afrikaners. He sought the day when "the burden of three hundred and fifty years" of colonialism would be "lifted from our shoulders," a time when he and his fellow whites would be able to "greet all our countrymen without guilt or fear . . ." Already, some were doing so. Like so many white South Africans, De Klerk's wife, Marike, "privately had a difficult time accepting the reforms instituted by" her husband, but one of their three children, Willem, had announced his intention to marry a "colored" (mixed-race) woman, Erica Adams, a few years before. Ironically, it had been none other than De Klerk who in 1985, as minister of the interior, had stood up in Parliament to scrap the prohibitions on mixed marriages and interracial sex. (Marike would press Willem to end the engagement by, among other things, telling him that it could jeopardize his father's political reforms by undermining white people's confidence in him. Newspapers reported that she also sent the amorous twenty-four-year-old off to London to "cool down his love" and threatened to commit suicide if he didn't break off the engagement. Adams later said she ended the relationship after being summoned by the president and told that it was not in anyone's interest for them to stay together.)

Now the democratic transition was underway. The previous year had been torrid, with major political events such as his controversial "whites-only" referendum (which he had called to get a "mandate" from white voters and to prove that white extremists did not have as much support as they claimed, but for which he was criticized by the ANC as evidence of racism), the Boipatong and Bisho massacres (forty-five and twenty-eight killed respectively), major marches and business boycotts by the ANC, and a nine-month hiatus in the negotiations.

Just two weeks before, on March 24, De Klerk had told Parliament that South Africa had during the previous decades developed seven nuclear bombs similar to those that had destroyed Hiroshima. Now, South Africa had become the first country ever to dismantle its own nuclear weapons capability.

He was amply rewarded, with many across the globe praising this extraordinary step. The ANC was skeptical of De Klerk's assertions that all the bomb-grade uranium had been eliminated and opposed the destruction of documents that might be used by a future government to track down the truth about the weapons program. The action had given De Klerk some global credibility, a commodity he personally sought after white South Africa had been a pariah for so long. That, and the fact that the multiparty negotiations were now back underway, gave him reason to believe that some progress would soon be made. By Easter weekend, De Klerk believed, he'd later write, "that we could take a well-earned break." Everything, he told himself, seemed to be going quite well.

Until the local policeman arrived.

Dave Steward, a veteran English-speaking diplomat whom De Klerk had recruited to his office six months before, had been frantically calling the farm number for a while with no success. Steward, a former journalist, was not one to call the president about small matters. He had served as South Africa's ambassador to the United Nations from 1981 to 1982, at the height of the country being a pariah in world affairs. With the apartheid government largely isolated, he had been brought back to Pretoria to head the internal propaganda machine, the South African Communication Service, as the iron claw of apartheid tightened. De Klerk, needing an experienced communicator as the democracy negotiations unfolded, had drawn Steward into his inner circle at the end of 1992.

That Saturday, Steward was on a rare Easter break with his wife and two small children in the picturesque town of Knysna, famous for its oyster festival and lagoon, when he received a call from a journalist asking him if he had heard the news. He'd immediately gone to his desk and started trying to reach De Klerk. He couldn't, so he did the next best thing: he called the local police station to get a message to the president at the Van Rooy farm.

After receiving the policeman's message, De Klerk called the local switchboard and was connected through to Knysna just as his family was preparing to sit down to a hearty Karoo lunch, usually roast lamb from one of the sheep that grazed among the unique local fragrant shrubs and grasses, served with mint jelly, gravy, pumpkin, and roast potatoes.

Steward picked up the phone and told the president that Hani had been assassinated. "[T]he news is already on the radio," Steward said.

De Klerk told me he was "extremely shocked" by the news of Hani's murder. He did not delude himself about Hani the man—the two were polar opposites politically. Yet Hani was at the negotiating table, a fact that De Klerk knew was a path to him achieving his goal of shepherding his flock to a new South Africa beyond apartheid. One cannot, after all, make peace by oneself. You make peace with an enemy, and you cannot do that if they are dead.

De Klerk said he knew that Hani's "assassination had the potential to ignite a major crisis." He'd have to start working immediately.

He never did find out what was served for lunch that day.

12 p.m.
Dawn Park

Back at the Hani home, ANC leaders stood around in shock. Gill Marcus, who had made a few calls to key leaders and then rushed to the Hani home, arranged for an impromptu press conference.

Tokyo Sexwale, Hani's jogging partner, was the first to speak. Sexwale had joined the ANC's military wing in the mid-1970s. He received military training in Ukraine, then a part of the Soviet Union, and was arrested on his return to South Africa after a skirmish with the police. In 1977, he was sentenced to eighteen years' imprisonment and sent to Robben Island to join Mandela and others, where he remained incarcerated until 1990. Blessed with a powerful voice and commanding presence, he wore military fatigues for public appearances. At many ANC events, he would act as Hani's militant second-in-command.

This time, however, Sexwale called for calm, not war. In front of reporters and photographers from across the globe, Sexwale broke down and cried. "It is a time to cry," he said. "I saw Chris Hani dead." It was a moment never seen before on South African television: a Black militant, demonized as a warmonger, was vulnerable, in tears. "Just two days ago," Sexwale continued, Hani "preached peace, which made him dangerous. He said let's get away from the violence . . . he died for peace. I beg all our supporters to remember this."

At David O'Sullivan's radio station, Radio 702, the telephone lines flashed, with callers desperate to talk about the extraordinary—and emotional—eulogy they'd just heard.

Immediately after the press conference, the ANC deputy president, Walter Sisulu, arrived. Soon thereafter, former ANC president Oliver Tambo arrived with his wife, Adelaide. Hani's body was already in the police morgue van. The van stopped so Tambo—who had over twenty-five years nurtured Hani and Thabo Mbeki, the suave ANC head of international relations, as his potential successors—could pay his respects.

In 1969, when Hani was detained by the ANC's security department for his memorandum excoriating the party leadership, Tambo had ordered his release. He had promoted him to the National Executive Committee, appointed him head of MK, and then to the ANC's negotiations team. Now he lay dead in a van.

Adelaide reached over and closed Hani's eyes.

Around the van, the many ANC supporters and neighbors wept. A slow, mournful dirge, all too familiar to many in that area, swelled up from the crowd: *"Hamba kahle, Mkhonto we Sizwe!"* (liberation movement, Spear of the Nation!)

12 p.m.
Jan Smuts Airport, Johannesburg

There is another man whose fame and popularity in South Africa could perhaps match or even surpass that of Chris Hani and Nelson Mandela. That is the former world boxing heavyweight champion Muhammad Ali, the American activist and slugger whose razor-sharp banter and antiracism stance had enthralled Black South Africans and given many hope that one day freedom would come to their land.

Ali had landed in South Africa that morning as part of a tour to fulfill a promise to Mandela, made in 1990, that he would one day visit him. Ali was a global superstar and the organizers of his visit wanted to ensure he got maximum publicity while in South Africa. So, by midday, Ali—who styled himself "the Greatest"—was ready to go out to the makeshift stage inside the airport building (then still named Jan Smuts after the prime minister voted out in 1948 to make way for the National Party) prepared for him to meet the press and greet his fans.

Mandela had been a keen boxer in his younger years and had kept up a punishing exercise regime while a lawyer in Johannesburg in the 1950s. He was notorious back then for asking guests to his Soweto home to join him for exercise and then putting them through the wringer.

Mandela had met Ali in California during his whirlwind tour of the US following his release from prison in 1990. The two men were smitten with each other, and Ali had promised to visit South Africa as soon as time allowed. Now Ali was about to spend two weeks traveling through Johannesburg, Durban, and Cape Town.

The arrivals hall at Jan Smuts Airport in Johannesburg exploded with excitement as Ali appeared. More than a thousand eager fans had turned up.

"Ali! Ali! Ali!" the crowd chanted.

News of Hani's murder—which was already spreading across South Africa—could not dampen the mood. When Ali's "famous, fatter, but still-handsome face" (as the *Weekly Mail* described it) came through the arrivals gates, the crowd roared and "pressed in, reaching out," trying to touch the man who was a legend in the land where Blackness had been demonized for centuries.

A stage had been set up and Ali shuffled to a chair. The man had become famous in the 1960s and 1970s not just for his prowess in the ring, but for his poetic, alliterative speeches outside of it. Yet on this day, that Ali was not present. When it came for his turn to speak, he did so in a "painfully slow, quiet whisper." He told the crowd about how he had longed to come to South Africa and his gratefulness at finally having made it. The "Louisville Lip," as he was called, had been diagnosed with Parkinson's disease in 1984 and his speech had slowed considerably. The crowd did not care—there was clapping and ululating at everything he said.

Then he flashed a smile.

"Let me take on one of your boxers now," he said.

A wildly popular young Soweto boxer, the lightweight Dingaan "Rose of Soweto" Thobela, jumped up to join the former heavyweight champion onstage. It was all show, of course. Ali sprang to his feet and "began pumping out his fists in fast combinations, grinning broadly in his enjoyment at his own joke. The punches all stopped just short of Dingaan's head. The lightweight fired back similarly, and Ali blocked in mid-air, sprightlier than any of us expected."

American boxing had given succor to Blacks during apartheid. Muhammad Ali was a hero: fast-talking, articulate, and unafraid to speak truth to power in the showreels that would play at cinemas before the feature film. His stand against going to fight in Vietnam was followed closely by Black magazines around the world. In October 1979, at the height of apartheid, a hint of his magic had come to visit South Africa. That month, World Boxing Association champion "Big" John Tate, an African American, had traveled to the country to fight an Afrikaner, Gerrie Coetzee, for the title vacated by Ali when he retired. It was a historic match—white and Black athletes were not allowed to compete against each other in SA except by special permission. For this match, however, the government even allowed Blacks into the "whites-only" Loftus Versfeld rugby stadium.

As with virtually everything in South Africa then, the showdown had racial overtones. Black South Africa was fully behind Tate while the 80,000 whites who packed the stadium were rooting for Coetzee. All three judges declared Tate the winner on points. Afterward, in the streets of Pretoria, whites attacked Blacks. In my village, we danced in the streets. We did not care that Tate—who had steadfastly refused to condemn apartheid—had broken the informal sports boycott that antiapartheid organizations had been campaigning for (and which was only adopted by the United Nations in 1985). He had spoken in the ring, where it mattered.

Now the real McCoy, Muhammad Ali, was in the country for the tour many had hoped for over the decades. But it was not to be the tour the world's great icon had anticipated. Never would he have thought when his plane touched down in Johannesburg that he would end up joining with protesters to pay tribute to a man whose commitment to equality and justice equaled—and perhaps outstripped—his own.

1 p.m.
Swaziland

General Bantu Holomisa was being feted like a king that Saturday, blissfully unaware that one of his closest friends had been murdered. He did not know that because of Hani's assassination he was now very much in the thoughts of both Nelson Mandela, who loved him, and F. W. de Klerk, who loathed him.

Holomisa was part of the despised "homeland system," designed by apartheid not just to keep the races apart but to keep various Black ethnic groups separate from each other. It had forcefully removed Blacks from areas designated white—selling the land at cheap prices or giving it for free to white farmers—to bleak, poverty-stricken parcels of land identified by the government as the supposed site of origin of various tribal or ethnic groups. The system had been developed in the 1950s and 1960s as the next step in the idea that every race and ethnic group in South Africa could have their own "homeland" where they could, the apartheid government claimed, thrive. This theoretically meant that Nelson Mandela, for example, being of Xhosa origin, could be forced to move out of Johannesburg, where he lived and practiced law, to live "among his own people" in the purportedly independent father country of Transkei.

The Transkei received its "independence" from South Africa in 1976. But it was a toy country. The state's entire budget was funded by the South African government. Nine more homelands were created on a similar basis: Bophuthatswana for the Tswana people, KwaZulu for Zulu people, Lebowa for the Pedi, KwaNdebele for the Northern Ndebele, Venda for Vendas, Gazankulu for the Shangaan and Tsonga people, Ciskei for another set of Xhosa-speaking people, and QwaQwa for the Basotho. More than three and a half million Black South Africans were forcibly removed from cities to the homelands between 1960 and 1990, and their land allocated to white South Africans.

When the Transkei was established, the homeland immediately formed its own army, which, like everything else, was trained, funded, and run by the apartheid state. Holomisa enlisted in 1976. Smart, savvy, a keen rugby player, and as the son of a chief, educated at elite schools, he was officer material. He quickly rose through the ranks to become a brigadier and then general. In 1987, he engineered a coup d'état, getting rid of the homeland's leaders after finding evidence of large-scale bribe-taking and other corruption. Holomisa was by his own admission a tin-pot dictator, but once in power he aligned himself with the ANC and other liberation organizations, stopping the persecution of their leaders. In 1989, Holomisa unbanned liberation organizations in Transkei. He held a massive welcome-home party for a group of ANC members released from jail in October of that year, with tens of thousands of people packing in the homeland's Independence Stadium in Umtata.

Holomisa became a favorite of Mandela's from their first meeting in 1990. "Madiba was like a father to me," Holomisa would later write. He said that Mandela, despite the two discussing important political matters such as De Klerk's policies toward Holomisa's Transkei or the safety of ANC leaders, still treated him the way a village elder treated a young boy. Mandela would summon Holomisa to come and see him: "I would obey."

In August of 1990, for instance, Mandela ordered Holomisa to fly to Johannesburg to meet with him. Chris Hani's indemnity against prosecution, which had allowed him and other members of the ANC to return to South Africa, had suddenly been revoked without explanation, leaving him at risk of arrest. "De Klerk wants to scupper the negotiations," Mandela told Holomisa. As Transkei was a nominally independent state, Holomisa proposed that Hani be taken there immediately. They snuck Hani out of South Africa that night. (Hani's indemnity was later restored after pressure from Mandela.)

At other times, Mandela would send Holomisa off to serve as his representative. That Easter weekend, he had needed an emissary to travel to the tiny neighboring kingdom of Swaziland, where he'd been invited to the wedding of a brother of King Mswati III. Mandela's daughter Zenani was married to another brother of the king, so he could not snub the royal family. As Mandela's representative—and being the son of a chief himself—Holomisa was ushered to the VIP platform and shown a reserved chair.

As Holomisa enjoyed the ceremony, thoughts of the homeland leader were gaining prominence in both Mandela's and De Klerk's minds. The reason for their concern was simple. The general had something that no other Black leader in South Africa who had been close to Hani had—a professional army with a proper armory, courtesy of the apartheid government. All the homelands were kitted with security establishments that mirrored the central apartheid state—an army, intelligence services, and a police force. The Bophuthatswana homeland even boasted an air force with one lone combat aircraft. The security arrangements served a double purpose. First, many of these homeland leaders served as agents of repression of their fellow Blacks, with draconian laws such as indefinite detention of political activists without trial. Secondly, the homelands were used as a propaganda tool to try and show the world that South African Blacks had "freedom and independence in their own countries." No country in the world recognized them, although the apartheid government established "embassies"—replete with diplomatic staff—in four of them. (Take note, dear reader: systems based on hate are hard work to maintain.)

Mere hours after Hani's assassination, threats of war and boasts of pending attacks were already being uttered by various groups. But although the Afrikaner Weerstandsbeweging (AWB) and the Azanian People's Liberation Army could plant bombs and cause some havoc, not many had the firepower to lead a substantial uprising. Only Holomisa—on the ANC-supporting side—had the capability to start and end true wars. Waluś and his coconspirators wanted people like Holomisa to act and trigger a response from hard-line generals in the state. And Holomisa had been a close confidant of Hani's. The two men had held an all-day meeting just two days before the assassination.

The general was the one person in the ANC—other than Hani—that Mandela went out of his way to keep close at hand. According to Barbara Masekela, Mandela's chief of staff, and the writer Stengel, Mandela would not make a move in the Transkei without inviting Holomisa along. Stengel recalled that Holomisa loved Mandela's attention, but Stengel saw it as a stratagem to keep the volatile young leader on their side. Their relationship was sincere, and was to endure and strengthen throughout Mandela's life, but Mandela also knew the devastation that an angry Holomisa could cause.

If Mandela was nervous, his worries were nothing next to De Klerk's. Holomisa had for years put the apartheid government in a quandary: If the Transkei was a puppet state, how could they allow the ANC to operate freely there? But if it was an independent country as they claimed, then how could they dictate to its leader? It was ironic: a product of apartheid, Holomisa and his Transkei could, by the early 1990s, potentially be a serious irritant or even a threat to the apartheid government.

De Klerk had long seen in Holomisa someone who could ignite a tinderbox. The two men had been having meetings since 1990, but there was no love lost between them. The last meeting had been just ten days before Hani's murder, when De Klerk had excoriated Holomisa for allegedly harboring members of the Azanian People's Liberation Army, which continued to attack white civilians. The meeting did not go well. De Klerk recalled telling Holomisa that he would hold the Transkei government responsible for any harm done to South African citizens or property.

But what might Holomisa do if harm was done to his friends?

1 p.m.
Steynsburg

F. W. de Klerk later told me that he knew that Hani's assassination "had the potential of igniting a major crisis in South Africa." There would be grave consequences for what had taken place that morning.

"We realized that it would be necessary to calm things down, that there was a great risk of things getting out of hand, causing severe protests, even riots, and had to decide how best to calm things down," De Klerk said in our interview in 2018.

At this point, De Klerk did not seem to realize that he was as much a target of the assassination as Hani was, that Waluś and his coconspirators were hoping that the riots De Klerk contemplated as a danger to the country could eventually be used to oust and replace him with a hard-line regime.

It was generally accepted that De Klerk's securocrats—with or without his knowledge or blessing—had been running an extensive disinformation campaign against Hani; it was no coincidence that the communist leader was constantly on the front pages of the conservative press internationally and locally, implicated in conspiracies he knew nothing about. Minister of Law and Order Hernus Kriel had in recent months circulated an eighteen-page disinformation document entitled "New political development—formation of South African People's Party (SAPP)," claiming that Hani and Winnie Mandela were preparing to establish a secret "Black People's Army" in Zimbabwe. Hard-liners in De Klerk's cabinet briefed opposition politicians in the Conservative Party about Hani's alleged shenanigans, and stories were leaked to international news outlets, notably the London *Sunday Times'* South Africa correspondent—without a shred of proof. The *New York Times* would call Hani one of De Klerk's "favorite bogies."

Yet this history was probably not the foremost issue on De Klerk's mind that Saturday afternoon as, lunch now abandoned, he made another call to his chief of staff, Dave Steward. One thing was clear to De Klerk: if he tried to put out this fire by himself it was likely only to blow up in his face.

On Steward's advice, he arranged for a statement to be issued in his name, expressing shock and conveying condolences to Hani's family. "[Hani] and I were at opposite poles of the political debate," the statement read. "But we were both prepared to resolve the problems of our country through the process of peaceful negotiations . . . He can no longer do so, but we who remain must rededicate ourselves to peaceful negotiations and to the creation of a society in which brutal acts such as this will no longer occur." That South Africa was obviously not yet such a society was the reason for his appeal for calm: De Klerk feared riots breaking out.

One of De Klerk's next calls was to his young minister of constitutional affairs and communications, Roelf Meyer, who was now leading the government's negotiations. Meyer had already spoken to former chief of intelligence Niël Barnard, one of the architects of the democracy talks through his secret meetings with Mandela in prison. Barnard was no longer in De Klerk's inner circle (their personalities clashed too much for that), but he was still the second most senior government negotiator after Meyer.

Barnard had told Meyer: "Tell De Klerk to speak to the 'old man.'" Only Mandela could calm the situation down.

Meyer passed this on to De Klerk, who'd already had the same conversation with Steward and others. He had to speak to Nelson Mandela.

It would not be an easy conversation. On many occasions Mandela had accused De Klerk of failing to act against members of his government who were fomenting violence; he was likely to hold the same view now. But what else could De Klerk do? He did not want the newly revived negotiations to come to an end again, as they had in June 1992 after the Boipatong Massacre. At that time De Klerk had tried to show his sympathy by visiting the bereaved at their homes. His visit was to be the first by a South African president to one of the country's many recent massacre sites. (There had been sixty-one incidents where at least thirteen unarmed, defenseless people had been killed by armed groups since 1990.)

De Klerk's heavily guarded motorcade had driven through the township, watched by angry crowds, until it came to a stop where the attacks had taken place. The posters carried by the protestors made clear their mood: "To hell with De Klerk—go away, go away!" or "Go away murderer!"

The crowd, perhaps some 3,000 strong, had surged. The security detail pushed back. De Klerk stared out of the back window of his silver-gray BMW, described as "stony-faced" by one journalist and "terrified" by another. He was there to give his condolences; he was supposed to step out, to address the mourning crowd. But some teenagers were clutching rocks in their hands.

After a tense fifteen minutes of confrontation between the crowd and the president's security team, De Klerk was forced to leave, the crowd chasing his convoy away. After his departure one person was shot dead by the police. Clashes between police and residents went on for days afterward.

The next day Mandela had visited the township, standing on the field where the police had fired on protestors. He was apoplectic. "I am convinced we are no longer dealing with human beings but animals," he said. "I have never seen such cruelty."

The relationship between the two men had deteriorated further as the ANC embarked on a campaign of rallies, marches, stayaways, and other forms of peaceful protest. In a letter soon after the massacre, Mandela accused De Klerk of relying on "white supremacist mechanisms" to provoke unrest in the townships. "The continuing direct and indirect involvement of the government, the state security forces and the police in the violence . . . has created an untenable and explosive situation," Mandela wrote.

The Boipatong Massacre forced the ANC to walk out of the negotiations, accusing De Klerk of doing nothing to stop the endemic political violence of the time. Now, just nine days after resumption of those talks after a nine-month hiatus, they were threatened again.

De Klerk was faced with a profound choice. He could step forward and do what he had attempted to do after Boipatong: speak to the mourners, give condolences, make it clear he mourned too . . . It would be as risky as it had been last time, and if he failed it could lead not just to a breakdown in talks but heighten the risks of racial conflagration.

No. He'd have to try another approach.

If there is one lesson we can take from De Klerk in the events of that week, it is this: he recognized that he had to step back and let Mandela lead.

And so De Klerk picked up the phone.

2 p.m.
Johannesburg and Cape Town

From being a pariah of the international community for decades, the South Africa of the early 1990s had attracted major attention from the rest of the world as political reforms ensued. South Africa's sometimes dizzying political developments—progress in the talks on some days followed by massacres or walkouts of the negotiating process the next—were reported in the world's media daily. Countries such as the newly minted Russia, reborn out of the collapse of the Union of Soviet Socialist Republics, had in the previous year opened up diplomatic missions in SA after decades without a presence in the country. The United Nations had, in 1992, set up an observer mission. The eyes of the world were on the SA transition, and on that Saturday news of the Hani assassination reminded many just how fragile that transition was.

Victor Zazeraj, director of the foreign affairs ministry in South Africa and himself a son of Polish immigrants, was one of the apartheid state's key diplomats. Zazeraj, who would later serve as democratic South Africa's ambassador to Poland and then Chile, was working in the ministry's parliamentary office on Plein Street, Cape Town, when his phone rang. It was the Polish ambassador, Stanisław Cieniuch, and he was distraught.

"His government was in a state of shock and had instructed him to contact the SA Government as a matter of urgency and convey their extreme outrage and sense of shame that a man of Polish origin was presumed to be the perpetrator" of the assassination, recalled Zazeraj.

The president of Poland at the time was Lech Wałęsa, a name well known in South Africa for having fought communism. Wałęsa was, however, a devout Catholic like Hani and wanted the South African government and the ANC to know that he condemned the murder.

Zazeraj called his boss, Pik Botha, the minister of foreign affairs, who was "stunned and dismayed," not just by the crime but because, as Zazeraj put it, there was "no Plan B" if the democracy talks halted yet again, perhaps for good this time. "The murder of Chris Hani was a potential nail-in-the-coffin for the democratic transition, and for the NP's negotiating position in the ongoing democracy talks," he explained.

In most of the international statements of grief, there were frantic and heartfelt calls for peace. The UN Security Council said the assassination underscored the need for the talks—which had gridlocked on what a transitional structure from apartheid should look like even before it had got to the brass tacks of writing a nonracial and democratic constitution—to continue. The council president, Jamsheed Marker, Pakistan's ambassador to the UN, said "negotiations leading to nonracial democracy must not be held hostage by the perpetrators of violence." The Russian foreign ministry concurred. The international observer missions of the UN, the Commonwealth, the European Community, and the Organisation of African Unity that had descended on South Africa to oversee the negotiations issued a joint statement expressing shock—and appealing for calm.

The appeals for peace came from within the country too. The Nobel laureate Archbishop Desmond Tutu would call Chris Hani's murder "the worst moment of my life." He was in no doubt that the assassination had been intended to tip the scales from peace to war. Hani "was a very positive influence on the young," Tutu would later say, a man who knew how to calm the anger and impatience that was growing after three years of peace talks, with little to show for the efforts. "Of all the ANC leaders, maybe all the political leaders we have, he had the credibility among the young to rein in the radicals. Clearly, someone wants to do all they can to sabotage the negotiations," he said.

What many feared but did not express was that the killing would lead to reprisals. Tutu was more explicit in his appeal for restraint that afternoon when called by journalists: "I want to make a call to our people. Please . . . Don't let them manipulate us. Don't let this tragic event trigger reprisals. It is what somebody wants to see happen."

Sexwale, in Johannesburg, was issuing calls for peace and calm as Tutu and Mandela would have wanted him to. Yet Mandela knew that Sexwale and other militant ANC leaders could go the other way. The antiapartheid movement had become a three-sided entity after the banning of the ANC and other organizations in 1960. Mandela and others were revered and respected in the thirty years since their arrest and incarceration in 1962 and 1964—but they were in prison, largely voiceless. The ANC as an organization was in exile, its guerrilla camps in various parts of Africa and its members scattered across the world. Within SA, various organizations aligned to it had taken root, led by trade union and civic leaders. Although Mandela and others were revered, it was still a loose formation rather than a united, well-oiled machine. Further, many youngsters in the townships were given "crash courses" in the use of guns and bombs by ANC commanders and formed into self-defense units or neighborhood militias. They were itching for action, leading to their hero Chris Hani saying just weeks before that the units were getting out of control and some were engaging in crime. He said this was endangering the peace process.

Their anger at his killing could derail the fragile path South Africa was on. On the streets, the violence that Waluś and his associates had hoped to unleash was beginning.

2 p.m.
Qunu and Steynsburg

In the end, it was not a long conversation. De Klerk's office gave him the number for Mandela's home in Qunu, and the local telephone exchange put him through.

De Klerk and Mandela's relationship had rarely been smooth. And yet back in February 1990, as he stood before thousands of people in Cape Town and gave his first speech as a free man after twenty-seven years, Mandela had described De Klerk as "a man I could do business with."

"From the first I noticed that De Klerk listened to what I had to say," he wrote after meeting De Klerk in late 1989. "This was a novel experience." His friend Archbishop Desmond Tutu also praised De Klerk and others like him for "acknowledge[ing] that they have been perpetrating a system of domination, racial domination."

Over the following three years, however, the admiration had cooled and the compliments dried up. Mandela was not a man given to bouts of public fury. He had, however, displayed rage in December 1991 when, at a public ceremony to signal the opening of the historic talks for a new South Africa, De Klerk launched a scathing attack on the ANC's refusal to hand in weapons stored in arms caches around the country. Mandela was particularly incensed as he had met with the president several times in the week before the ceremony and De Klerk had given no indication that he would raise the issue publicly. And as the two men had agreed that De Klerk would speak last, Mandela had kept his own speech perfectly civil. When De Klerk finished his speech, Mandela had stood up and demanded to answer De Klerk's attack. He had got on the podium and accused De Klerk of bad faith.

"Even the head of an illegitimate, discredited, minority regime as his has certain moral standards to uphold," Mandela charged, speaking off the cuff except for a few glances at notes he had made while De Klerk had attacked the ANC earlier. "No wonder the Conservative Party has made such a serious inroad into his power base . . . If a man can come to a conference of this nature and play the type of politics [he's played] . . . very few people would like to deal with such a man." No one had ever witnessed such a thing in South Africa: a Black leader standing up and upbraiding a white leader, on live television. De Klerk was shocked.

Mandela had, however, always held out an olive branch to De Klerk—and the man took it. After this moment of anger Mandela had the next day pointedly stood up and walked across the massive convention hall—there were more than three hundred delegates and observers in the room, all watching—to De Klerk and shook his hand. He had repeated the gesture the following day. After that, De Klerk thawed, although he said at the time that he felt that "there was no longer any possibility of our ever again having a close relationship."

After excoriating De Klerk following the Boipatong and Bisho massacres of 1992 and the walkout from the talks, Mandela had called De Klerk despite having called off formal negotiations. He was worried to find him "sounding so down" and tried to cheer him up by saying they would find a way through the impasse in the negotiations.

When the call was publicized, the national mood over the public spat changed "at a stroke from one of deep despondency to hopefulness." Yet despite these overtures, over the years there would be more public rows, angry calls, and walkouts. Mandela had come to regret the "man of integrity" line, admitting that "these words were flung at me many times when Mr. De Klerk seemed not to live up to them."

Whatever warmth there was between them had dissipated slowly in the grind of the interminable negotiation process. They understood, however, that they needed each other. Barbara Masekela, who had called Mandela in Qunu to tell him the news of Hani's assassination, told me that Mandela had one very clear objective throughout the period she worked with him between 1990 and 1994: to hold free elections and achieve freedom for South Africans. "Nothing would divert him from that goal. Even at the very worst times of his relationship with De Klerk, he held his own views back and never took it to the point where it would cause diversion to a settlement because that was the main thing."

Princeton Lyman, a career diplomat who served as US ambassador to South Africa in the early 1990s, remembered a dinner at the home of the liberal MP Helen Suzman, who had been for years the lone outspoken opponent of apartheid in the whites-only South African parliament. Asked what his view of De Klerk was as the negotiations continued, Mandela replied: "My worst nightmare is that I wake up one morning and he is not there." The fate of the country depended on the two of them finishing what they had started.

Now the two men were talking. In that conversation between the rolling grasslands of Mandela's Qunu village and De Klerk's arid Steynsburg it became clear that they were at one about what they faced: whoever was responsible for the assassination wanted to derail the negotiations.

According to De Klerk, both were "in shock." But there were no accusations, no recriminations. "The wonderful thing about my relationship with Mr. Mandela," De Klerk told me in 2018, "is that although we had these big tensions . . . when real crisis loomed, we both found ourselves able to rise above those tensions and to shake hands and to put our hands and heads together in order to find solutions." To De Klerk, it seemed the two men agreed that "the situation carried a serious threat of things getting out of hand."

"It was necessary to calm things down and to reassure people and to prevent activists from misusing this to disrupt the negotiation process," he said. "But more importantly, to prevent riots and situations where people's lives would be under threat, and where race relations should become extremely tense."

Despite their ability to transcend their differences, from De Klerk's description it is clear the pair did not see eye to eye on where danger emanated. Chris Hani lay dead, yet De Klerk's first thought was that people like Hani—activists—would "misuse" his death to disrupt the talks. Mandela, on the other hand, feared that the right wing wanted to push "the country to a racist war." For Mandela, the challenge was to frustrate this ambition. De Klerk saw the issue as one of law and order.

De Klerk recalled having discussed what steps to take next with his

aide Dave Steward. Roelf Meyer had also been in touch. They had ban-
died around the idea of De Klerk addressing the nation, but that was out of
the question because, according to De Klerk, "it would have been difficult
for me to get to a TV studio." De Klerk also knew that he had absolutely no
influence on the people who were most angry about the killing of Hani:
Black youth. "This was Mandela's moment, not mine," he later wrote.
"Only he would be able to calm his enraged followers. Any high-profile
appearance by me—no matter how well intentioned—would probably
have the opposite effect." So he asked if Mandela would go on television
to try to put out the fire that threatened to engulf them both.

In the aftermath of the crisis many were to write that this was the
moment that power shifted from De Klerk to Mandela. It was an "unprecedented move that underscored the government's eagerness to de-
fuse tensions from the killing," the *New York Times* wrote the next day.
Mandela, who had been banned from being quoted, photographed,
or having his image or likeness shown in any form in South Africa for
twenty-seven years, was now being asked by the president of the country
to take charge of a crisis in a role that was akin to what a leader of a free
country would do.

2 p.m.
Port St. Johns, Eastern Cape Province

The great South African writer Alan Paton opened his classic novel *Cry,
the Beloved Country* with a powerful, haunting description of South Africa's KwaZulu-Natal Midlands. "There is a lovely road that runs from Ixopo
into the hills," Paton wrote. "These hills are grass-covered and rolling, and
they are lovely beyond any singing of it. The road climbs seven miles into
them, to Carisbrooke; and from there, if there is no mist, you look down
on one of the fairest valleys of Africa."

Just south of the Midlands is another breathtaking piece of country:
the Wild Coast, a three-hundred-kilometer stretch of coastline between
the Great Kei River and the town of Port Edward on the country's eastern

seaboard. From its wild sea to the "soft hills" that rise into the interior, the Wild Coast is a rugged, beautiful untouched part of the world. It is notorious for its sudden waves, with hundreds of ships sinking along the coast over the centuries, gaining the region a reputation as South Africa's own Bermuda Triangle. Maps still warn of "possible 20m freak wave phenomena." The coast is home to hundreds of kilometers of empty beaches, huge swathes of untouched countryside, and spectacular cliffs that feed waterfalls directly into the ocean. It is dotted with small villages and towns with quaint names such as Hole-in-the-Wall and Coffee Bay.

It was a place that forty-four-year-old Alastair Weakley loved. He was visiting on Easter weekend 1993 with his brother Glen, four years older than him and working as an engineer in the resort city of Durban. Glen had two children, Trevor and Debbie, who had stayed home, but Weakley's partner, Chloë O'Keeffe, and her eleven-year-old son Thomas had come along on the holiday. Their friend Keith Rumble and his son, Brett, had come along too.

Weakley loved this land. When he was a young teacher in the 1970s, he had taken a group of his pupils on a ten-day field trip along the coast. They camped on the beach, hiked on the endless sand dunes, and visited the homesteads of the Xhosa people of the region, learning about local customs and practices from the villagers. "Ally brought it all to life, explaining the traditions to us with vivid words and images as we sat around a campsite fire on the beach," one of his former students remembered. "There was no facet of Xhosa life that did not fascinate Ally. He was so enthused that he carried us along with him by sheer force of character."

So that was the plan for the week of April 10: hikes, fishing, food, family, and laughter.

It is possible to be totally cut off from the world in the Wild Coast. Radios have poor or no signal and newspapers aren't delivered. The Weakley party was not even aware that Chris Hani had been assassinated. Had he known, Ally Weakley would have been devastated by the news. He participated in the local peace committee—largely interceding between different political groups and ensuring that volatile situations such as protest

marches did not descend into violence—in Grahamstown. There was another reason Weakley would have been devastated. He had grown up in
Cofimvaba, the same area as Chris Hani, where he had learned the Xhosa
language while Hani pursued Latin, two curious young men separated by
apartheid's bitter laws.

2 p.m.
Sabalele, Eastern Cape Province

How does one react to the slaying of one's son? There were two men that
Mandela treated as though they were his own flesh and blood: Bantu Holomisa and Chris Hani. And yet in his memoir Mandela simply writes,
blandly, that Hani's death "was a blow to me personally and to the movement." He must, surely, have been devastated. But he describes Hani
matter-of-factly as "a soldier and patriot for whom no task was too small."
Instead of personal testimony, Mandela puts the political first: "He was a
great hero among the youth of South Africa, a man who spoke their language and to whom they listened. If anyone could mobilize the unruly
youth behind a negotiated solution, it was Chris. South Africa was now
deprived of one of its greatest sons, a man who would have been invalu-
able in transforming the country into a new nation."

Still, those who knew Mandela remember his pain. "He was so sad,"
his personal assistant, Jessie Duarte, recalls when she saw him that evening. "He really loved Chris."

Nine days after the assassination, in his funeral oration, Mandela
would admit: "You lived in my home, and I loved you like the true son
you were." Using the plural but clearly referring to himself, he continued,
"In our heart, as in the heart of all our people, you are irreplaceable. We
have been struck a blow that wounds so deeply that the scars will remain
forever." Yet neither his tears nor his devastation were visible to even those
closest to him.

There are many descriptions of how Mandela took the news of the
slaying of his protégé and sometime irritant. His biographer Stengel says,

"In the days after the assassination there were press reports and stories cir-culated even within the ANC that Mandela had been 'broken up' and 'fran-tic' about Hani's death. In fact, he was icily calm and analytical, reckoning with plans for the immediate future and consequences of the murder. In the moments that I have been with Mandela in a crisis, he has always been intensely calm, entering a kind of Zen state that seems to slow down the events swirling around him." The fresh-faced ANC media manager Carl Niehaus, an Afrikaner recruited by Mandela into his office, described him to me as being "stoical." Another of his biographers, John Carlin, writes that the loss of Hani rivaled his divorce from Winnie, the woman he had loved for decades, for the heartache it caused him. And the *Sunday Star* described him as "emotional" later on in the evening, reporting that he wiped a "tear from his eye."

What are we to make of all this? Tokyo Sexwale, the first of the party leaders to arrive at Hani's house with Gungubele, had seen Mandela emo-tional in ANC meetings. But these were rare public displays of emotion. In Sexwale's view, Mandela found himself "trapped from time to time in the emotions of being . . . the head of the organization, head of the people—the best statesman in the world." During a crisis, a statesman has little time to grieve.

ANC leaders were congregating at the Hani home, while others like Pallo Jordan and Gill Marcus had returned to the ANC head office in cen-tral Johannesburg preparing the speech Mandela would deliver to the na-tion that evening. The calming messages from the ANC were not being heeded; Mandela knew this. He described the state of the country as "frag-ile." He later wrote that he was fielding concerns and opinions that "Hani's death might trigger a racial war, with the youth deciding that their hero would become a martyr for whom they would lay down their own lives."

"We could have ignited dynamite on that day," Sexwale told me, sketching a scenario where people like him and others chose vengeance instead of negotiation. "By the time Nelson Mandela arrived from the Transkei, there would have been an armed fight. Yes, we were command-ers of the army at the time. Yes, people would have followed us . . ."

By Sexwale's reckoning, Mandela's leadership was absent on the day of Hani's assassination. There was a power vacuum that he, and others, could have filled in a negative manner: "We could have caused hell for him [Mandela]. He might have arrived and found the country burning."

Was Mandela so overcome by grief that he gave himself over to it? Or did he trust that the younger ANC leaders would choose to wait for him, filling the void with calls for calm?

Instead of immediately flying back to Johannesburg after his conversation with De Klerk, Mandela arranged for a helicopter to fly him to Chris Hani's village of Sabalele, a thirty-minute ride away in the district of Cofimvaba. Mandela knew the place well, as it was the home region of his relatives, the Matanzima family. The Matanzimas and Mandela came from the same royal family, although the Matanzimas were later to align themselves with the apartheid government and become the founding powerhouse of the Transkei homeland system. Did Mandela decide to fly to Hani's home because of his grief, or was this a sign of an indecisive politician who didn't know what else to do?

Cofimvaba was a harsh place, as Mandela knew: lack of running water and electricity, poor housing, and general poverty. He marveled at how such a poor place had produced a man like Hani and understood that Hani's concern for the poor and his passion for justice were rooted in his childhood there.

By the time Mandela arrived in Sabalele the news had already reached the village. Hani's older brother Victor had hurried to his parents' house as soon as he heard from friends at around midday. Nomayise and Gilbert, Hani's parents, were devastated, with Gilbert contorted by grief. Both had feared for their son's safety since his return from exile. Gilbert had wanted him to come back to the rural Eastern Cape or, if he had to live in Johannesburg, to at least live in a "Black area." He never liked Dawn Park. Whenever Hani visited, Gilbert—himself an activist who had in the 1960s been banished from his work in Cape Town and sent back to the poverty of Sabalele for five years because of his opposition to the homeland system—would raise the subject.

In his telling of that afternoon, Mandela said Gilbert spoke eloquently of the pain of losing a son, yet with satisfaction that Hani had died in the struggle for liberation. As Hani had been an ANC leader, the party would take charge of his funeral. They discussed arrangements to get the Hani family to Johannesburg and for a bus to ferry other bereaved villagers to the funeral.

And yet after this visit Mandela still did not rush to Johannesburg. Led by Gill Marcus, the preparations for him to appear on television that evening were underway. But instead Mandela flew to Umtata Airport in Transkei, where he sat in the VIP lounge and waited.

In Johannesburg, the clock was ticking toward the prime-time 7 p.m. news bulletin on the CCV-TV channel and the 8 p.m. news on TV1. The ANC leadership was waiting for Mandela, and Mandela was waiting for the other man who was often referred to as his son: Bantu Holomisa.

3 p.m.
Johannesburg

Only hours after the assassination, four white men in a white pickup truck cruised past the SACP headquarters chanting, "Up with the AWB!" The Afrikaner Weerstandsbeweging, or Afrikaner Resistance Movement (AWB), was the whites-only organization led by a former policeman, Eugène Terre'Blanche, whose fiery rhetoric had made him a central figure in ultraconservative politics. The organization routinely beat up Blacks it encountered in the streets, referred to Blacks using the SA equivalent of America's N-word, and was distinguished by the proud display of its Nazi-style swastika symbols and khaki quasi-military gear.

In Khayelitsha township just outside Cape Town, at least one house and a car were set alight. Rioting broke out in Crossroads, one of the fastest-growing shack settlements in the city, and more than a hundred protesters marched through the streets, carrying SA Communist Party and ANC symbols. They gathered outside President De Klerk's official residence (one of two, the other being in Pretoria due to the fact that SA has two capitals), singing freedom songs and holding up slogans. "Nine Thousand Killed Under FW's Rule" said one. Another said: "Interim Government Now!"

There was also violence in the Eastern Cape. In industrial Port Elizabeth, two cars allegedly belonging to white businesses were set on fire. In Elliot (now Khowa in the Chris Hani District Municipality), young people carrying SACP banners marched through the town until they were dispersed by the police. On the east coast of South Africa, in the resort city of Durban, students protesting Hani's murder clashed with holidaymakers.

5–6 p.m.
Umtata, Transkei

It was evening when Holomisa's plane from Mbabane, the capital of Swaziland, landed. He was not expecting to see "the old man," as he affectionately referred to the ANC leader. He assumed Mandela would be home in Qunu. As his plane landed, Holomisa noticed that a jet was parked on the apron, ready to take off. This was unusual. Umtata's was a small airport. There were two flights a day to Johannesburg, and the second flight would have left already.

When he saw Mandela, seated in the lounge, Holomisa knew immediately that something was wrong. The leader gestured to him to sit down. Holomisa was used to smiles and jokes whenever he met Mandela. Not on this day. Mandela was somber, "almost in tears."

"He sat there with a still face, his eyes fixed on one place for a few seconds before he spoke . . . When he opened his mouth, he spoke with a lump in his throat, his voice unusually hoarse, as he broke the news to me that Chris Hani had been assassinated," recounted Holomisa later. This doesn't tally with the idea of a Mandela who was cold and calm and clinical, ready to do what's necessary. The man described by Holomisa was stricken with grief. Despite this, it appears that he was carrying out the beginnings of his plan.

Holomisa believes that Mandela waited for him because, knowing how close he was to Hani, he wanted to deliver the bad news in person.

"It was a sign of his respect, though I felt it was not necessary," Holomisa would say later, "but that was just like Mandela." It is also true that if there was a man he had to keep by his side on this day of utmost provocation, it was Holomisa. Many, like Sexwale, could speak of igniting "dynamite on that day," but only Holomisa had the standing troops and the weapons to do so in a meaningful way.

Mandela asked Holomisa to accompany him to Johannesburg. He did not give him a chance to say no, or to go home, shower, or even grab a change of clothes. They proceeded to the waiting jet and headed for Johannesburg and the ANC leaders waiting impatiently for him to address a nation on the edge.

In Dawn Park, the young ANC spokesman and speechwriter Saki Macozoma harbored another fear: With nightfall looming, what would happen? What if another leader were assassinated?

5 p.m.
Pretoria

When Janusz Waluś had left at 7 a.m., he had told Maria Ras he would be back around 11 a.m. As 11 a.m. came and went, he did not return, nor did he call. She waited, unworried.

The two had been together for ten years. She knew the story of the man she and her friends called by his nickname, Kuba. As a boy back in Poland he had consumed the Voice of America radio station voraciously and clandestinely, developing his deep hatred of the communism that held sway in his homeland under the Polish United Workers' Party, the Polish communist party, from 1948 through to 1990. He had told her about his uncle, the same man who had taught him how to shoot, a survivor of Buchenwald concentration camp during World War II. He told her he had asked his uncle what was worse, communism or fascism. His uncle had replied: "Communism."

In South Africa he had found a home in right-wing politics, becoming a member of the Conservative Party, the Afrikaner Weerstandsbeweging, the international far-right group World Apartheid Movement, and

Derby-Lewis's Stallard Foundation, launched to lure South African English speakers into far-right politics. The couple frequented barbecues at the homes of politicians such as Clive and Gaye Derby-Lewis. Ras was smitten with him and was to later say that she considered Waluś sensitive, cultured, nonviolent, and religious.

That day, though, he did not return at the time he had specified. She waited.

At around 2 p.m. the phone rang. It was Clive Derby-Lewis. He asked where Kuba was and she said she expected him home soon. Did he have a message for him?

"Tell him to call me the moment he arrives," Derby-Lewis answered.

By this time the airwaves were dominated by news of Hani's killing and the arrest of a suspect. Spontaneous protests were erupting across the country. Ras, in her own telling, knew nothing of this. She was becoming worried and so decided to call a few hospitals and the police and ask if there had been an accident involving a blond, blue-eyed white man.

Toward 3 p.m. the phone rang again. It was Derby-Lewis.

"I am afraid something has happened to him," she told him.

He told her not to worry. He said he was calling to invite Ras and Waluś to a barbecue at his house the next day.

Frustrated, Ras decided to leave the apartment and go visit some friends.

When she came back in the late afternoon there were police cars outside the building. She walked in and saw the apartment cordoned off. A full-scale search was on.

The police took her aside and began interrogating her about Waluś, asking her about the murder of Chris Hani.

6 p.m.
Pretoria

An hour after Waluś's arrest, police sergeant Mike Holmes had arrived at Boksburg Police Station, hustled him into a police car, and drove him for half an hour to the police station at the nearby city of Benoni. He took him straight to his office and threw him in a chair. He told Waluś to tell him "everything."

"If you don't talk you will make big trouble for yourself, your family, and your friends," he said. "Talk."

Waluś said nothing.

Holmes tried again and again.

"Speak to me!" he shouted.

But Waluś kept quiet.

Someone came in with some information for Holmes.

Waluś was handcuffed and thrown in another car, and a convoy of wailing police cars took off for Pretoria, heading toward Waluś's apartment in the shadow of the Union Buildings.

The apartment search had yielded far more than the police team had expected. In the top drawer of a desk they found a typewritten three-page document that contained nine names. At the top was Nelson Mandela, followed by Joe Slovo. The list continued with Chris Hani's name, followed by that of Mac Maharaj, the former Robben Islander, Mandela confidant, and one of the ANC's top negotiators at the democracy talks. These names were followed by Afrikaans investigative journalist Karin Brynard; Foreign Minister Pik Botha; a judge who was leading investigations into political violence, Richard Goldstone; the editor of the *Sunday Times*, Ken Owen; and liberal Afrikaans journalist Tim du Plessis. Except for Joe Slovo, under each name there appeared the address of the person listed. The whole of the first page was devoted to Nelson Mandela. Below his address were lines of notes that read:

NOTE: THE HOUSE, SITUATED IN OAK LINED ROAD, IS
DELIBERATELY NOT NUMBERED, BUT IS EASILY RECOGNISABLE
BY THE WROUGHT IRON BLACK FENCE WHICH HAS HAD
BLACK METAL SHEETING PLACED BEHIND IT TO LIMIT THE
VIEW FROM THE ROAD.

IT HAS HIGH TECH ELECTRONIC SURVEILLANCE SYSTEMS
THROUGHOUT, INCLUDING A TELEVISION CAMERA
17 MOUNTED AT THE GATE BEHIND A GLASS PANEL THE
GATES ARE ELECTRONICALLY CONTROLLED.

The lower half of the first page contained a color photograph of a two-story house under a red-tiled roof. The document contained handwritten additions in ink, with numerals added to each name. Mandela, Slovo, and Chris Hani were numbered 1, 2, and 3. Next to the name and address of Hani had been added the make and registration numbers of a friend's car the political leader had used several times: "BMW 525i, PWY 525T."

After the police search, Holmes and his sidekick, Detective Sergeant Anton Grimbeek, got back in the car with Waluś and headed back to the police station in Benoni. It was nearly three in the morning.

Waluś smiled at Holmes. "Mike, I think something made you happy," he said. "You found something."

It was as if Waluś had planted the evidence there himself.

7 p.m.
Port St. Johns, Eastern Cape Province

ANC Youth League member Phumelele Civilian Hermans had been an activist since the mid-1980s, when he was in his teens. When the ANC was unbanned in 1990 he was one of the first in Port St. Johns to sign up and receive the black, green, and gold card that set him back R 12 (about US$4 in today's money) to be declared a fully paid-up member of the organization. In 1992, he had joined the local self-defense unit (SDU). These units—which had grown out of the paramilitary groups that were part of the ANC's attempts in the 1980s to render Black areas ungovernable for the apartheid government—evolved, in the early 1990s, into groups to defend communities against state-orchestrated violence such as the massacres that racked the townships around Dawn Park. Just a week before, Hani said some SDU members had gone out of control and were committing crimes in the name of the antiapartheid struggle.

Hermans was with his comrade Fundisile Guleni, the twenty-three-year-old secretary of the ANC in the small town of Port St. Johns on the Eastern Cape coast, 860 kilometers from where Hani was murdered, when they first heard the news. They didn't believe their hero could be dead.

Hermans was unemployed, spending his time at the ANC office, doing whatever work needed to be done for the party's youth wing, of which he was secretary. He had spent his childhood in the small rural community of Mpande, forty kilometers south of town, where his uncle had a trading store. The beautiful Mpande, with its thick green forests and massive empty beaches, remains to this day a magnet for a particular type of holidaymaker—those who want to commune with nature and do not seek the expensive resort life. It attracts backpackers who rent its cheap cottages, bring their own food, fish, and swim.

Despite its beauty, lack of jobs and opportunity in the area had forced Hermans's family to seek a better life in the urban Port St. Johns, where he now lived, but it was a small town and Hermans had, like so many others, ended up being part of the country's 29.8 percent unemployed.

Port St. Johns was a study in racial segregation. The picturesque town center was reserved for whites, while Blacks lived in the impoverished Mthumbane township just two kilometers away on the road to Second Beach, the most beautiful of the numerous picturesque beaches around the Umzimvubu River mouth. Mthumbane was a labor reserve. In the mornings, workers threaded the two-kilometer distance on Mthumbane Road to the bed-and-breakfast hotel and backpacker establishments that formed the backbone of Port St. Johns's economy. The combined population at the time was about 6,000 people, mainly Black and living in Mthumbane. While Mthumbane township was made up of cramped mud huts and an impoverished populace, the town of Port St. Johns looked more like a small, quaint British colonial town. Because of its beautiful beaches and spectacular waves, it attracted various kinds of tourists: hippies, eccentrics, and backpackers. Although the Port St. Johns of today is dilapidated and the municipal authority is perpetually facing criticism of neglect, the beauty of the region remains and the areas outside the town center still remind one why it's known as the Jewel of the Wild Coast.

Like so many other young men and women in transitioning South Africa, Hermans was waiting for freedom, waiting for the negotiations to conclude, waiting for his life to get better and for the grinding poverty of his area—the Eastern Cape was South Africa's poorest region—to be tackled by a government that cared for him and his people.

After a day of shock, confusion, and anger in which they had milled about listlessly with other comrades, at 7 p.m. Hermans and Guleni sat down to watch the main news bulletin on television. The assassination and its aftermath dominated the coverage. Hermans and Guleni were angry as they watched the bulletin. Although the SA Broadcasting Corporation (SABC) was changing from being a National Party propaganda tool and covered the assassination in largely objective terms, political activists at all levels were in no doubt about the genesis of the political violence that had gripped the country since 1990 or the assassinations of ANC leaders since the 1970s.

"People are dying and the government is involved," Hermans was to explain later. The whites were hiding the truth, he believed.

Their anger and impatience were exactly what those who had assassinated Hani were hoping to trigger. These were the young people that Mondli Gungubele, the Hani protégé in Dawn Park, dealt with almost every day: angry at the system, suspicious of the government they considered to be responsible for ongoing political killings, and incensed that their comrades and heroes were dying daily in senseless violence. They were the tinder that Waluś wanted to set on fire.

Yet on hearing the news, the two young men did not know what to do. They did not have any way to express their frustration. They felt impotent.

For now.

7 p.m.
Umtata, Transkei

As the jet pierced the night sky and headed toward Johannesburg, Mandela reflected on the democracy negotiations that were now imperiled by the callous killing of Chris Hani. The negotiations had started publicly in 1990 with the release of Mandela and others from prison and the return of the ANC and other liberation organizations to the country from exile, but the actual, delicate moves to end apartheid had been going on for more than a decade. An assassin's cruel bullet could bring all that work crashing down.

It had been a long and hard journey. The previous year, 1992, had been particularly disheartening for Mandela. When he was released in February 1990, things had moved quickly as the ANC's identified obstacles to full constitutional negotiations—unbanning of all political parties, return of exiles, ending of the four-year-old state of emergency—were removed. After two years of direct talks between the ANC and the government, in December 1991, the first session of the multiparty forum called the Convention for a Democratic South Africa convened near Johannesburg, signaling that things would move at an even more rapid pace. But they had dragged. There were actions Mandela considered reversals: in early 1992, De Klerk, worried that he needed to show that he had a strong mandate for reform, called for a referendum for white people only to vote for or against continuing negotiations. Thankfully, De Klerk won, with 68 percent of the white electorate voting "Yes" for him to push ahead with the reform process.

Then that May, talks had broken down over disagreements on majority rule and power sharing. De Klerk demanded a veto power for the National Party in an interim government that would oversee the writing of a constitution. Mandela refused. The talks ended in deadlock. The ANC and its allies launched a program of rolling mass action: marches, sit-ins, stay away from work campaigns . . .

When the Boipatong Massacre occurred the following month, the ANC accused De Klerk of doing little or nothing to end violence while wanting to hold on to a veto right over a future interim government. The

ANC suspended all talks, including those aimed at repairing the breach in trust.

It had taken nine months of secret talks between the ANC's chief negotiator, Cyril Ramaphosa, and the National Party's Roelf Meyer, meeting in hotel rooms, to iron out a way to discuss the differences over a veto power and the rifts of the Boipatong Massacre. Just ten days before Hani's assassination, on April Fool's Day, they had congratulated themselves on managing to bring together almost all political players in the country back to the negotiations room. The ANC and the NP had convinced twenty-six parties to join what they agreed to call the Multi-Party Negotiating Forum. For the first time the radical Black nationalist Pan Africanist Congress, the Conservative Party, and the "Afrikaners must get their own homeland" Volksunie sat together at the negotiations table. Only the African nationalist, far-left Azanian People's Organisation and several extreme-right Afrikaner parties refused to join.

Now this. From the Hani home, where he was still grieving with other comrades, Mondli Gungubele felt down, bleak about the future. Peter Harris said he was petrified that the youth of the country, who idolized Hani, "will rebel and attack the cities, stripping them like locusts, angered at the murder of one of their most charismatic leaders." All these men held the same view—Hani's murder was the ultimate provocation of a constituency that had suffered unprecedented violence since negotiations began. Mandela believed this was the moment when SA was "closest to a race war of Black against white on a scale never seen before." In Steynsburg, F. W. de Klerk had come to the same conclusion. Everything they had worked toward since 1985 could blow up from the anger triggered by Hani's murder.

8 p.m.
Johannesburg

Ask most political leaders in South Africa when the Hani crisis came to an end and they will point you to the evening of the assassination when, they claim, Nelson Mandela gave one of the most significant speeches of his life, bringing angry young Black militants and fearful whites together while isolating the far right who wanted to stoke war.

In his memoir De Klerk writes: "Mandela rose to the occasion in a statesman-like manner. That evening—in a broadcast that was repeated three times—he said . . ." before going on to quote a speech that Mandela did not give that evening.

In *Long Walk to Freedom*, Mandela says he was "asked to speak on the SABC that night to address the nation" and that "with all the authority at my command," he appealed for peace. He, too, goes on to quote the same speech referred to by De Klerk—but that was not the address that he delivered that night. Richard Stengel, David O'Sullivan (the journalist who read out the first bulletin that alerted the world to Hani's murder), even Hani's biographers—all praise the speech Mandela supposedly gave mere hours after the assassination. Even I and many of my colleagues who have written about South African politics have, for a long time, held the memory of Mandela giving a majestic speech that evening.

But it's odd how our memories work, confusing the details of even those events we thought would be seared in our minds forever. Because there was no such speech on the evening of April 10, 1993.

9 p.m.
Johannesburg

After landing in Johannesburg, Mandela and Holomisa made their way to an airport lounge where a large ANC delegation was waiting. Four people were ready to give Mandela a briefing: Cyril Ramaphosa, the young, bright party secretary-general who was also the lead negotiator in the democracy talks; Gill Marcus; Pallo Jordan; and Joe Slovo. Other leaders waited outside the lounge while Mandela was briefed on the day's events.

Arrangements had already been made, after talks between the government's chief negotiator, Roelf Meyer, and Ramaphosa alongside Gill Marcus, for the special broadcast at the SABC. However, having insisted on waiting for Holomisa, by the time they landed at Jan Smuts Airport it was already past the main "Black" news bulletin at 7 p.m. and the main English news bulletin's 8 p.m. broadcast. Television was introduced to South Africa late—in 1976—after vociferous opposition from the government for decades. The minister for posts and telegraphs at the time, Dr. Albert Hertzog, said television would come to South Africa "over my dead body." He charged that "South Africa would have to import films showing race mixing; and advertising would make Africans dissatisfied with their lot."

TV1, introduced in 1976, was for white audiences, broadcasting in Afrikaans and English. In 1981, a "Black channel" was introduced with Black American sitcoms such as *Sanford and Son* dubbed into local languages. By 1993, TV1 remained TV1, still broadcasting in English and Afrikaans, while CCV (Current Community Values) served a Black audience, although the rebranding did not want to say so.

Mandela had missed the biggest audiences of the day. The killing of Chris Hani, it turns out, attracted a bigger television audience for the 8 p.m. news than anything the SABC had yet shown—bigger even than the release of Nelson Mandela on February 11, 1990. We can only take the temperature of the nation by the 8:00 p.m. bulletin because even by 1993, the SABC still did not measure Black Audience Ratings—only whites, coloreds, and Indians—as the advertising industry considered Blacks not to have an "addressable income." Still, the Audience Ratings for the 8 p.m. English bulletin on the day Hani was assassinated were described as "eye-watering" by a veteran SABC audience analyst.

An AR is a time-weighted average—it counts the people as well as the time (every second) they contribute to that quarter hour. On that evening the ARs were forty-five. This means that the equivalent of 45 percent of the adult television universe (4.5 million in the case of 1993 South Africa) watched every second of the first fifteen minutes at the top of the hour without a break. That is unlikely, meaning that it took many more than these 2 million people to make up forty-five AR.

"Apparently the only other show ever to produce these kinds of ratings was the 1970s American TV series *M*A*S*H*," the analyst told me. In simple terms, the entire nation had been glued to the television at 8 p.m., wanting to know about Hani—and waiting for Mandela's reassuring words. At 8 p.m., Mandela was still flying from Umtata.

Marcus and Jordan decided to take Mandela straight to the SA Broadcasting Corporation's studios in Auckland Park. Mandela had not seen or read the statement that had been prepared for him. Ordinarily, Mandela was a dream to work with on speeches, speechwriter Saki Macozoma recalls. Once the key messages had been discussed, one could almost leave Mandela alone to extemporize. Not so with this speech. He may have tried to read the statement in the car, but he did not have much time to practice on the forty-minute journey to the SABC studios.

On arrival in the studio the speech was put on autocue, but it was difficult for Mandela to read it smoothly, as he suffered from several eye conditions. He had cataracts in his left eye. Even worse for his reading, he could literally not shed tears—leading to irritated, scratchy, and burning eyes—because of damage to his tear glands caused while breaking rocks on Robben Island during his eighteen years in the penal colony. The island was battered by intense, incessant winds that filled prisoners' eyes with grit, while tear glands were burned out by the alkaline nature of the limestone.

He also could not see well enough at the distance from the autocue. Mandela used spectacles when he read, but in most public engagements he preferred not to use them. This time, however, as Pallo Jordan put it to me years later, Mandela had to wear "his glasses because he literally had to read, rather than speak, the statement." But the autocue was still too far away.

It wasn't just the studio setup that was wrong on that evening. Mandela's suit was a light, bright tan—almost a festive yellow. Mandela, as the *Financial Times* pointed out, was a man who "took clothes—and their power—seriously." As a young lawyer in the 1950s he had worn the finest suits, going out of his way to frequent the same tailor that was used by Harry Oppenheimer, the country's richest man. George Bizos, his longtime friend and personal lawyer, first met Mandela in the 1950s in a tailor shop, where Mandela was being fitted for a suit. According to Bizos, "I had never seen a Black man in there before, much less being fitted for a suit."

With his tall, athletic frame, Mandela was a handsome man who enjoyed dressing properly and appropriately for whatever occasion he was attending. "He's a vain man. He knows he's a handsome man. He knows the image that he cuts. He likes fine things. He's incredibly neat about his things, and cares for them. That was the dandy side of him," said Stengel.

This time, however, Mandela was in the only suit he had taken to Qunu that weekend, a suit that looked slightly too big for him. For a man who enjoyed ceremony and had a sense of occasion, it was not the somber, dark color Mandela would have ordinarily chosen. He did not look like he was mourning a man he regarded as a son.

By the time Mandela was ready to go on the air it was just after 10 p.m. In a halting voice, stopping often, and moving slightly forward as if to get a better look at the script, Mandela started with a cough. His voice was hoarse. It was clear he was reading. There had not been enough practice, or any revision, of this speech.

The speech Mandela read out was unadorned. It was a cold statement, almost without the most important aspect of great speeches: nothing that touched the heart, the emotions. The words themselves were delivered in a flat monotone.

Mandela's eyes looked straight into the camera as he read, but his glasses gave off a glint. His eyes moved with the autocue. It was as if he were looking through the camera, not at the audience. It didn't feel at all like the Mandela whose humanity one could usually feel through distance and time. His posture was stiff. Not once did he move his hands or his body.

There were no greetings. He simply started with the first paragraph: "Today, an unforgivable crime has been committed. The calculated, cold-blooded murder of Chris Hani is not just a crime against a dearly beloved son of our soil. It is a crime against all the people of our country. A man of passion, of unsurpassed courage has been cut down in the prime of his life."

From this introduction Mandela went on to herald Hani, saying he had spent his life "fighting for freedom, democracy and justice" and situating him as someone whose love for freedom "persuaded him, at an early age, to commit himself fully to the African National Congress and the South African Communist Party." He said that Hani's "death demands that we pursue the cause [of liberty] with even greater determination." But Mandela had still not gotten to the point.

He pointed a finger at the killers but did not endeavor to name them or isolate them, a curious omission because by that time the country knew that a white right-winger had been arrested. The story of the arrest had been on the news in the afternoon, and the Sunday newspapers, whose early editions were usually on the streets of Johannesburg by 10 p.m. the previous evening, had even identified the woman who saw him kill Hani and called the police. It could be that at this time the ANC was not convinced there was no larger conspiracy that had murdered Hani. Whatever the reason, Mandela's speech continued on in a generalized, rather than specific, accusatory tone: "We are a nation deeply wounded by callous, uncaring men who plot such heinous crimes with impunity. The cries of our nation are heard from old men who bury their sons and daughters, wives who weep for their husbands, communities who endlessly bury young and old, infants and pregnant women. This killing must stop."

It was at this point, toward the end of his speech, that Mandela at last called for calm. It was a powerful summation: "We are a nation in mourning. Our pain and anger is real. Yet we must not permit ourselves to be provoked by those who seek to deny us the very freedom Chris Hani gave his life for . . . Let us respond with dignity and in a disciplined fashion."

He promised that Hani would be buried in "a manner befitting a hero of our people."

"No one will desecrate his memory by rash and irresponsible actions," he vowed.

The statement was just under six minutes long. When he came to the end, Mandela seemed exhausted. He looked down, away from the autocue and the camera, to the right. There was a glint in his right eye—could a tear have been wrung out of the eyes that doctors said couldn't be shed?

The *Sunday Star*, which described Mandela as "looking drawn," reported that at the end of the live broadcast, he "pause[d] to wipe a tear from his eye."

Mandela walked out of the studio, seeming relieved, toward his colleagues. There was a tender, telling moment.

"It was fine," said Gill Marcus, touching Mandela's arm.

Mandela's entourage left the ugly monolithic building of the SA Broadcasting Corporation, hoping the message had been heard and that it would be heeded. For some of Mandela's aides, such as the young speechwriter Saki Macozoma, holding the press line at the Hani home that night, the hope was that nothing would happen overnight to exacerbate the crisis.

Yet it was not just the night that held danger. It was the next eight days.

In the public eye, Mandela is the great man who stood up against apartheid and won. He is superman, he is indestructible, he survived twenty-seven years in a penal colony. He is fearless.

Few want to believe that Mandela also suffered, also faltered, also despaired. Just because Mandela was so brave in so many instances doesn't mean he never felt terrified. He did. But he taught himself to control these fears, to present a picture of equanimity and stoicism even though inside he was in turmoil.

In 1992, Mandela took a small plane to speak at a rally in a violence-torn area of KwaZulu-Natal, where ANC and Inkatha members were involved in a near all-out war. Twenty minutes from landing, one of the propellers stopped working.

Mandela noticed. He asked his bodyguard to alert the pilot.

The pilot knew. The bodyguard told Mandela that the pilot had called ahead to ensure there were ambulances and fire engines ready when they landed.

"Mandela just nodded," the bodyguard later told Stengel, who was waiting for Mandela at the small airport. "And went back to reading his newspaper."

The bodyguard revealed to Stengel that he was never as frightened at any time in his entire life as he was on that plane. The only thing that would calm him, he said, was looking at Mandela, who was "calmly reading the newspaper like he was on the commuter train into Grand Central."

When the small plane landed, Mandela shook hands with the many people waiting for him, calm as a snowball, and then he went to join Stengel.

"How was the flight?" Stengel asked.

"Man, I was terrified up there," Mandela replied.

As Stengel was to put it, Mandela illustrated that courage is not the absence of fear. Mandela often said that on Robben Island when he was terribly sad or frightened, he had to pretend to be strong and stoic and bold. "I had to put up a front," he said.

Why? Because he knew that other people were looking to him for inspiration.

When Hani was assassinated, though, Mandela found himself challenged. His actions that first day tell us he was in deep mourning. It seems to me that he tried to go deep into the stoicism that he had often displayed, but he could not always sustain the front he tried so desperately to put up. He was deeply hurt—and it showed in some of his actions that day. Despite his external, "icy" calm when he received news of Hani's murder, he had chosen to tarry in Qunu and then visit the Hani family home in Sabalele.

Mandela knew what it was like to lose a son. In 1969, in his seventh year in prison, he received a telegram informing him that his eldest son, Thembi, had died in a car accident. He had gone to his cell and lay down for a long time until his friend Walter Sisulu came in, knelt by his bedside, and held his hand silently. Thembi's death, he said, "left a hole in my heart that can never be filled."

Mandela had waited for his "other" son, Holomisa, in Umtata for hours, thus missing a key opportunity to address the nation at prime time.

To see these as failings rather than as the signs of a grieving human being and a vulnerable leader is to miss the point. Mandela, despite the pedestal we have put him on, was human—and was a grieving leader that day. It is perhaps such *ubuntu* (a South African word meaning humanity) that made him special as a leader. But had Mandela, in his moment of grief and pain, done enough to avert disaster—or were things about to get worse?

EASTER SUNDAY

April 11, 1993

Danger knows full well
That Caesar is more dangerous than he:
We are two lions litter'd in one day,
And I the elder and more terrible:
And Caesar shall go forth.
    Julius Caesar, Act 2, Scene 2

5:30 a.m.
Benoni Police Station

Back in his prison cell, Waluś was woken up at 5:30 a.m. and taken to an office where three plainclothes policemen started questioning him. It was still dark outside.

"I won't give any answers without my lawyer and without legal advice," Waluś said.

But under the Internal Security Act, he could be held for up to twelve months in preventive detention without access to a lawyer—ironically one of the many laws Hani was fighting to eradicate. There was also an option for police to hold a suspect in "indefinite interrogatory detention." According to the Human Rights Committee, some 80,000 antiapartheid South Africans had been held under these laws since 1963.

After a few hours the men gave up and took him back to his cell. At 10 a.m., Mike Holmes, the lead detective who had interrogated him the previous day, signed him out of his cell and took him out to a squad car.

"We are going to Dawn Park," Holmes told Waluś. He drove him around: to the shopping center where Hani had bought two newspapers, to an industrial suburb called Apex, asking him about distances and times from one to the other. Waluś asked again for a lawyer.

Holmes took Waluś back to his cell at 2 p.m. He had got nothing out of him.

Holmes had put the gun through the forensics lab. Tests showed that the bullets that had entered Hani were fired from the Z-88 found on Waluś. And there was blood spattered on Waluś's clothing and shoes and it matched Hani's blood type. Forensically, it was becoming a watertight case. Holmes had a killer, but no motive, no sense of whether he was part of a wider conspiracy.

There were forty detectives now working on the case. The instructions had come from the very top, the president's office: the case had to be cracked.

In the meantime, Holmes had ordered a Sergeant J. Slingerland to do a thorough of search Waluś' Ford. More evidence came to light: a bag containing adhesive plastic "Snapstix" letters and numerals that Waluś had meant to superimpose on the registration plates of the red Ford Laser in order to falsify them. Slingerland also found the receipt for the Snapstix and headed to the hardware store in Sandton where they had been bought. The shop assistant, a Mr. M Sebeko, confirmed that the "Snapstix" found in the red Ford had been purchased on the afternoon of March 2. It was clear that Waluś had been planning the hit for at least six weeks. So why hadn't he used the Snapstix to at least hide his own number plate on the day of the hit? He was later to confess that he had used them once before and most of them had lost their adhesion.

Things were moving fast. The gun's provenance had been ascertained. It was one of a large arsenal stolen from the SA Air Force base in Pretoria in April 1990, when emotions were running high in the wake of Nelson Mandela's release from prison. More than seventy weapons and thousands of rounds of ammunition had been stolen in that heist. Although the police had arrested the kingpin—a right-winger called Piet "Skiet" Rudolph (*skiet* is Afrikaans for shoot)—and recovered most of the weapons, some had already been distributed.

At the time of the arms heist, Hani had told colleagues he was certain that the guns had been stolen by people on the right. "I remember him saying that those weapons were just being shifted into different hands for covert operations," Tokyo Sexwale told reporters. "It has turned out to be all too true."

For Holmes, it meant he had to get something out of Waluś fast.

Midday
Central Johannesburg

If Mandela's historic televised speech and the press statements by De Klerk, the ANC, and numerous other parties and leaders were supposed to calm the anger that was brewing across the nation, then they failed.

Although there were no major incidents of violence overnight, impromptu protests and attacks continued to break out across the country, with at least five people killed on Sunday, two in clashes involving police. Police shot dead a man in a Soweto shack settlement after a crowd gathered to commemorate Hani. Residents said three people had been killed, but the police denied that. In the Phola Park squatter camp, east of Johannesburg, the ANC said another man had died fighting police.

Elsewhere in the Johannesburg region, a police sergeant was shot dead in his vehicle, three policemen were injured by a petrol bomb, and gunmen fired on white motorists. Police believed the incidents were in response to Hani's death.

An angry crowd attacked two white men, set them alight, and cut out part of the tongue of a third in Lwandle township, in the Strand near Cape Town. On the streets, anger escalated. Paul Njikelana, a civic association member from Dobsonville, Soweto, told the *Sunday Times*: "Now that the government is talking peace while killing our leaders, negotiations should be suspended. We are back to square one."

The front pages of the Sunday newspapers all carried gory pictures of Hani, blood pooling around his dead body. Those were the pages the men and women who filed into the twenty-two-floor building located at 51 Plein Street, Johannesburg, the head office of the ANC, had read that morning. Emotions were still raw. Virtually everyone who had gone to the Hani home had wept at the scene. Many of the newspapers carried pictures of Sexwale, held by Gill Marcus and trade unionist Mbhazima Sam Shilowa, weeping. Other pictures showed Winnie Mandela sobbing at the crime scene. That morning the SA Communist Party chairman, Joe Slovo, had stopped a radio interviewer in a trembling voice because he was "shocked and shaken" and needed "time to collect my thoughts."

There was no time for the Easter Sunday church service. Shilowa, at the time an avowed communist who only wore red socks, had been on the N1 motorway to the north to attend southern Africa's biggest Easter weekend gathering (the Zion Christian Church's mass gathering that attracts between three and five million pilgrims every year) when he heard that Hani was dead. He immediately turned around and headed to Dawn Park and was at the ANC head office early on Sunday morning.

The ANC had asked South Africans to use Easter services to remember and honor Hani. Yet for the ANC's leaders, church would not be a priority.

Indeed, while in most Black congregations there were prayers for Hani and his family, in other congregations there was no mention of the Hani name. At the Dutch Reformed Church, just ten minutes' drive from Hani's home, the priest did not mention the fallen communist and resident's name. Instead, Dominee Johan Orsmond related the story of the death of Christ and asked his hundred parishioners to pray for their country and its political leaders.

"The death of Christ was probably the worst day in the lives of many of His followers," Orsmond said. After the service he said he had not referred to Hani because it would have put the focus on the "political violence and vendettas that plague this country."

The meeting of the ANC's National Executive Committee (NEC)—usually made up of fifty members plus six top officials—that took place at noon the day after Hani's death was a somber affair. If Hani could be gunned down in so brutal a manner, what about the rest of the people in the room? The ANC was unbanned, but it had no power in the transitional phase between 1990 and 1994. None of its leaders had state protection of any kind, and most of them lived scattered across the country, far from their comrades. They were sitting ducks.

The convener of the meeting was Cyril Ramaphosa, who had taken over the party machinery in 1991 when he won the secretary-general's position, making him the third most powerful person in the ANC. A lawyer and founder of the country's biggest trade union, he had been at the head of the ANC's leaders at the gates of the prison when Mandela was released in 1990 and had become the ANC's chief negotiator.

According to Joel Netshitenzhe, the bearded, soft-spoken former exile who was one of the party's key strategists, there were no sharp differences in how to respond to Hani's death. But his words were carefully chosen: "There were a few in the leadership who, during the discussions, questioned the utility of negotiations . . ."

Others were not as delicate. Harry Gwala, the ANC leader from the violence-racked KwaZulu-Natal Midlands where the Inkatha Freedom Party's paramilitary groups were assisted by rogue police elements in attacking ANC supporters, had already called for the suspension of the talks. Gwala was famous for his fiery oratory. A teacher who switched to union organizing, he was banned by the apartheid government for political activities in the 1950s. In the sort of casually cruel manner things happened back then, the government refused to give him legal permission to work in any field. He continued his underground activism but was rearrested in the 1970s and tortured together with a comrade who died during the "interrogation." He was sentenced to ten years on Robben Island, was released after serving it in full, then sentenced again to life in prison. The authorities refused him permission to attend his wife's funeral. In prison he developed a motor neuron disease that left his arms paralyzed. He was released in 1988 and immediately got back into the fight against apartheid. His neck was always encased in a brace. He struck an imposing, postapocalyptic figure when he gave his speeches.

Gwala was disdainful of many of his comrades in leadership, believing that they were not attentive to the extent of the brutality of the war against the ANC in the townships, particularly in KwaZulu-Natal. "Every weekend," he told one ANC leader in 1992, "we are burying comrades. You people in Johannesburg head offices . . . don't understand what is really happening down there on the ground."

He told a mass rally: "We have come here to take power from the hands of the fascist Boers. If our freedom depends on blood-shedding so be it."

Gwala was not alone in his militancy. Winnie Mandela was a known critic—if not outright opponent—of the ongoing negotiations process. Months before, she had written in the two most influential and biggest English-language newspapers in the country, the *Sunday Times* and the *Sunday Star*: "The NP elite is getting into bed with the ANC in order to preserve its silken sheets." Her meaning was that De Klerk and company aimed to preserve their hold on economic and political power—and the ANC's leaders such as Mandela were selling out.

Among those who would give the meeting a fair amount of pushback about continuing with negotiations would be Peter Mokaba, the ANC youth leader. Gwala, Winnie Mandela, Mokaba, and the ANC's Western Cape secretary, Tony Yengeni, shared similar traits: they were charismatic, mesmerizing public speakers who harbored very strong suspicions about the National Party and the negotiations process. Like Hani, with whom they were closely associated, they were extremely popular among the ANC's radical youth who expressed impatience with apartheid and the protracted negotiations process and sought revolution rather than reform. In public speeches these leaders were uncompromising, striking fear in the hearts of conservative commentators and often profiled as the "hawks" of the ANC as opposed to the "doves" such as Mandela.

The classification was largely misplaced: those who were often tagged as "hawks," such as Chris Hani, were at the negotiating table beside "doves" such as Mandela and the chief negotiator, Ramaphosa. In large measure, the ANC's "hawks" spoke the language of radicalism onstage and made peace in meetings.

As the NEC members filed into their conference room, Mokaba, the leader of the youth league, told reporters outside the meeting that ANC supporters in the townships were angry. "We're always being told to be calm when we want to hit back," he said. "For three years now we've been negotiating. The leaders talk of a political solution. But the so-called peace process is not on. What is 'on' is war."

As the meeting deliberated, the ANC Cape leader, Tony Yengeni, was leading a march commemorating Hani through central Cape Town. He had already received word from Johannesburg that there would be commemorations on Wednesday, so when he took to the podium he announced in the Xhosa language: "The police must know that on Wednesday we are going to town in our thousands. If they shoot one of us the town will be burned down."

Yet, later on when ANC supporters started shooting into the air, he took the bullhorn: "We are asking people not to shoot so close to the police station because the cops will be provoked and fire at us."

His reasons for not wanting confrontation were interesting: "We don't have too many guns to defend ourselves."

At the NEC meeting, discussions continued. In situations where there was major discord about the direction of negotiations (the likes of Mokaba felt the ANC leadership was being "soft" on the government by agreeing in August 1990 to suspend the armed struggle, for example), Mandela always chose to keep quiet and let criticism of him and the party's leadership flow. According to Ronnie Kasrils, the SA Communist Party and Umkhonto we Sizwe commander who was among those seeking faster concessions from De Klerk and often profiled as a "hawk," Mandela typically allowed those who were angry to fully "vent" in meetings. In this meeting, too, there was despair, confusion, anger—and venting.

For Mandela and many others in the room, the call for negotiations to be suspended reminded them of the Boipatong Massacre. At the funeral of the forty-five victims the thousands of mourners had sung: "Mandela, you are leading us like lambs to the slaughter." The reprimand had stung. Mandela had taken the issue of the increasing political violence in the country—and what he believed was a lack of appropriately tough action by De Klerk—to the United Nations and had briefed African leaders on his plans for an ANC walkout, seeking their counsel.

Julius Nyerere, the president of Tanzania, who had been one of several generous host countries of the ANC during its years in exile, had disagreed with Mandela's decision to suspend negotiations. Nyerere pointed out to Mandela that the ANC and other liberation organizations had always contended that the apartheid state was inherently violent. "Now how could it be cogently argued that violence could be totally eliminated before the apartheid state itself was abolished?" he asked.

Now, two of the ANC's key point men on the negotiations pushed for the talks to go on. Joe Slovo argued that calling off the negotiations would play into the hands of the assassins.

"This is their purpose: to spike the negotiations process. And we must defeat that purpose," Cyril Ramaphosa agreed, adding that Hani's death "should act as a catalyst, to make sure the negotiations process gathers momentum. It is what Comrade Chris would have expected all of us to do."

Still, Mandela knew the depth of pain felt not just by those in the room but by ordinary people because of the assassination. When, toward the end of the meeting, it came to his turn to speak, Mandela said the ANC "had to do something to channel away that anger . . ." In his view, "the only thing we can do is to have demonstrations throughout the country so that the people can find expression for their anger."

The men and women in the room had very few viable options on the table. They had no state power, so the investigation would be led by the ANC and Hani's enemies in the security forces. The ANC could not declare that it was reinstating its armed struggle—what would be the point of that when negotiations had restarted just ten days before after nine months of protests and boycotts? It could not tell its angry supporters to stay at home, either. It had to lead them in their anger.

To channel the anger, the ANC decided to stage marches, memorial services, rallies, and other gatherings where leaders would speak, express their condemnation of the act, and yet underline the message of negotiations with a militant stance.

The matter of personal safety was also deeply felt at the meeting. The news that Mandela and Slovo had been first and second on Waluś's hit list was already known to those present. And Hani was merely the latest in a long line of antiapartheid leaders to be shot and killed in broad daylight by apartheid assassins. ANC leaders were still investigating the murder of Dulcie September, the party's Paris office representative, who was opening her office in March 1988 when an assassin shot her five times and killed her. Her murderers were still at large. The lawyer Griffiths Mxenge was killed by apartheid hit squad leader Dirk Coetzee and others in 1981 in brutal fashion—they stabbed him forty-five times, beat him with a hammer, slit his throat, and dumped his body on a soccer field. Four years later they shot and killed his wife, Victoria, also a lawyer and activist, in front of her children. In 1978, academic, trade unionist, and philosopher Rick Turner was shot through a window of his home and died, in a scene almost like the Hani assassination, in the arms of his thirteen-year-old daughter. The last of the high-profile assassinations, the murder of University of the Witwatersrand antiapartheid lecturer David Webster in May 1989, was still "unsolved." De Klerk had assigned two white officials to conduct a closed inquiry into the killings but refused to release their report.

Death was a real and present danger for everyone in that room. Virtually all of them had been detained, jailed, tortured, or had their close comrades and family harassed by the government they were now negotiating with. They were extremely worried, and no one could blame them.

The men and women in the room knew one thing, though, and it was that they had a very powerful tool and ally in their hands: the people of South Africa were behind them. Niël Barnard, the apartheid spymaster who had played a significant role in the secret negotiations of the 1980s, has pointed out that of "crucial significance for the ANC were the supportive masses . . ."

The "masses of our people," or simply "the masses," was how the ANC referred to its supporters—in the positive sense that Marxists used it. Other interpretations of the masses, such as Barnard's, were on the more condescending side. Barnard was quick to recognize that mass support for the ANC, if used properly, almost guaranteed Mandela's party victory in the negotiations. He said in engagements, from the ANC's side, "[a]ll negotiation on the peace process had to focus on rescuing the masses from oppression. This permeated virtually every discussion . . ." But it wasn't just that the masses were the focus of conversations. "[T]he masses were the ANC's excuse," in Barnard's view. "When the organization was forced into a corner in a debate, the escape route was to declare that the 'masses would never agree to it.' Time and again this proved to be an effective tactic: a support base of this size could not be ignored."

Barnard might not have liked it, but the objective fact is that the ANC did have the support of the masses. And if ever there was a time to channel the people of South Africa's anger into productive protest that would garner concessions from the government, this was it.

The ANC leadership's insistence that "the masses would never agree" to certain things wasn't an excuse. The party knew their supporters wouldn't agree to any old order from on high. In 1989, for example, Ramaphosa and other leaders of the antiapartheid opposition organized in the United Democratic Front had formally called on the Black community to "distance" itself from Mandela's wife, Winnie. The leaders held her indirectly responsible for the beating and murder of a fourteen-year-old child activist, Stompie Seipei, by members of her notorious "football club"—a front for her recruitment of activists that became feared for meting out rough justice in Soweto and being implicated in killings of activists accused of being collaborators with the state. Winnie's bodyguard—secretly an informer for the police, he later revealed—was convicted of the boy's murder. After the doctor, Abu Baker Asvat, who examined the badly beaten boy was murdered, the ANC leaders called for the nation to steer clear of her. It was an extraordinary call—made after the leaders had consulted Mandela in prison—about a longtime activist revered as "the mother of the nation." It didn't work at all. Winnie's popularity skyrocketed and in 1991 she was elected to the ANC's National Executive Committee.

It was in this Sunday morning meeting that the skeleton of Mandela's plan for the week emerged. Mandela was acutely aware that many of the ANC's detractors believed that "the leadership of our people could not control 'young militants'" and so a key challenge would be containing the anger that was already spilling out on the streets. Mandela did not just want to save lives and preserve the talks; he wanted to prove the skeptics wrong and show the ANC could indeed control its militants when the cause was justified. It was perhaps why, already, he had brought along one of the most militant among them—Bantu Holomisa—to Johannesburg. Mandela was always eager to point out that he had the militant wing of the ANC on his side, or that on some issues he took a tougher stance than the so-called hawks. In May 1991, when he wanted to break off talks because political violence had become too much for him to bear, he said he was overruled by the "militants" Joe Slovo and Chris Hani.

The first thing the ANC had to do was organize disciplined demonstrations to ensure that there was no excuse for the government's armed forces to inflict a massacre on protesters. Mandela and others used the word "discipline" several times to indicate that violence had to be averted. If tit-for-tat violence with the police and right-wing elements was allowed to happen, it would lead to a downward spiral into the civil war they suspected the killers wanted to trigger. Yet they could not allow the pressure in townships and villages to simmer and fester without any action—it might blow up in a manner they could not control.

The ANC's second objective was to exploit the crisis: "Use the moment to extract concrete concessions from the regime and move the entire negotiations process to a qualitatively new stage," as Netshitenzhe put it. The ANC would make two key demands to the National Party government, the meeting agreed. These were not new. First, that an election date be set immediately. The negotiations process had become bogged down in details, many, such as Ramaphosa, argued in the meeting.

Uncertainty that the country was heading toward a new nonracial democracy had to be ended. An election date would focus the minds of negotiators and send a strong signal to the right-wing forces and laggards such as the Inkatha Freedom Party that the freedom train was moving with or without them. There was another reason. If an election date was not set in the next round of negotiations, the ANC would find it difficult to convince ordinary people that the negotiations should continue. The mood in the country was pessimistic enough: a Gallup International poll carried out by the Markinor Research Group found that 41.7 percent of whites and 40 percent of Blacks felt that 1993 would be a far worse year than 1992 because negotiations had stalled while political violence had spiraled. Optimism was the lowest among Blacks since 1989, when it had risen due to political reforms started by De Klerk with the release of several of Mandela's comrades from twenty-six years' imprisonment.

The second demand was for the immediate establishment of a transitional executive committee, a multiparty structure that would oversee the security forces, public broadcaster, and other key areas of government in the run-up to a fully nonracial election. The demand was grounded in the ANC and Mandela's belief that the security forces were out of control and "a level playing field for all parties" was needed to mount a free and fair election.

These demands had to be made to De Klerk and his cabinet with vigor, resoluteness, and speed. Or, as the veteran negotiator Ramaphosa put it, the ANC had to go "for the kill."

The meeting agreed on the demands and the implementation of a series of protests across the country. It was not a unanimous meeting, however. Mokaba, the young firebrand, reluctantly agreed that negotiations should continue but said the youth "must be able to return to the barricades. We must be able to make our 'mass action' bite." This was, on the surface, a reference to how township youth erected barricades of burning tires in the streets to enforce "stay away from work" campaigns and economic boycotts of white businesses (to pressure them to, in turn, put pressure on government to reform) and to prevent police from entering communities during the State of Emergency of the 1980s. It could also mean returning to the armed struggle, but there is no witness to this being said directly by Mokaba or others. Even Mac Maharaj, the fiery Mandela associate who had been arrested by the government in 1991 for stockpiling arms in the country as an insurance measure in case talks collapsed, or any of his close MK comrades did not raise the issue.

Immediately after this meeting broke up, the top twenty leaders of the ANC present met with the central committees of its alliance partners, the SA Communist Party and the Congress of SA Trade Unions, for further discussions. Among a plethora of decisions, the three organizations appointed Thabo Mbeki, an astute and suave Sussex University economics master's graduate whose father had spent as much time in prison as Mandela (the two had worked together and bickered incessantly throughout their decades-long incarceration over ideology, at some point not speaking to each other for three and a half years), as its chief liaison with external organizations. Mbeki was an experienced negotiator who had been one of the key initiators of the ANC-government talks from outside South Africa. Now Mbeki had the hard task of ensuring that the police did not incite violence. His execution of this task was to prove crucial.

Then the leaders went out and held a press conference. An agitated Mandela detailed how Walter Sisulu had, in his capacity as deputy president of the ANC, written to the law and order minister, Hernus Kriel, the previous year asking for special protection for Hani. Kriel, who was regarded as one of the most fiercely right-wing members of the De Klerk cabinet, had failed to heed the warning.

There had been "continuous signals," Mandela said, that attempts could be made on Hani's life. He told of an incident some months before where Hani had been followed when he left his office on Rissik Street in Johannesburg and another when Hani's bodyguards had been shot at in

Soweto. Although police had not been expected to provide Hani with a continuous guard, Sisulu had asked for increased security around his home in Dawn Park. Sisulu had also requested firearm licenses for ANC security personnel, which were refused.

Ramaphosa reserved his greatest anger for the deputy minister of law and order, Gert Myburgh, and the police spokesman, Craig Kotze. In comments to reporters the previous day, the two men had stated that Hani's death might not have been politically motivated. Preliminary investigations "would seem at this stage to indicate that Mr. Hani's death could be the result of an individual operating on his own," Kotze had told reporters hours after the murder.

Ramaphosa said it was "blatantly clear" that Myburgh and Kotze had prejudged the assassination before the conclusion of an official investigation. Unbeknownst to Ramaphosa, Kotze—a former journalist who had secretly been a paid police informer in the *Star* newspaper's newsroom under apartheid—was a friend of Gaye Derby-Lewis and had been a regular at Truckers, the bar she managed in the 1980s.

The spokesman Kotze confirmed later that day that Sisulu had indeed warned that Hani's life was in danger, but, Kotze said, police could not "provide protection to politicians over and above that we give to ordinary members of the public," an extraordinary answer. He also said that while police would take various steps should they be informed of a specific assassination plot, the SA Police could not "as a blanket measure" provide protection to high-profile public figures—essentially saying the ANC had to have hard evidence of an assassination plot before the police would step in.

Of course, that assumed the police weren't behind the plot. Just three months later, in July 1993, an unmarked car carrying four men in plain clothes would try to ram into Sisulu's motorcade, killing one bodyguard and hospitalizing another. The police would admit that the car belonged to them but claimed it had police license plates and a blue light and the entire episode was an accident. They were lying again—a German television crew had been following the Sisulu car and the footage showed clearly that the police car had no markings, no blue lights, and gave no warning to Sisulu's motorcade.

As the afternoon wore on, Mandela's new message slowly spread through the country, primarily through news bulletins on the SA Broadcasting Corporation. The SABC was in the process of talking about transforming itself from being a state broadcaster—taking instruction from politicians—to being an independent public broadcaster and was keen to be seen to be providing comprehensive coverage of the assassination. The news was also being filtered in other ways. In townships in the East Rand, groups of activists gathered out of grief and sang the ANC's freedom songs. Leaders at such meetings disseminated whatever instructions they had heard over the radio: Mandela's directive was that people must mourn but do so with restraint and responsibility. As Mandela had told reporters at the press conference, memorials and marches would be held to channel this anger, to give it an outlet, instead of sitting and letting emotion express itself by means that might worsen the already volatile situation. Mandela was alive to his friend Desmond Tutu's warning: "Don't let this tragic event trigger reprisals."

Driving from gathering to gathering in the East Rand, Mondli Gungubele was getting snippets of the press conference from radio and the pager service (a microblogging device that was popular in the 1990s to transmit news and messages) that he was hooked into. He was still in shock from the previous day's events, still operating on adrenaline. When he heard Mandela's voice on the radio announcing that the ANC wanted immediate agreement on an election date, Gungubele felt himself being restored. Mandela's demand came like a staff to hold on to. "I connected with the sentiment immediately," he told me: this is too good not to continue fighting for. "It became something new to live for. It became something to say to our people," he said.

Yet the wheels of tragedy were already turning.

Midday
Port St. Johns, Eastern Cape Province

Chris Hani's office was spartan—no adornments or personal touches except a few potted plants near a modest desk, a bookcase with Leninist books, and two posters depicting the ANC's struggle on the wall. On the desk that Sunday was a notepad Hani had been using in the week before he was murdered. Two words were scrawled across the pad: "Peace Corps."

It had been Hani's obsession over the previous few months that the angry young members of the ANC's self-defense units and the rival Inkatha's self-protection units could be molded into a "peace corps" that encouraged them to start community-building, employment-creating projects. On his last day at his desk, Hani had been thinking of young men and women like Phumelele Hermans and Fundisile Guleni, the two SDU members in Port St. Johns who had been so shocked by his murder.

The two spent Sunday morning in a desultory mood. They were angrier than they were the previous day. They wanted action. Yet they felt impotent. They were looking for direction, for an outlet for their anger.

Hermans knew that his comrade was a man who was always ready to jump into action. Guleni had received basic training—hand-to-hand combat, basic usage of whatever firearm was available, and information-gathering and assessments to be made before staging an attack—from an MK cadre six years before, but it had not been put to use at all. With Mandela's release in 1990 and the commencement of the democracy talks, it was possible that it never would be. (In fact, in the next twelve months Guleni, nicknamed "Moods," would participate in the killing of four members of another liberation organization, the Azanian People's Liberation Army, as well as in the killing of an ANC political rival in Port St. Johns. But they did not know that this was what the future held.)

On that Sunday morning Hermans and Guleni walked to the local ANC office. It was usually shut on Sunday but had opened because of the news about Hani. The two fell to work. They wrote letters to all branches under their jurisdiction, informing them to be ready to attend a memorial service or even travel to the funeral in Johannesburg when a date was announced. For the two, it was something to do while many of the families in the township either attended traditional family celebrations (when the many migrant workers from the area, who worked largely in the main cities of Cape Town or Johannesburg, would return home for visits after three months away) or went to the several Christian churches in the area.

Yet something was burning underneath. There was suspicion and mistrust between activists such as Hermans and the white townsfolk. Hermans remembered that the year before he and Guleni had reported to the subregional office of the ANC in Flagstaff that they suspected that there was right-wing activity in Port St. Johns. They had no evidence, but they were suspicious. Workers in the area had reported being harassed by whites. He remembered that employees of a local businessman had reported problems with their boss, claiming poor wages and asking the ANC to help. There were stories that sometimes the businessman would receive material in boxes that he would not allow his workers to help him with. The workers reported that they suspected there were arms in the boxes. But they had no evidence.

There were rumors that the businessman was a member of the right-wing organization the AWB. Hermans remembered that a few months before, local activists had organized the launch of a Communist Party branch in the town. During their meeting, cars had arrived at the hall, surrounded it, honked, and then driven off. They suspected that these were right-wingers.

Yet his most powerful memory was from Christmas 1992, four months before Hani's assassination. He was accompanying his father to Durban, riding the long-haul bus for the five- to six-hour drive along South Africa's eastern coastline to the north. One of the passengers was a white man dressed in khaki shorts and shirt he'd seen leave the Port St. Johns businessman's house. Hermans regarded the house as the businessman's, but it was actually a bed-and-breakfast and the businessman—who owned several other businesses, including a market—used it as his office.

Anyone could stay there. In Hermans's reckoning, though, whoever stayed at the guesthouse had to be an associate of the businessman.

On the bus to Durban the white man was feeling boisterous. He was drinking from a clear bottle, what Hermans identified as "white spirits," possibly vodka, gin, or the notorious *witblits* (Afrikaans for white lightning), a cheap and popular moonshine made from fermented peaches with a very high alcohol content. As the spirits sank in, the man started talking to the passengers in Afrikaans. Hermans could not understand everything he said properly, but the key message was that he was an AWB member and he had been on a mission in Port St. Johns.

Hermans, on his return home, had reported this and other incidents to the ANC office in Flagstaff. The comrades in the leadership of the ANC in the subregion had told him and Guleni to go back to Port St. Johns and get some evidence. They had gone back home, become engaged in other campaigns, and never really did any investigating. So, nothing ever came of it.

As they worked in the ANC office that Sunday, faxed statements and messages started coming through from the Eastern Cape regional office of the South African Communist Party. Unlike its national counterpart, the regional SACP took a hard-line stance. Despite the ANC and SACP's dogged adherence to the Marxist-Leninist principle of "democratic centralism" that dictates that all decisions adopted by the highest structures of the organization are binding on all lower structures and members, regional structures often held strong views on issues that had a direct impact on them. In one famous incident in 1990, Mandela had been told by the ANC in the violence-racked KwaZulu-Natal region to cancel a peace rally he had planned with the rival Mangosuthu Buthelezi of the Inkatha movement. Archie Gumede, an ANC national leader who also held leadership positions in the region, said pointedly at the time that ANC leaders "fresh from prison" were "lost": "They are excluding themselves from obtaining information from people who they ought to know are in contact with the situation." Mandela canceled the meeting.

So, in its fax statement to the branches, the regional SACP said that the "suspension of the armed struggle is to be reviewed." It also called for the "immediate establishment of defense units/protection units" where they did not exist. Given that the ANC itself called the SDU's paramilitary units, organized in platoons and companies, this was a call to be combat-ready.

For Hermans and his comrade, it was exactly what they wanted to hear. Someone was expressing their anger. Yet they still had no plan to translate their anger into action.

While Hermans and Guleni stewed, they were being thought about by another angry member of the ANC. One of the comrades they had reported their suspicions to in Flagstaff was Mlulamisi Maxhayi, a teacher and leader of the ANC's subregional committee comprised of four local branches that included his town and Port St. Johns. On the Sunday after Hani's murder Maxhayi had met with another self-defense unit member, Vuyani Nyalukana. They were angry, just like their comrade Hermans and others across the country.

"We should retaliate," Maxhayi said. "We should avenge Comrade Chris."

They already knew from their two informants in Port St. Johns that there was possible right-wing activity in the seaside town. The two of them were too few to carry out an attack, though. They needed reinforcements, but they needed to keep things tight. So they called on their comrade, Lungile Mazwi, who lived in Port St. Johns.

Three was just enough to do something.

Midday
Pretoria

Nelson Mandela and F. W. de Klerk had decided back in 1992 that they needed to keep a channel of communication open no matter how dire the situation. The "channel," as it came to be known, was made up of two young men that both leaders trusted. Mandela had chosen the ANC's secretary-general, the charming, quiet, yet extremely sharp forty-year-old trade union leader Cyril Ramaphosa.

De Klerk had chosen a rake-thin, tall, forty-five-year-old lawyer with a perennially optimistic face and ready smile by the name of Roelf Meyer. He was a *verligte*, Afrikaans for a liberal, and was detested by the hard-liners of the National Party and De Klerk's cabinet.

On the evening of Sunday, June 22, 1992, Meyer had sat down in front of the television at his home in Pretoria to watch the main news broadcast of the day when Mandela came on the screen. That winter evening was not a great time to be watching the news in South Africa. Six days before, the latest and worst of the massacres, the bloodiest of the cycle of mass killings in South Africa since the 1976 Soweto student shootings, had taken place in Boipatong.

What Mandela had to say that evening was devastating. He said the massacre had turned the clock back three decades to the bloody confrontations between the white government and oppressed Blacks. "The gulf between the oppressed and the oppressor has become unbridgeable," said Mandela.

Talks with the National Party government would be stopped, he said. Meyer was stunned.

"Oh, damn it!" he recalled thinking later. "All the hard work up to that point appeared to be over. It seemed everything had been for nothing."

He was disappointed not to be told of such a momentous decision by his ANC opposite number, Ramaphosa, before hearing it on the news. That's when Meyer's telephone rang. It was Ramaphosa.

"What the hell are you doing?" Meyer asked.

"When can we meet?"

"But your boss said talks were over."

"Oh, don't worry about that. He says you and I should continue talking," Ramaphosa answered.

It is a story that Meyer has told to illustrate that in the two men's estimation, in the brittle and fragile process they were involved in, both sides knew they had to keep talking.

They also knew they had to trust each other. This trust had its genesis on a weekend the previous year when they were invited to a trout lodge by the millionaire Sidney Frankel, chairman of the largest stockbroker on the Johannesburg Stock Exchange at the time. Ramaphosa, raised in the hard-knuckle township of Soweto, hardly a place known for trout fishing, had picked up the sport some four years before while on holiday in the Drakensberg Mountains. He had come upon a fly fisherman casting. "I looked at the way he was flicking his rod and the artistry of it all attracted me. I approached this person and said: 'Can I try?' I didn't catch a fish, but I was hooked," he later told a reporter. He bought some tackle, caught twenty fish on his first trip, and became a fisherman.

Meyer, on the other hand, had never fished until the weekend they came together at the trout farm. On his first try at casting he caught a hook in his finger. The only way to remove it was to yank it out with a pair of pliers. It would be painful. There was no anesthetic, so Ramaphosa poured a stiff whiskey down Meyer's throat.

"Don't say I don't trust you," Meyer told Ramaphosa before the makeshift surgery.

That was the first of many times when the two would have to trust each other.

When the heated emotions following the Boipatong Massacre had abated, the two men had established small teams to work on a series of steps (streamlining the negotiating process to ensure smaller parties did not have veto powers and that the ANC–National Party delegations set the pace; setting up deadlock-breaking technical committees trusted by all parties) that would enable both sides to resume formal talks. Between June—when Ramaphosa placed his call to Meyer—and September 1992, "the channel" met forty-three times in hotel rooms and different venues as they hammered out a deal to revive the negotiations. The deal itself was simple: they set up the processes to speed up substantive steps to agree on a transition to democracy.

Throughout this period the ANC staged marches, sit-ins, political rallies, and other forms of protest at government offices, businesses, foreign embassies, and other institutions. In many instances Ramaphosa led these protests. He talked tough on television in the daytime while remaining in almost nightly contact with Meyer, seeking a solution.

With the murder of Hani, both Ramaphosa and Meyer knew that the talks they had assiduously nursed back to life faced a new hurdle. Personally, Meyer says he felt a "deep loss."

"The country has lost a great man," he remembers thinking at the time. Meyer released a statement as soon as he got the news of Hani's killing. "The murder of Chris Hani is a setback for the constitutional negotiation process," he acknowledged, adding that Hani had been a committed negotiator. His statement revealed his deepest fear that the negotiations could collapse. "There is only one solution for SA—negotiations," it almost entreated. "Mr. Hani's death must encourage all those involved to succeed with constitutional negotiations."

On this Sunday, with reports of the escalating violence coming in from across the country, it was clear that the statements from both sides and the television address had not worked. The channel had to start working again.

Afternoon
Umtata

The first time Holomisa had time to reflect properly on the weekend's events was when he sat down on the plane from Johannesburg to head back home to Umtata that Sunday afternoon.

In his seat at 10,000 feet, with no distraction from Mandela and the many ANC leaders he had had to interact with over the previous twenty-four hours, the sheer enormity of having lost Hani began to sink in. Hani and Holomisa had become close over the last three years and now, alone for the first time in twenty-four hours, the horror of what had happened started to "eat me inside like a worm." He was overtaken by sadness and anger. The soldier broke down and sobbed for a long time. It was the first time the thirty-five-year-old had cried since he was a child.

Holomisa's mind was roiled by emotions that were obsessing other ANC leaders that day: anger, fear, guilt, self-doubt. His guilt drove him to ask himself whether Hani would have lived if he had stayed in the Transkei, under Holomisa's protection. Why Hani and not other leaders?

Crucially, how did the assassin know that Hani's bodyguards had been given the day off?

He felt haunted by the murder as the questions swirled in his mind. There were no answers. Fear and hopelessness crept into his mourning. He recounts that he was in an agitated state and felt he could not think straight. He felt unsafe.

"At that moment I lost hope in the whole negotiation process. With anger reaching boiling point among ANC members and supporters, the country was on the brink of a bloody catastrophe . . . There was no way that the talks in Kempton Park could go ahead."

It was in this frame of mind, angry and suspicious, that the military leader began to interact with the world when he landed at Umtata Airport that afternoon. The assassination of Hani was part of the alleged operation sanctioned by the South African government to eliminate activists in the Eastern Cape, Holomisa told the influential provincial paper the *Daily Dispatch*.

"The murder of Chris Hani cannot be divorced from the ongoing implementation of Operation Katzen approved by the Cabinet of President FW de Klerk," Holomisa said.

Katzen was a clandestine black ops initiative set up in 1986 by the South African Defence Force (SADF) to overthrow the homeland governments of Ciskei and Transkei and establish a regional resistance movement aligned to the apartheid government—led by Black puppets of the government—to counter the influence of the banned ANC. Coordinated at Defence Headquarters in Pretoria, Operation Katzen was approved at the highest echelons of the security establishment—the chief of the army, General "Kat" Liebenberg, and his superior, the chief of the SADF, General Jannie Geldenhuys. It had the blessing of the cabinet of the apartheid security apparatus, the State Security Council, which was led by the president of the country, P. W. Botha.

Holomisa had thrown down the gauntlet. He was blaming the government for Hani's assassination and refusing to investigate the Azanian People's Liberation Army (APLA) for similar action.

In reaction, De Klerk's chief of staff, Dave Steward, said the South African government had taken note of Holomisa's "irresponsible outburst in which he alleges that the government was involved in the assassination of Mr. Chris Hani." "The SA government will not tolerate the instigation of violence from any quarter and will take appropriate steps to address any threats in this regard," he said. He didn't say what those steps might be, leaving the door ominously open for anything.

While this war of words was going on, the region around Holomisa's Transkei was slowly turning violent in reaction to Hani's assassination. Waluś's hopes of Black anger spiking were being realized.

9 p.m.
Dawn Park

For Retha Harmse, the woman who had witnessed Hani's assassination and called the police, the threatening calls had started as soon as the Sunday newspapers had hit the streets—around 9 to 10 p.m. on Saturdays in the major metropolitan areas. She was featured prominently in the highest-circulation Afrikaans Sunday newspaper and in the biggest English Sunday newspaper recounting what she had seen. Overnight, she had become a star.

The callers were all speaking in her native Afrikaans.

"Is it Retha?"

Harmse remembered the voice, describing it to one interviewer as a "beautiful Afrikaans voice."

"Ja?" she answered.

Silence. Harmse could hear that the person was still on the line. The woman said nothing.

Click.

It went on like that for the rest of the evening.

"Take the phone off the hook," Daan said, after the 12:15 a.m. call. "I'll call the police from the neighbor's house."

When the police arrived later with a guard, their advice was the same: pull the phone cord out; otherwise you won't sleep.

In the morning they plugged the phone in again. It was 7:30 a.m. The phone rang almost immediately when the plug was in the socket. It was the beautiful Afrikaans voice again.

And again, the silence.

Again, they pulled out the plug.

When they put the plug back in later, the calls started again. This time it was not the silence or heavy breathing down the line.

"You white dogs are going to die," one said.

Another, a man who introduced himself as Viljoen from Pretoria, wanted to congratulate Retha. "You are fantastic," he said. "You did a remarkable thing. You have just signed your death warrant."

When somebody whispered, "What is the color of your skin?" a lightning bolt hit her. She answered, pretending to be a cop stationed at her house, "Captain Nel, can I help?"

The person on the other end put the phone down quickly.

Respite, at least for a while.

Afternoon
Pretoria

All hope for a restful weekend at the farm was gone and so De Klerk followed Mandela's lead and headed back to Pretoria.

Steward had arranged for him to give a television interview on the murder. Unlike Mandela's address to the nation, De Klerk was interviewed on the current affairs program *Agenda*, on TV1, a station that broadcast in English and Afrikaans and was aimed at a white audience.

The interview did not have the stature accorded to Mandela's broadcast the previous evening. It was not a direct address to the nation. It could have been an interview at any time of the year. De Klerk struck a somber note by first telling the interviewer that Hani's murder was a real loss, as the man had played a constructive role in the negotiations and had gone out of his way to warn people against violence. He voiced the hope that the "shock wave" the assassination had sent through the country would have a positive impact by convincing all parties of the seriousness of the negotiation process. "People who aren't serious about negotiation don't deserve to be a part of it," he said.

De Klerk knew that there was danger ahead. It would have been a mistake to underestimate the potential of right-wing extremism, as some of these groupings were well trained. He saw it as a "real threat." But he didn't say just how serious this threat was. The National Intelligence Service believed that the neo-Nazi AWB had some 127 training camps within South Africa where 5,700 people were trained to operate as military units. Participants were trained in everything from self-defense to explosive techniques. Tienie Groenewald, the former military intelligence director, apparently claimed that he and other former SA Defence Force generals who supported the cause of the Afrikaner Volksfront (AVF) had addressed 140,000 rightists in just two months of clandestine meetings across the country.

De Klerk must have had intelligence briefings on this threat. Yet in his interview he outlined only the threat of retaliatory anger from ANC supporters and was quick to give the assurance that "we are in a position to maintain law and order especially in the coming days where unrest might spread."

In the South Africa of the previous forty-five years, "law and order" was code for suppression of people's legitimate demands and preservation of the white minority's racial privileges. Bringing in the police and the army would merely worsen the situation, not help it.

Still, like Mandela, De Klerk emphasized that emotions shouldn't be stirred up in such a way that they slow down negotiations. He addressed himself to ANC "militants" directly as he said this. He did not address himself to right-wing groupings, one of whose members had pulled the trigger of the gun that killed Hani. Even with the evidence before him, he still could not bring himself to see where the problem really lay: among those who did not wish to see South Africa truly free.

This blind spot was the beginning of the widening gulf between De Klerk and Mandela. By the time the TV show ended at 9 p.m. it was thirty-five hours after Hani's death. Violence had flared in various parts of the country, but nothing serious yet.

EASTER MONDAY
April 12, 1993

Their understanding
Begins to swell, and the approaching tide
Will shortly fill the reasonable shore
That now lies foul and muddy. Not one of them
That yet looks on me, or would know me.
  The Tempest, Act 5, Scene 1

Daytime
Benoni Police Station

For Waluś, Monday, April 12, was a blur of interrogations. He was taken out of his Benoni Police Station cell and taken to Boksburg's Murder and Robbery Squad offices, where he had been held when he was first arrested on Saturday. Policemen arrived from various places, and he was questioned, again and again. Sergeant Mike Holmes came in and made him sign that he had been on the trip to Dawn Park and the suburb of Apex the previous day. He signed. No one spoke about the trip to Pretoria and the search of his apartment.

Another policeman, a Sergeant Vorster, arrived and cleared everyone out. He started asking Waluś about the Stallard Foundation—the extreme right-wing group founded by Clive Derby-Lewis. The policeman also asked Waluś if he was a member of the Afrikaner Resistance Movement (AWB). When the policeman's questions about the Stallard Foundation persisted, Waluś snapped: "Read between the lines, but don't ask me further about it because there is a lot at stake."

The policeman did not understand what he meant, and Waluś refused to elaborate. He would not sign anything further. He asked for his lawyer. Except for the smoking gun, the ballistics report, and the red car, the state had a "lone assassin" and nothing else.

They let him see a lawyer obtained by his brother Witold.

Lunchtime
Krugersdorp

It was two days after Waluś's arrest, but Clive and Gaye Derby-Lewis still seemed strangely unconcerned that a man Clive had given a gun and a list of names to was in custody for the murder of Chris Hani.

Arthur Kemp, the journalist at the conservative newspaper the *Citizen* who had drawn up the hit list and helped Gaye procure addresses and descriptions of the houses on the list, came for lunch.

That morning, Gaye Derby-Lewis had bought a copy of the Afrikaans daily *Beeld*, which had published despite the public holiday. The paper detailed the finding of the hit list at Waluś's flat and revealed the names of those on it. The journalist clearly had sources within the police services, as the information had not yet been disclosed to the public.

Later, Gaye related how she had confronted her husband about the list. "What happened to it?" she asked. "Did you give it to Kuba?"

"I gave it to him," he answered.

Strangely, she did not ask about the gun, or how deeply he was involved in the plot. Gaye, a major ideologue of the extreme right in South Africa, seemed oddly incurious (from her recounting) about the fact that a gun that was brought to her house may have been used to murder the country's most popular left politician after Mandela and that her list was used to get to his house.

Gaye claimed Kemp came to her home that day to install a software program on her computer. Curiously, six days previously, another friend of hers, Edwin Clarke, had been in the house "fixing" her computer while Janusz Waluś had come to pick up the gun that killed Hani. And now the man who had provided her with the addresses of the people on her list was popping in to help her with her computer too. Clarke was the man, it would later emerge, who drove her to the Johannesburg bus station where Kemp had given her the list of targets.

"Look," Kemp told her. "I've put two and two together and I realize that my list has been used."

At first the couple said they denied the charge. Then Gaye changed her mind.

"It looks as if it was," she admitted.

Clive Derby-Lewis suggested that they go to the police, but she said that they should wait and see what happened.

And so, with a murder hanging over their heads, Gaye and Kemp went to her computer and tried to "sort out a problem." They did not, they say, discuss coordinating their stories even if the police came to question them. However, Gaye would later let slip that they *had* discussed the list that day, but that Clive had assured Kemp: "Not to worry, Mr. Waluś would not speak..."

Kemp had a new baby at home. And yet on Easter Monday, a public holiday, rather than spend time with his young family, he had gone to have lunch and sort out a computer problem with a couple he had given a by now highly compromising list—already referred to in newspapers such as *Beeld* as a "hit list"—of names to. When he left their house at 3 p.m., he did not pick up the phone and inform the authorities that he had crucial information on how the hit list found in the assassin's apartment had come into being. Neither did the Derby-Lewises.

Instead, that afternoon Clive retired to his bed for a nap. Gaye later said the Derby-Lewises were probably Waluś's "closest friends," but they seemed in no hurry to find out why he was being held by the police.

But Hani's assassination was causing consternation among some other right-wing white leaders. The leader of the AWB, Eugène Terre'Blanche, told the *Citizen* that "he condemned the assassination but that he understood the motive any white would have for killing Mr. Hani." Still, "He disapproved of the attack because it was an assassination and not a kill in a real war, adding, 'if it had been a proper battle, I would have killed Mr. Hani myself.'"

Daytime
Umtata

If Holomisa was worried about his own safety and those of other ANC leaders in the wake of the Hani assassination, events in the days after the bloody act did not help calm him down. The press was beginning to excavate its records, and reports littered the country about attempts on the former MK leader's life, making Holomisa even angrier and despondent about what had happened.

It was becoming clear that Hani had been marked for assassination and he had known it, even if he did not have concrete information about a specific attempt. "I know that there are plans to kill me, emanating from certain elements—and I know them—in military intelligence, Special Branch, the NIS [National Intelligence Service]," he'd said. Hani had also told the *Sunday Times*: "These guys see me as someone who is bad news. I fear that there are people who have the capacity to eliminate me. I am frightened about what they are planning."

These new revelations of Hani's premonition of his own death were feeding into the anger nationally. Incidents of cars being stoned by angry crowds were reported in Holomisa's region. An Umtata magistrate reported his car had been pelted with beer bottles. It was the government of De Klerk that Holomisa was most angry at, though. It was one thing to speak to reporters, but he wanted to show his fury.

By the perverse logic of the apartheid government, Transkei was an independent country. Holomisa was the man in charge there. He could do what he pleased. And so, as the leader of a sovereign state, puny and funded by the South African treasury as Transkei was, Holomisa fired off a diplomatic note to the president of South Africa.

The five-page note repeated Holomisa's suspicion of state involvement in the slaying of Hani and accused De Klerk of allowing Eugène
Terre'Blanche's "white terrorist group, the AWB . . . free rein to mobilize,
openly train and arm whites to launch ruthless attacks on Blacks."

Holomisa said the government's security apparatus was involved in
stoking the ongoing political violence in the country. De Klerk was furious with the note, but he decided to respond with a terse statement saying
the SA government would study the note and respond at an "appropriate
time." He wanted to send a tougher message to Holomisa.

Daytime
Katlehong

The shock that had seemed to immobilize Hani's supporters was beginning to wear off. It was replaced by anger and a demand for some sort
of action. In Katlehong township, six kilometers from where Hani had
been murdered, two delivery trucks were set on fire as ten thousand angry
mourners gathered at Huntersfield Stadium. Mondli Gungubele was
among the leaders on the stage trying to calm things down. He repeated
the messages from Mandela's press conference on Sunday: "the people"
had a right to show their anger, but it had to be done in a disciplined manner. The signs around him did not bode well. One leader sitting on the
stage next to him wore a T-shirt bearing the words: "You cannot die alone.
They must also die."

Gungubele knew the anger of the people in his region. Since 1990
some of the worst political killings in South Africa had occurred in the
area. Gungubele always knew he had to invite a militant speaker to ANC
rallies, funerals, and vigils in these situations. When "credible," radical,
fiery leaders such as Hani told the many young people organized in self-
defense units to calm down, they tended to be listened to.

Sometimes, however, words went awry. Once, Gungubele had invited the fiery ANC Natal leader Harry Gwala to come and motivate the
young militants in the townships to fight for peace. Gwala had referred to

Peter Harris's organization—the National Peace Accord—and its logo of two white doves signifying peace. He asked the crowd: "Who told you a dove can bring you peace? Where I come from we eat this thing. You must fight!"

Gwala was important—he addressed the anger of the crowds. "But," says Gungubele, "I would never take his directive."

Yet this was the dance at these rallies: fiery rhetoric coupled with an instruction to listen to and follow the directives of the leadership. Sometimes the lines got blurred.

One of the main drawcards at ANC rallies was the youth leader Peter Mokaba. Along with Winnie Mandela, Chris Hani, Harry Gwala, and a handful of others in the provinces, he was revered by the militant youth. Stadiums erupted with adoring chants when any of them entered. Mandela was revered wherever he went, but this grouping was enchanting in an altogether different way. At the many rallies I had seen them speak, they seemed to encapsulate a basic truth that went unsaid in South Africa: If our cause is just, if we are human like any other humans across the globe, why are we having to "negotiate" our humanity and freedom? The thirty-four-year-old Mokaba popularized a call-and-response chant that incorporated the words "kill the Boer, kill the farmer." Government and Afrikaner leaders were outraged, saying it was a call to murder whites. It was a slogan he repeated many times—and various bodies were to lay charges against him about it. He did not care. He used it, to much adulation and applause from his supporters, even when senior ANC leaders later asked him to tone it down. It is a chant that continues today, still triggering lawsuits and legal challenges.

On this day Mokaba was his usual charismatic self—speaking tough but calling for talks to be preserved. He had told the crowd inside the stadium: "We must make sure that whenever they take action like this they will live to regret it . . . We must become disciplined, cool, but hit back. Chris Hani should not die in vain."

On the surface the words seem to be implying some form of vengeance, yet they could also mean that the peace Hani sought should be delivered to the people of South Africa; that would be another way of ensuring he did not die in vain. Like so many ANC leaders, Mokaba was doing his best to hold the crowd in check, to speak the language of war and yet have those listening act in a disciplined fashion. It was impossible to talk peace in those forums. The speeches were performance art: speak like a militant, then call for patience while the leaders fix the problem. But such nuance of interpretation was not available that day. The words were taken to mean "Hit back!" The crowd seemed like it was lost to Mokaba.

Gungubele, like so many other ANC leaders there, told me later that by the leaders' reckoning, the rally was over after the speeches. The crowd had other ideas. As the gathering dispersed, some in the crowd fired into the sky and above police and journalists with machine guns. The crowd converged again, with about 6,000 people now in the throng. As some people left the stadium, others were arriving on foot, in chanting groups, and in packed minibus taxis from other townships. They decided to march to the Hani home in Dawn Park.

Mokaba, having lost sight of his own transport, flagged down a well-known journalist, John Carlin, from the *Independent* in London. Mokaba, despite his militant talk earlier, was a worried man. He claimed some anti-white radicals from the Pan Africanist Congress seemed to have infiltrated the march, bringing their far more militant rhetoric and race-baiting slogans and inflaming emotions. He feared police would open fire on the crowd as they had done in an incident in Soweto the day before.

"Chris Hani is the only man in the ANC who could have handled this situation," Mokaba told Carlin. "That's why I have to do this. No one knows who most of the leaders at headquarters are." "This" was to talk down his own militants. With his head sticking out of Carlin's car window, Mokaba spoke to groups of ANC supporters and policemen along the way, telling them not to allow radicals to cause a bloodbath, calming them down. The militant was calming the militants; the radical taming the radicals.

Gungubele was doing the same, marching with the crowds. At some point he had to restrain a section of the crowd from setting alight a house near the Hani home. Finally, the marchers reached the Hani home, "jammed the leafy residential streets, sang songs, shouted slogans, and listened to more speeches." A speaker reminded the congregated marchers that anyone who "did harm to white people could not call himself a member of the ANC."

Then everybody trooped off home. It was nighttime. Gungubele sighed and walked to his home too.

Daytime
Bruma Lake

By Monday, Retha and Daan could not take it anymore. Thousands had arrived in the neighborhood to mourn their hero, but radio chat shows and letters to newspapers were filled with hate for the Afrikaner woman who had called the police. What if someone in the crowd was there to shoot them?

They needed something to calm their nerves, so they went to see a pharmacist. He recommended some tranquilizers. He recognized Retha from the pictures in the newspaper—and gave the couple the pills for free.

4:40 p.m.
Johannesburg

Clive Derby-Lewis would have been proud of the sight. His plan to bring chaos to the country was playing out perfectly. Just under two hours after Arthur Kemp left his house, plumes of smoke covered a police helicopter flying over the Kagiso Mall, a shopping center outside Derby-Lewis's hometown of Krugersdorp on the West Rand. Sixteen stores were on fire. About sixty youths, armed with petrol bombs, were methodically setting fire to the place while members of the police's riot squad, the euphemistically named Internal Stability Unit, tried to arrest them.

There were only two members of the unit at the burning mall. Other unit members were putting out fires elsewhere.

It was the end of a brutal day of escalating violence and chaos in South

Africa's Black townships. If anything was needed to illustrate that Mandela's speech to the nation on Saturday evening—or the numerous other statements from everyone ranging from F. W. de Klerk to Archbishop Desmond Tutu—had had no effect on the situation, it was the events of Monday, April 12. The Easter celebrations were done—and the enormity of the news was sinking in, goading young people into action. Many spoke of disillusionment with the government, which they said had a hand in Hani's assassination.

The death toll was rising, with police reporting that day that an unknown number of people had died across the country in violence linked to the assassination. The third white man attacked on Saturday in Lwandle, outside Cape Town, had died in the hospital.

Police described townships around Johannesburg as "chaotic" after a shopping center was gutted, cars were burned, roads were barricaded by youths, shots were fired at police and journalists, and shops were robbed. In the East Rand, near where Hani had lived, youths stoned and attacked cars and buses. Houses of Blacks linked to the government, such as policemen, were petrol-bombed. A post office and other government buildings were set alight.

In Mamelodi township outside Pretoria, calls were made by local youth leaders for "arms to be taken up against whites in retaliation" for Hani's assassination.

At a rally attended by 50,000 people in Port Elizabeth in the Eastern Cape, ANC regional deputy chairman Thobile Mhlahlo called for the creation of a "revolutionary climate."

In Cape Town, the ANC's regional secretary, Tony Yengeni, accused Mandela and other ANC and SACP leaders of behaving "as if it is business as usual." He said there should be a serious and thorough consultation process with ordinary members about an appropriate way forward.

"It is the masses who should call the shots on what action is to be taken in the wake of Hani's assassination. It should not be clever leaders who are negotiating on behalf of the people in smoke-filled rooms," he said. Yengeni wanted the leaders of the SACP and ANC to not only feel anger but display it to their members. "It is only when the leaders express their anger that the people will listen to calls for calm," he said.

Realizing the damage that was being done by the spiraling anger and violent acts, the ANC leadership, led by Tokyo Sexwale, in the region of Pretoria-Witwatersrand-Vereeniging (PWV), which included Johannesburg, issued a statement saying it had not called for any "armed activities" directed at whites. "While the ANC understands the anger of our people in this time of grief . . . [c]olor does not play a role in this instance and we therefore call on our people to refrain from racial attacks and hijacking of cars."

If there was Black anger, there was also white hate. On the country's first-ever talk station, Radio 702, most callers were angry at the murder but said they were glad Hani was dead. Brian from Johannesburg said: "This is a war we're involved in and we've wiped out one of their top generals. It's the survival of the fittest. And let me tell you, it's difficult to say this because it's difficult to see a man lying with his brains blown out, but he's one of the enemy and we wiped him out. This is a racial war and there's only going to be one winner."

"This is the best thing that could have happened. Not everyone is sad about Hani's death," said a man who identified himself as a "white male."

A "colored" man—"colored" was apartheid's official designation of mixed-race people—from the area around Hani's home said the murderers should be given a medal and that they should start working on getting rid of another popular leader, the Congress of SA Trade Union's general secretary Jay Naidoo, as well as F. W. de Klerk.

Peter from Boksburg said he was "happy in a political way" that Hani was dead but offered his condolences: "I am a family man too . . . I've got children like he has."

The biggest complaint was the fact that TV1 had interrupted the biblical film *King David* starring Richard Gere to show Mandela's address to the nation. One caller asked if it meant the station considered Hani as being above God.

·   ·   ·

As all the violence and mayhem and the expression of fear and angst unfolded, it became clear to Mandela and the ANC that a new and powerful intervention was needed.

The late-night speech to the nation that Mandela had delivered on Saturday had been historic in many ways. In a divided society, in a difficult and contested transition, a man who had no state power had been the key figure to step forward and attempt to assuage Black anger and fears, temper white angst, and hold out a beacon to a peaceful future. The act of appearance itself was a breakthrough moment, a key turning point for South Africa. De Klerk held and controlled the machinery of the state, but popular power, it was clear, lay in Mandela's hands. Without title or ceremony, he was very near to being the leader of the country.

That power was not enough to quell the violence and staunch the deteriorating situation. Something else needed to be done.

None of the key players interviewed for this book can remember how it came to be that Mandela decided that he needed to address the nation again. However, that evening he used the communication channel between Ramaphosa and Meyer, which was the main form of communication between the ANC and the government, to request another appearance on television the next day. Gill Marcus would liaise with the SABC.

His mind was made up that this second address would be done in his own way. If his usual need to be fully involved in his speeches had been subsumed by the fast-moving events and his grief on Saturday, it was back on again.

TUESDAY
April 13, 1993

Let me have war, say I; it exceeds peace as far as
day does night; it's spritely, waking, audible, and
full of vent. Peace is a very apoplexy, lethargy;
mulled, deaf, sleepy, insensible; a getter of more
bastard children than war's a destroyer of men.
> *Coriolanus*, Act 4, Scene 5

5 a.m.
Mandela home, Houghton

Tuesday the thirteenth marked the first working day following Hani's murder after the long Easter weekend. Nelson Mandela, usually up at 4 a.m., overslept and was a few minutes late for his 5 a.m. meeting with his biographer, Stengel, the first since leaving him behind in Qunu on Saturday after receiving the news of the assassination.

Mandela was back in the house in the leafy Houghton suburb that he had bought in 1992. He had bought it through his attorney, Ismail Ayob, for R 525,000 after his separation from Winnie and his departure from their Soweto home. Mandela had been advised by the ANC to separate from Winnie the year before. He was still totally in love with his wife, but their marriage had been on the rocks for a variety of reasons after he returned from prison in 1990. The breaking point came when newspapers published lurid details of her love affair with an ANC lawyer twenty-five years her junior (she was fifty-six at the time). His confidants Walter Sisulu, Oliver Tambo, and others pressed him to walk away from the marriage.

This new house had been reconnoitered by Waluś and found to be too secure. It was not. Just days after Hani's murder, Stengel drove up to the house, pressed the bell at the gate, and it swung open. He drove in and parked his car. There was no one around. He walked to the front door, opened it, and walked in. Silence, even when he shouted a "hello." He walked upstairs to Mandela's bedroom. "All without seeing a single soul," he wrote in his diary that evening.

The ANC was at once paranoid and cavalier—even comically so— about the security of its leaders. For example, in June 1990, Hani's contingent of bodyguards was dispatched from Lusaka, Zambia, to Johannesburg to ensure his safety. They had no money on them. Arriving at Jan Smuts Airport, the guards only had enough to make one phone call to the ANC head office asking to be picked up. Hani's office said he was busy. No one bothered to help them out. They hung around the airport for hours until they were rescued by one of the government's Security Branch members stationed at the airport. He alerted the ANC to the men's predicament. The organization ordered them to get on a plane back to Lusaka.

Just after 8:30 a.m. Mandela was on the phone, making his customary early-morning calls, rallying the troops. The ANC response to the Hani murder was in full swing. He was trying to get hold of the Transkei general Bantu Holomisa but could not. According to Stengel, Mandela left an "elaborate message to the effect that he wanted the general to tell Hani's family that the ANC would be providing tickets for them to come to Johannesburg on two separate occasions." Further, for the funeral the following Monday, the ANC wanted to have a busload of people from Cofimvaba present. The ANC would be providing the bus.

Why was Mandela concerning himself with such minutiae? Stengel wondered. Two of the newspapers in front of him that day carried reports out of Sweden that should have worried him considerably. The Swedish government had announced that its long-standing funding of the ANC of $14.5 million per year would be stopped as soon as the ANC started campaigning for office. Swedish law prohibited the funding of foreign political parties and, by going on the election trail, the ANC would have transformed from liberation movement to political party.

Yet Mandela chose to indulge in administration, even though his chief of staff, Masekela, said to me that Mandela knew when to let go, that he did not feel he had to control everything. Mandela's efforts at administration were too late, anyway. Ramaphosa's office had already made arrangements with the Hani family to be transported to Johannesburg, and Gilbert, Hani's father, was already in the city.

Mandela then called his fellow former Robben Island prisoner and one of his closest confidants, Mac Maharaj. Without greeting, he went straight into the conversation: "Mac, I wonder if you have a draft yet of my funeral speech . . ."

Mandela was only then informed that Hani's father was in the city. He was to accompany Gilbert Hani to his slain son's home at midday.

The key event of the day, though, was to be Mandela's address to the nation on television again that evening. It was being written by the Department of Information and Publicity team of Pallo Jordan and Gill Marcus. Marcus was negotiating a spot on the news with the head of SABC News, Johan Pretorius. After the visit to the Hani home, Mandela would need to return to the ANC head office on Plein Street, Johannesburg, to properly prepare for it.

8 a.m.
Boksburg Magistrate Court

It was a bitterly cold morning. After three days, Janusz Waluś was still not talking. The police had to present him to court that morning. The law demanded that unless the state decided to invoke the Internal Security Act, he must be presented before court within forty-eight hours of arrest or no later than the end of the first working day after a weekend arrest. And so, as Mandela started his day, the police woke Waluś up. They expected protests outside court, so they took him out of the cells at Benoni Police Station at dawn and had him in the cells below the Boksburg Magistrate Court before sunrise at 6:23 a.m.

Waluś appeared before a magistrate promptly at 8 a.m., his application for bail was swiftly denied, and he was remanded into custody for further police investigation. The entire hearing happened in just a few minutes. When reporters and ANC leaders and supporters started arriving to see the man who had allegedly murdered Hani, the hearing was done. The police drove him out of the court precinct just before 8:30 a.m.

The ANC in the PWV region had issued a statement the day before saying pickets would start at 6 a.m. across the region, but specifically indicated the Boksburg Magistrate Court protests would start at 9 a.m. when courts generally started work. The suspect was gone by the time the crowd swelled to about 5,000, chanting freedom songs, at 9 a.m.

Two members of the Afrikaner Weerstandsbeweging—its leader Eugène Terre'Blanche had announced proudly on Sunday that Waluś was a member—arrived outside court in their full khaki and red-beret regalia, sporting Nazi-style swastika markings, and stood with the substantial police contingent. They were armed with pistols that were clearly visible in hip holsters. They stopped near four uniformed policemen, with whom they chatted and cracked jokes, and were not confronted about their guns until a reporter asked if it was legal for them to be displaying their weapons in public.

"I am not sure," replied one of the policemen. "I'll call my captain on the radio and find out."

After a while the captain turned up and explained to reporters that it was "perfectly all right" to carry openly. But, the captain offered helpfully, he would ask them "to do him the favour of hiding them under their clothing," according to the *Independent*. South Africa had very lax laws for white gun owners, but until 1983, Black people were prohibited from owning guns. After that, only a handful—mainly policemen or government functionaries in Black townships—were granted licenses.

This was to be a major theme for the week as De Klerk, policemen, and government officials turned a blind eye to flagrant transgressions of the law (mainly illegal gatherings, gun-pointing, and threats of violence) by armed white right-wing elements while coming down hard on Black protesters. Later in the week Mandela was to repeat many ANC leaders' assertions that the right wing and whites who threatened violence were being treated with kid gloves by the government.

Barend Strydom had gone on a racially motivated mass shooting spree in a public square in Pretoria in 1988, killing eight unarmed Black people and injuring sixteen others. Strydom was convicted and sentenced to death for the attack but was released in 1992 by De Klerk alongside 150 other political prisoners from all political parties. After Hani's murder, Strydom released posters saying his Wit Wolwe (White Wolves) organization would take up arms against the ANC. Strydom, who was on parole, was only sent a letter in the mail on April 15 by the Department of Prisons saying that his parole could be canceled, as his "veiled threats" did not "promote the process of peace and reconciliation." (Police would also find that the Wit Wolwe had no members apart from Strydom himself.) There was no other action taken.

This was typical. In 1990, Terre'Blanche had visited Law and Order minister Adriaan Vlok in his office. Afterward, Vlok's office and the AWB issued a "joint communique." "It was as if the Federal Bureau of Investigation in Washington had invited the Ku Klux Klan around for a chat," wrote the *New York Times*. Max du Preez, the fiercely antiapartheid editor of the Afrikaans liberal newspaper *Vrye Weekblad*, said at the time: "It's a reluctance on the part of the Government to accept that white people can be terrorists, because in our book terrorists are Black people and the ANC."

This was the context within which the gathering at the courthouse took place. The police had deployed marksmen on the low roof of the court building, and one of them occasionally trained his rifle on the ANC crowd. People responded by gesticulating at him. He smiled, taunting them.

For the ANC, there were two key players at the court appearance: Tokyo Sexwale and the ANC's most visible Afrikaner, Carl Niehaus.

Aware of the rising racial tensions in the country, Mandela had called upon Niehaus to be present at court and to give an address alongside Sexwale. Sexwale told the crowd that the ANC was "rooted in nonracial democratic principles." He said people should simmer with anger inside at Hani's slaying but maintain their dignity and discipline during the next few days of "rolling mass action."

To huge applause, Niehaus declared: "We will not rest until we find all those responsible for Chris Hani's death."

Then the crowd became restive. Two more armed white men drove up to the courthouse in a pickup truck as Niehaus was speaking. The man in the passenger seat waved a gun at the crowd. Howls of anger arose.

The truck stopped. The driver stepped out of the cab, leading his dog to a police cordon separating the two men and their car from the crowd. The police opened for him without question, and he approached the crowd.

When the man reached for his gun, the police did nothing. As the crowd advanced on him, ANC crowd marshals subdued him and dragged him away, handing him over to the police. Only then did they arrest him.

Niehaus continued his speech, reclaiming the Afrikaans language, his mother tongue, from its users massed on the police side. He exclaimed in Afrikaans: "This racist city will become multiracial. We will chase the AWB away from here."

Sexwale took the microphone again and called for peaceful protest: "Nobody may say that the ANC have fired the first shots in a race war."

But Sexwale and Niehaus could see that the crowd was angry. They had to do something to calm their supporters down. Both men told me later in separate interviews that angry as they were, perhaps even angrier than the crowd in front of them, the facts of the ANC's situation were also stark to them. If the talks broke down, Niehaus said, "What would we do? We couldn't go back to exile. That was gone. Take up arms? What then? We had to keep this train on the rails. There was no other plan."

Incumbent on them, and on every leader of the ANC, was ensuring that every gathering avoided bloodshed, including the one in front of them. The two had an urgent problem on their hands: What to do with the restive crowd? "The crowd wanted to burn," said Niehaus. They had to channel the anger elsewhere.

"We march them until they are exhausted," Sexwale told Niehaus.

Sexwale was angered and pained at the assassination of his friend Hani. Yet he considered other factors that made him want the talks to succeed. Just a year before, Sexwale had gone to a whites-only voting station when De Klerk had called a referendum to ask the white electorate whether he should continue with talks. The reason Sexwale went to the voting station was because he was with a white person—his wife, Judy, the paralegal who had come to see him on Robben Island while he was serving an eighteen-year sentence for terrorism alongside Mandela and others. Sexwale and Judy had fallen in love. When Sexwale was released in 1990, the couple had moved into the house down the road from Hani's home together. When Sexwale had accompanied her to vote, she joined the queue and said loudly: "Where do I queue to vote 'Yes'?"

Like Niehaus, Sexwale says the ANC was on the ropes. "De Klerk was our interlocutor. We were negotiating with him. We wanted De Klerk to defeat the right and continue to talk to us."

For De Klerk to win, the ANC had to help him stay in power by avoiding a bloodbath—and then out-negotiate him. So Sexwale took to the bullhorn again and told the crowd that they would march to Hani's house in Dawn Park. It was a ten-kilometer march and, accompanied by the police, they trudged the distance, singing and doing the *toyi-toyi*, the ANC dance made up of high-kneed kicks and foot-stomping accompanied by call-and-response chants.

Two hours later, around lunchtime, the crowd reached the Hani home. As Sexwale and Niehaus had hoped, most marchers were drained of energy and went home peacefully.

Niehaus and Sexwale, however, had other tasks. Mandela needed them to help him deliver his new message of peace to the nation that evening. The two men had to be in Johannesburg that afternoon to help with arrangements to get his message out.

10 a.m.
Cape Town and Port Elizabeth

While Sexwale and Niehaus were leading the long march from court to Hani's home, groups of angry youth attacked police stations in Zwide and KwaZakhele, two Black townships outside Port Elizabeth in the Eastern Cape. The main Port Elizabeth–to–Uitenhage road was closed due to petrol-bomb attacks on cars. There were reports of at least three deaths linked to the violence in the Eastern Cape. In the Cape Town area to the west, stonings, petrol bombs, barricade burnings, and torching vehicles were reported throughout the day. More than a hundred incidents of violence linked to the Hani assassination were reported in just the Western Cape areas. The unrest was concentrated in the urban centers around Johannesburg and Cape Town, which were traditionally very political and where the ANC was most dominant and radical—Mandela's, Hani's, and Holomisa's home province of the Eastern Cape. The pressure to calm things down was increasing, both for the sake of saving the negotiations and to safeguard lives.

It wasn't just Mandela mulling over the increased violence. De Klerk was facing similar pressure.

9 a.m.
Union Buildings, Pretoria

President F. W. de Klerk started his week back at his desk with a meeting with the two men overseeing the Hani investigation. They were not ideal candidates for the delicate task of keeping peace in a transitioning South Africa. The two, both in the steel-framed glasses fashionable among the gray-suited, dour, middle-aged civil servants of the time, were the B-team of De Klerk's cabinet and security structure. Deputy Minister of Law and Order Gert Myburgh was a quiet, unremarkable man who was in the shadow of the man he was deputy to, Hernus Kriel. Kriel was an ultraconservative, loudmouthed, belligerent member of the cabinet who often challenged De Klerk's reformist agenda. The second man, Police Commissioner General Johan van der Merwe, was drenched in the sins of apartheid—he had been party to torture, detention without trial, and murder of ANC activists in his role as head of the feared Security Branch of the apartheid police in the 1980s. He once complained to an interviewer that apartheid was hobbled by, among other things, the fact that the law made it very difficult to detain children who participated in antiapartheid activities.

The two men's reports to De Klerk made for depressing reading. There had been 222 separate "unrest-related" incidents reported by the police between Saturday afternoon, following the murder of Chris Hani, and Tuesday morning as his alleged killer appeared in court. More chaos was to come, according to Van der Merwe. He claimed he had information that radical elements wanted to use Hani's death to foment further violence and derail the democracy talks. "They aim in particular to focus their attention on the destruction of property and attacks on security forces culminating in large-scale public violence," he said.

Myburgh and Van der Merwe represented a conservative wing of De Klerk's cabinet (and the country's top civil servants) that argued that the protests across the country were the result of "uncontrolled vandalism." They wanted to clamp down hard on the protesters. The pair asked for permission from De Klerk to grant police extra powers of search and arrest in three areas in the Eastern Cape Province around Bantu Holomisa's Transkei to combat what they classed as "a serious deterioration in security." De Klerk agreed to their request.

Then they discussed the ANC's marches planned for Wednesday. Both Van der Merwe and Myburgh were adamant that De Klerk deploy extra police and soldiers. This, too, De Klerk agreed to. Immediately afterward, Van der Merwe called a press conference and announced the deployment of 23,000 active police, reservists, and soldiers to monitor proceedings the next day and to spread to "hot spots" across the country. He told reporters that "political leaders" had to exercise control over their followers during Wednesday's gatherings and stressed that his officers, assisted by the military, would maintain law and order. He repeated his claim that he had information that radical elements wanted to use Hani's death to foment further violence but did not produce evidence to back this up—or indicate what action he had taken to deter those who planned these unlawful acts.

The areas around the city of Port Elizabeth and the towns of Cradock and Uitenhage were declared unrest areas; curfews and de facto martial law were imposed.

Midmorning
Elangeni Hotel, Durban

Muhammad Ali had had no idea who Chris Hani was when he left the US. But his days since his arrival had been dominated by the assassinated leader's name. ANC leaders in Cape Town announced that Ali would attend commemorations for Hani even before they had asked him, and his ticker-tape parade in Johannesburg was under threat of cancellation. His historic visit had become a footnote, garnering at best a single paragraph in the inside pages of the daily newspapers.

On the morning of April 13, before he left Durban for Cape Town, Ali wrote to Mandela offering his condolences. The assistant to the general manager of the seafront Elangeni Hotel typed out the letter on hotel letterhead. He was so nervous "about typing a letter of such historical importance," he later recalled, that "I misspelt the name Muhammad, replacing the last 'a' with an 'e.'"

2 p.m.
Johannesburg

The ANC had very little investigative capacity in the period after its unbanning, when it was repatriating thousands of its members from across the globe, reestablishing itself within a fast-paced South African political environment while political violence spiked across the country. The ANC

National Executive Committee's appointment of Mathews Phosa, a fast-talking lawyer who had been on its constitutional committee in exile, to lead its investigation into the Hani assassination was really nothing more than a gesture. He had to rely on the SA Police investigators for all his information, and these were men—and a few women—who were "raised in the service of apartheid," as one reporter put it.

His liaison within the police was Deputy Police Commissioner Lieutenant-General Basie Smit. Phosa had a cordial relationship with Smit, whom he had met right at the beginning of his return from exile in March 1990. At the time, Smit—the head of the security police that had through the 1980s chased, kidnapped, blackmailed, detained, bombed, and assassinated ANC activists like Phosa—had remarked on how thin the ANC lawyer was.

"It's because your police have been chasing me so hard," Phosa joked.

By 1993, there were few jokes. Smit was now known as the "Third Force General," as he had been linked in newspaper reports to the funding and arming of Inkatha Freedom Party supporters who, as in the Boipatong Massacre, then went on to attack ANC-supporting township residents. A year after Hani's murder, the nickname was to be confirmed as true when an interim report of the Goldstone Commission, which probed allegations of a Third Force—in the SA context, a manipulator in what seemed overtly to be turf battles between political rivals the ANC and the Inkatha Freedom Party—in political violence, implicated him and ten officers in the arming and funding of attackers of township residents. He would be suspended.

For now, Phosa had very little to work with. The ANC had received a few tip-offs by anonymous callers to its head office, with one claiming that Waluś had worked at a gun shop and had connived with some fellow employees. An ANC intelligence operative, a burly former rugby player from the Eastern Cape named Ronnie Watson, was following up that and other leads—particularly suspicions that there had been a second person with the assassin. Phosa had also dispatched an ANC lawyer, Tefo Raditapole, to review police evidence as it was brought to the party's attention.

Raditapole was later to recall that there was so much distrust of the police that even the relatively scientific ballistics report was "viewed with suspicion."

Hours after Hani's assassination, Deputy Minister of Law and Order Gert Myburgh announced that it had been "the act of a lone gunman without political motive," a remark repeated by police spokesman Captain Craig Kotze to journalists. At that point there had not even been an interrogation of Waluś, and the search of his apartment in Pretoria was still ongoing. Phosa fired off a press statement charging that "at the highest levels of the police force and through their spokesperson, Captain Craig Kotze, the waters around the assassination are being muddied." He slammed Myburgh's initial declaration that the assassination had been the work of a lone gunman.

Newspapers had also reported that some witnesses claimed there had been a second car at the murder scene and that it had sped off after the killing. Dudu Kraai, a nurse who lived nearby and had been walking home at the time of the shooting, had called the police a few times and told them she had seen two cars.

"They then called me once to identify the red car. I asked if there was no white car to identify, but they said there wasn't. When they held an identity parade of suspects I offered to help identify the driver of the red car, but they didn't want me to," she later told investigative reporter Evelyn Groenink. Then, two days later, something strange happened to Kraai. At 4 a.m. there was a commotion outside her house and aggressive knocking on the door. The banging and shouting was so loud it woke up her children.

It was the police. It was not a friendly visit.

"They said they had come to interview me, but it was more like they were scaring me. They asked me who I thought I was, why I wanted to be involved in this case, if I was a relative of Chris Hani," she told Groenink. Then they left.

Two other residents agreed with her that there had been a red and a white car at the murder scene. There were also reports of a can of soda and cigarette butts on the ground behind the neighbor's wall, also suggesting that there had been a second person at the scene.

The police had seemingly decided that these leads were not worth following up.

Although he had no investigative capabilities and no new evidence, the one thing that Phosa believed he could do, he told me, was to ask questions. He fired off a letter to the police commissioner, General Johan van der Merwe, and a press release that said a number of questions needed to be answered:

"Why was a man in the country for a few years and apparently not yet a citizen given an initial firearm licence and subsequently a further three licences for weapons of different calibres within two years of his arrival?

"What connection is there between the suspect and those involved in the robbery of arms from the Air Force base . . ."

This was all Phosa could do: ask questions. It reminded him that the ANC had still not won the freedom it had been fighting for.

5 p.m.
Port St. Johns, Eastern Cape Province

The 4x4 double cab pickup truck made its way up the hill, its occupants done with their day of fishing, heading home for dinner. It was around 5 p.m.; the sun was setting in the west. There were five people in the car: Alastair Weakley and his engineer brother Glen, both in their forties, Keith Rumble and his seven-year-old son Brett, and eleven-year-old Thomas O'Keeffe, who had his window down, elbow out, watching the trees flash past. There were many people in the South Africa of 1993 that one could have considered legitimate targets for the anger of young Black people who had just lost a hero to their cause. But one would have been hard-pressed to say anyone in that car was among them.

The legend of Ally Weakley stretched from the 1970s at the posh Anglican boys' high school in Grahamstown, where he had been a white guy teaching Xhosa, through to the dawn of South Africa's democracy where he was a well-known liberal lawyer and participant in a peace committee that mirrored the work of Peter Harris in the PWV area. To hear the boys at St. Andrew's College talk about Weakley, you would think he was a rock star. "He was a brilliant rugby player. He was funny. And he seemed to know all about things like women," Hamilton Wende, now a top international journalist, was to write about him in later years. He was also very different from many of the whites in South Africa back in 1975, the year that Wende was a fourteen-year-old who, like the rest of his class, idolized Weakley. Grant Fowlds, another of Weakley's pupils at St. Andrew's, wrote that Weakley was "a carbon copy of the inspirational teacher played by Robin Williams in *Dead Poets Society* . . . In those days there were few Black teachers in white schools and so it was not unusual to have a white guy teaching the home tongue of Nelson Mandela. But Ally was not your average white guy. Not only did he speak the language beautifully, but he was enthralled by Xhosa culture and traditions," wrote Fowlds. Weakley was "so far removed from most other whites of his generation that they could have come from different planets."

Unlike the rest of South Africa, where soccer dominates as a sport among Blacks while rugby is largely loved among whites in general and Afrikaners in particular, the Eastern Cape is different: there, rugby rules across race and class. It was loved by the likes of Mandela, and Weakley was excellent at it. He was captain of the regional first team that, according to Fowlds, was feared as the meanest, toughest players on any field across South Africa. And Weakley did not just play rugby. He cared that it stood for the right values. At Rhodes University in the 1970s, he had an annual intervarsity match against the University of Port Elizabeth canceled because UPE would not allow a student of Chinese origin to attend the post-match ball. In the late 1970s, at the height of apartheid, he defied Danie Craven, the notorious rugby administrator of the all-white South African national rugby team the Springboks, who had said: "Over my dead body will there ever be a Black Springbok." Craven threatened to ban Weakley from rugby for life if he played in a nonracial rugby match in Port

Elizabeth. Weakley defied the threat. He was later visited by the security police for his principled stand.

"Ally did not exactly have film star looks," said Fowlds, and yet he was "seldom seen without a gorgeous girl on his arm. So to us he was glamourous as a movie star, with wild long hair, flashing a gap-toothed smile and speeding around the town in a purple Volvo." Even more, "He had zero tolerance for the racism that was common and so accepted in our world then," said Wende. Some say he supported the ANC, while others remember him as a man who was a "new South African long before most whites began even to think about the morality of the system under which they prospered and others groaned."

During apartheid, Weakley would go from house to house canvassing for support for the liberal Progressive Party and its successor, the Democratic Party, as the new South Africa loomed closer. When political violence had restarted in 1990, he had immediately signed up to the local peace committee. Ally Weakley was the kind of person the new South Africa that Mandela was negotiating for needed.

He would not see it.

5 p.m.
Port St. Johns, Eastern Cape Province

Early on Tuesday, April 13, 1993, Mlulamisi Maxhayi, Vuyani Nyalukana, and Lungile Mazwi had headed for Port St. Johns. They wanted to obtain more information about the local right-wingers from their comrades Phumelele Hermans and Fundisile Guleni. Even without information they were ready for action: they carried an automatic rifle given to them by the MK man who had given them basic training. Nyalukana, who had a pickup truck, acted as the unit's armorer and driver. Among the arms he had for immediate use were a pistol and two hand grenades. Chris Hani was dead, but he would not die in vain.

Hermans and Guleni listened earnestly to Maxhayi and his crew and welcomed their mission. There were indeed right-wingers around, explained Hermans. But there was a problem: a police station and the Transkei Defence Force's troops, installed in barracks near the town, would intervene.

It would be better, Hermans advised, to target the remote area near Mpande. He had a relative in one of those villages, his uncle was the local shopkeeper, and they could case the nearby holiday resorts to check for white right-wingers there.

There was another hitch. Hermans and Guleni were envious of the Flagstaff trio's hardware. They also needed guns.

"We can get guns from a comrade in Majola. His name is Zongezile Mxhize," said Hermans.

The five men climbed into the pickup truck, but their trip to Majola was fruitless.

"He doesn't have guns. He doesn't even have one himself," Hermans reported. "But he can help us get two guns from some comrades in the area."

Mxhize, too, joined the group, so there were now six of them. They drove in search of guns to another comrade called T-Man. T-Man and a friend of his had two 9mm pistols, but there was yet another hitch: T-Man and his comrade did not want to give them to Hermans and Guleni.

"We want to join the operation," they told Maxhayi.

There were eight of them now.

They agreed to head to Mpande, to the loose spread of villages and backpacker lodges along the scenic Umngazi River. Hermans knew the area and directed the group to one of the built-up camping areas nearby, usually rented by white holidaymakers.

Someone in the pickup said there were just too many of them. A debate ensued that Hermans ended by saying one person should drive the truck to a certain spot while the rest of the group would cut through the bush to the meeting point. They agreed and split. At the meeting point the group parked the vehicle some distance away and Hermans, together with Guleni and Nyalukana, walked along the gravel road to the chalets. They were greeted by a Black woman, a worker.

"We are looking for work, Ma," they told her. "Is any available at the chalets?"

She answered that the place was virtually empty. There was only one woman there. The men had gone fishing at a nearby resort. The three men spotted a white child.

They chatted to the lady worker for a while longer, thanked her, and headed back to their comrades.

They now had a plan. They would drive down the road to the sea from the chalets. They would pick a vantage point from which they could see a long way down and spot an oncoming car. This would be where they would wait for the men who had gone fishing. Three men would do the shooting, and the rest would act as lookouts.

It was a great road for an ambush. It had been cut into the dense forest of the mountainside. A sheer cliff fell to the sea on the one side and green vegetation rose on the other. The road wound up the side of the mountain like a lazy snake. It was a clear, bright day.

The five watchers would stay with the pickup truck. They would have one gun and the two hand grenades with them. The five scouts would see the car from a distance, time enough for the three shooters, hiding in bushes around a curve in the road, to be ready. Maxhayi took the R4 rifle, given to them by the MK man. It was not exactly the popular Russian-made, more revolutionary AK-47 that was known as the ANC cadres' weapon of choice. This was the enemy's gun: manufactured in South Africa, the Vektor R4 assault rifle had been the standard service rifle of the South African Defence Force since 1980.

Guleni was hot for action. He would not agree to be left to guard duty. He wanted to be one of the shooters. He took T-Man's comrade's firearm.

Maxhayi told Vuyani Nyalukana, the driver who was his very first co-conspirator: "The signal is that you must hoot if it's whites in the car."

That's how it unfolded.

Maxhayi, Guleni, and T-Man went off and hid in the bushes. They waited. In the late afternoon, around 5:00 p.m., far in the distance, a white speck appeared, then the shape formed into a recognizable vehicle. A white 4x4 twin cab truck, winding its way slowly up the mountain road. Two people were in the front, three in the back. All white. The one nearest to them had the window down, his elbow sticking out, catching the wind.

Mlulamisi Maxhayi held the R4 in his hands and waited for the signal. His comrade Vuyani Nyalukana saw the white people in the car as it drove past the watch car.

Then Nyalukana honked to signal to his comrades to shoot.

It was not clear who shot first, but it was one of the pistols: Guleni or T-Man. Then a second shot, again unclear whose pistol it was. The car was still moving forward, headed for the bush where Maxhayi was hidden. He pressed the trigger on the R4.

Maxhayi wanted to shoot the car and derail it, making its stalled momentum overturn it down the cliff. He had put the rifle on automatic fire to get as many rounds off as he could. The car came nearer, unhindered by the first two shots. Maxhayi aimed at the front seat and squeezed the trigger. *Rat-a-tat-tat-tatatatat* went the rifle.

He saw the car jerk, come to a halt, and then slowly, slowly, directionless, move backward. Then it turned on its side, falling over the edge of the road, careening down the cliff a few meters before coming to a stop on its side.

The other men came running up the hill, shouting to go down and "finish the job."

"No! It's done. We made our point," Maxhayi shouted. "Let's go."

Evening
Pretoria

F. W. de Klerk was panicking. Reports of riots and deaths were coming in from across the country. In Port St. Johns, a pickup truck had been shot off the road, killing the driver and one of the passengers, although the two children in the back seat were reportedly unscathed. To his mind the unfolding violence was due to the ANC's failure to maintain a "responsible approach." He believed that the ANC's program of marches, memorials, and protests was the trigger for the violence that was consuming the country.

On the previous Saturday he had felt that only Mandela "would be able to calm his enraged followers." Now, just three days later, he had reached a turning point. "The ANC had failed to exercise control over its followers and it seemed as though we might return to the volatile days of August 1992," he reasoned. He claimed that "ANC demonstrations led to rioting and looting in several cities." Not once did De Klerk demonstrate a recognition of the deep, legitimate anger felt by progressive Black and white South Africans and the need to do *something* to let that anger out.

De Klerk was falling victim to the argument of the securocrats on his side, such as Law and Order minister Hernus Kriel, his most anti-ANC cabinet member. The argument had an interesting history. In 1990, Craig Kotze, a crime reporter on the liberal Johannesburg newspaper the *Star*, had revealed that he had for years been spying on his colleagues for the apartheid government. After his revelation, Kotze had joined the police as a spin doctor. He had devised the strategy, in 1992, to blame the ANC's demonstrations for the massacres in which the organization's members were being killed in townships. He had taken his plan to Hernus Kriel, the hard-line minister, who at first could not believe it would work.

"But how can we do that? We don't know that," Kriel had told Kotze.

"Haven't you been watching television? Don't you see shops being looted and burned because of mass action? Violence is a natural consequence of mass action. And that's what we have to tell the public," Kotze responded.

By the time Hani was killed, this was the dominant narrative among the hard-liners in De Klerk's cabinet: the ANC's mass action campaigns protesting against the violence were the cause of violence! And so, on this day, instead of reaching out to Mandela, De Klerk convened a meeting of his top security ministers, the State Security Council, for Wednesday the fourteenth "to consider the situation and to take steps to maintain law-and-order." This was a body whose participants were *hardegat* (Afrikaans for hard-core or stubborn) securocrats who had in the past lied to him about the continued existence and operation of "death squads" and had never allowed him into their world of espionage, torture, and murder.

Now, panicked, he turned to the body that had brought South Africa to the brink.

6 p.m.
Johannesburg

Mandela's address to the nation on Saturday had been approved through De Klerk's office, and arrangements, handled by the ANC's Gill Marcus, had been smooth even when the ANC president had missed the prime-time news slot. When Mandela decided to have a second go at a message to the nation to address specifically the ongoing bloodshed, his people again approached the South African Broadcasting Corporation. They were rebuffed.

According to Tokyo Sexwale, the government's view was, "Well, Mandela can have a press conference and it will be covered by SABC in the evening news." The ANC wanted Mandela carried on the main news bulletins of all major stations, in his own words, without editing. By 2 p.m. there was still no agreement, so Sexwale arrived at the SABC's main thirty-story building and demanded to get a hearing from someone in management and for a guarantee that Mandela's speech would be televised.

But there was no speech written.

The ANC wanted to be in control of all aspects of the speech this time around. The organization had put together its own camera and editing crew. Working from their studio on the sixth floor of the ANC head office, the team ensured Mandela changed from a white to a blue shirt, from an outgoing tie to a somber burgundy grenadine tie, a black jacket, and an ANC flag—black, green, and gold—discreetly placed to the right behind him.

When the speech was at last presented to him, Mandela insisted that "it had to be pointed out that although it was a white man who pulled the trigger killing Hani, it was also a white woman who courageously came forward and provided the evidence that led to the arrest of Waluś." This was to be the most quoted, most resonant, and most conciliatory line of his speech that evening. Where did it come from? Niehaus, who was in the room that day, says it was Mandela's idea. It is certainly a line that accorded with the nonracial values he was dogged about espousing and a line he may have used at the party meeting on the Sunday after Hani's murder, for he certainly wasn't the only ANC leader drawing attention to this detail.

The fiery KwaZulu-Natal leader Harry Gwala had alluded to this theme in a speech in his region the previous day, noting: "Apartheid is not a Black or white issue . . . It is a white woman who made it easy for Chris's killer to be caught." The firebrand's utterances had been quoted in the most influential business publication, *Business Day*, that morning in its front-page wrap of the day's events countrywide. Certainly, the dichotomy had been percolating in Mandela's mind earlier that day, because while at the Hani home standing next to Hani's father, Gilbert, Mandela had said: "A white man pulled the trigger of the murder weapon, but we should also remember that a white woman helped to catch Hani's murderer."

By the afternoon, the idea was clearly still on his mind.

And so, at his instruction, the speechwriters included the words that were to be quoted again and again in newspapers across the world, and which were to become the key takeaway from one of Mandela's most important and famous speeches. He scribbled them down himself at the top of the draft, making them even more graceful than his earlier remark: "A white man, full of prejudice and hate, came to our country and committed a deed so foul that our whole nation now teeters on the brink of disaster. A white woman, of Afrikaner origin, risked her life so that we may know, and bring to justice, this assassin."

The speech finished, it was time to record the segment. By then the SABC had agreed to run it, but there were conditions. It had to be no more than four minutes long, said the SABC's executives. The ANC was so suspicious of the SABC that it insisted that the prerecorded clip would not be touched by the broadcaster and no editing whatsoever would be done to it.

•   •   •

Many have remarked that when in deep pain Mandela became almost statue-like, his face still and unmoving, lacking in animation. Having to read the speech was to revisit the pain that he felt at Hani's assassination.

According to Niehaus, the ANC staffers were "shaken up and emotional" during the recording. Many of the people in the room were in tears, as if the recording had opened up the pent-up emotions of the past few days.

"What made it even more difficult is that Madiba dealt with his grief in a very stoic manner," said Niehaus. "It was as if he was bottling up all the grief and anger that he felt deep inside himself, with his face having become almost expressionless and his voice monotone."

There were several stops and starts. They couldn't have a repeat of what had happened Saturday.

"Cut!" the director would say. "Let's start again."

As Niehaus put it, to get the right balance between deeply felt—but controlled—grief and anger was difficult, and several recordings had to be made. Then, finally, with Johannesburg about to be enveloped by darkness, it was done. The recording was just over six minutes long.

Few of the ANC members present at the recording had cars. Niehaus did. He was dispatched to deliver the recorded speech. Time was running out. The tape was supposed to go on air at 7 p.m., 8 p.m., and 11 p.m. It was 6:30 p.m. when he and a few others headed out for the 3.9-kilometer drive to the ugly cluster of concrete buildings that house the SA Broadcasting Corporation to this day.

Getting into the SABC, then and now, is a mission. Arriving in 1994 to train SABC journalists on how to shed their apartheid training and deliver news, the head of TV journalism training for the Canadian Broadcasting Corporation, Tim Knight, described the complex as "clearly designed to keep ideas and values out."

"A sign orders us to leave firearms and explosives at the reception desk. We carry no firearms or explosives. Only ideas and values. Bags, wallets, keys pass through a metal detector. Guards armed with automatic rifles watch us like jackals watch rabbits," he wrote. Imagine what Niehaus, who just ten years before had tried to plant a bomb at a gasworks just four hundred meters from the SABC building, must have thought. After parking, they had to wait for the notoriously slow and bureaucratic security personnel at the SABC to check their IDs, call someone from the news studio to verify their legitimacy, sign them in, and then take them up.

Time was running out.

Their contact was the highest-ranking editorial executive at the public broadcaster, SABC-TV editor in chief Johan Pretorius, described by Knight as "all pink and smooth and unctuous."

Pretorius had described his job succinctly a year before: "It would be naïve to deny that the corporation followed a fairly strict government of the day line."

In 1987, for example, the former president, P. W. Botha, had called the SABC in the middle of the evening news broadcast and demanded a revised report on his firing of a cabinet minister. The SABC had immediately complied with his wishes.

Pretorius had been sweating as 7 p.m. approached. As soon as he was given the tape, he put it in the VHS player in his office and timed it. Six minutes long.

Niehaus, who describes Pretorius as "red-faced and hyperventilating" at that point, says the man told them he had been strictly informed that Mandela's message was to be four minutes long.

"If it's longer I cannot broadcast it," he said. There was no legitimate reason why not.

The ANC delegation was fuming.

"For less than two measly minutes this apartheid apparatchik was prepared to let the country go up in flames," said Niehaus.

For the ANC, failure to broadcast the message would be a disaster. It was not only that the security and political situation was deteriorating rapidly across the country. Throughout the afternoon the party had sent out messages on the radio that Mandela would address the nation on television. Given his stature and the unfolding events, many would have been making their way to wherever they could access a television to hear, as Niehaus put it, "what the message of our leader was." If Mandela did not appear as advertised, it would dent the ANC's and Mandela's reputation and stature—and frustrate what the ANC considered would be a key statement in calming the country.

Niehaus asked Pretorius for the phone and put an urgent call through to Mandela's office. He explained what the problem was. Mandela took his number and told him to wait.

It was 6:55 p.m.

Within minutes the phone on Pretorius's desk rang. Niehaus suspects it was F. W. de Klerk on the line, but this has never been confirmed. De Klerk has no recollection of such a conversation. Neither does Roelf Meyer, the ANC's main contact and the minister of communication. What we know is that Pretorius paled and stood up. He responded three times to the voice on the other end, in his native Afrikaans.

"Ja, meneer." (Yes, sir.)

Pause.

"Goed, meneer." (Right, sir.)

Pause.

"Ek maak so, meneer." (I will do so, sir.)

He replaced the handset, grabbed the video cassette, and ran to the broadcasting studio.

The rest of the ANC team followed him.

"There were now literally only seconds left to spare," remembers Niehaus. He was exhausted. He had driven up from Cape Town after hearing the news about Hani's assassination on Saturday. That morning he had been up at dawn to be at the Waluś court appearance in Boksburg. He plonked himself in the chair in Pretorius's office to see how the broadcast actually looked when it went out to the nation.

At 7 p.m. sharp the newsreader introduced the message of Nelson Mandela, president of the African National Congress.

7:02 p.m.
Johannesburg

For many, the address was a game changer. The celebrated British journalist and later Mandela biographer Anthony Sampson was to say Mandela's "statesmanlike speech, set against De Klerk's silence, suggested that he was already the real leader, and the protector of peace."

"This was the week when moral authority passed visibly from the Government to the ANC," wrote newspaper editor Ken Owen in his popular *Sunday Times* column the following weekend. "It was to Mr. Nelson Mandela that the country turned." Owen was one of those who had been named on the hit list found in Walus's flat.

"Power slipped visibly from the limp hands at Groote Schuur," De Klerk's Cape Town residence, he continued, "to the stronger hands at Shell House"—the ANC headquarters.

Business Day, required reading for the economic elite, said in an editorial that De Klerk had become defensive, preoccupied with claims that whites were threatened because a Black leader had died. "While the president deploys 23,000 troops to protect whites, it is ANC president Mandela whose utterances are more statesmanlike . . . [De Klerk] has sadly misjudged the situation," former newspaper editor and political analyst Raymond Louw said.

Archbishop Desmond Tutu said he believed that "had [Mandela] not gone on television and radio . . . our country would have gone up in flames . . . It would have been the easiest thing just to release the dogs of war . . . Mercifully, Mandela was there and held them all at bay."

As speeches go, Mandela's that night was a remarkably short one at only 759 words. He began with a direct, punchy introduction that aimed straight at the heart of every man, woman, and child watching. The speech first and foremost entreated the people of South Africa to listen, to give him their ears. "Tonight I am reaching out to every single South African, Black and white, from the very depths of my being," he said, humbling himself before them.

After this, he immediately redefined what had roiled the country over the past few days. This, Mandela seemed to be saying, was not a political assassination. It was instead beyond human comprehension and below human decency. The person who had done this deed was no ordinary person, but a man "full of prejudice and hate" who had come to "our country" to commit "a deed so foul that our whole nation now teeters on the brink of disaster."

In a widely circulated academic paper years later, Kenneth S. Zagacki, professor of communication and former head of the Department of Communication at North Carolina State University, wrote that Mandela "made it clear that Hani's assassination was no mere happenstance of war, no justified political maneuver."

"He described the murder in stark terms, confronting whites with the damaging effects of their 'prejudice and hate' and with the reality that not nearly enough had been done by whites to move the country away from apartheid," he said.

Immediately after this indictment of apartheid, Mandela then reminded his audience that it was Retha Harmse, "a white woman, of Afrikaner origin," who had "risked her life so that we may know, and bring to justice, this assassin."

Gungubele had, since the age of sixteen when he arrived in Johannesburg to work in the mines, regarded whites as the enemy. In the East Rand townships that he led, he knew that Hani's murder had sharpened Black animosity toward whites as Waluś and his coconspirators had wanted it to. When Mandela spoke of a white woman who saw the killing and called the police, Gungubele felt like "something went off in my head," confusing the certainties of South Africa's divisions. "This," Gungubele realized, "is how you paralyze racial hate." For the second time in three days, Mandela had given him something he could say with certainty to his own followers. He felt total and absolute trust in Mandela's words, and that people would trust him, too, when he repeated those words to them. He said he remembered something else, too, when he watched the news bulletin: Mandela clearly believed in his words. He was authentic in the saying of them— and that was why he, too, believed him.

In his televised address to the nation on the thirteenth of April, Mandela wanted to build a new patriotism of the good, peace-loving South African and create a bulwark against those who sought to derail the democracy project. Again and again, he used an inclusive "our," saying "our grief and anger is tearing us apart" and that what had happened was a "national tragedy that has touched millions of people, across the political and color divide." He was othering Waluś, his coconspirators, and those who sought to hinder the path to democracy.

In the same breath, he corralled the dastardly deed and put it squarely at the door of "the men who worship war, and who lust after blood." He asked for a coalition of the good against these dogs of war, declaring: "Now is the time for all South Africans to stand together against those who, from any quarter, wish to destroy what Chris Hani gave his life for—the freedom of all of us."

Mandela reached out to this coalition of the good, making them a partner in the quest for justice, democracy, and peace by saying: "This is a watershed moment for all of us. Our decisions and actions will determine whether we use our pain, our grief, and our outrage to move forward to what is the only lasting solution for our country—an elected government of the people, by the people, and for the people."

The speech is remarkable for how Mandela—who for the period before his release from prison in 1990 and afterward was routinely labeled soft or accommodationist or even a "sellout" by detractors—displays his most misunderstood characteristic: that militancy does not mean reckless rhetoric but rather winning the many battles that one's cause has identified. Like the US's Reverend Martin Luther King Jr., Mandela has been portrayed as someone who would bend over backward for peace and sacrifice justice in the process. This was a moment where Mandela illustrated that justice, democracy, and peace are all important—and none can be pursued at the expense of the other. He was no sellout.

Always a man of action, Mandela went on to punt the next day's nationwide protests, saying they were for "one of the greatest revolutionaries this country has ever known."

Young people were itching for action, and Mandela knew that he could not just tell them to go home and mourn Hani quietly. He needed to help them find expression for their pent-up anger. This is, perhaps, where the great difference between Mandela and De Klerk lay that week. De Klerk's view was that the ANC had to "control" its members. The idea that they had to grieve was alien to him. It was Mandela, as academic Kenneth Zagacki pointed out, who "encouraged them to transform" their grief and anger into productive "mourning and protest."

Again, Mandela addressed these young people directly—and placed the responsibility of discipline on their shoulders: "To the youth of South Africa we have a special message: you have lost a great hero. You have repeatedly shown that your love of freedom is greater than that most precious gift, life itself. But you are the leaders of tomorrow. Your country, your people, your organization need you to act with wisdom."

Mandela expected even more protests, more demonstrations, and perhaps even more riots and deaths in the days ahead. The days would be difficult, but he did not see how the process of mourning could be done in any other way—or done away with. "If we had not done so the right wing and these sinister elements would have succeeded in drawing the country to a racist war and incalculable loss of human lives and bloodshed," he was to say.

Mandela knew just how desperate Hani's murderers were to cast the march to freedom in racial terms, to portray themselves as victims. Again he sought to nullify their message, saying: "Now is the time for our white compatriots, from whom messages of condolence continue to pour in, to reach out with an understanding of the grievous loss to our nation, to join in the memorial services and the funeral commemorations."

It was all a delicate balancing act, and he knew the ANC needed partners in this endeavor. He reached out to the police: "Now is the time for the police to act with sensitivity and restraint, to be real community policemen and women who serve the population as a whole. There must be no further loss of life at this tragic time. We must not let the men who worship war, and who lust after blood, precipitate actions that will plunge our country into another Angola." Here Mandela was referring to a memory many white South Africans did not want to revisit—the apartheid government's raids into Angola between 1975 and 1988 as part of its "border war" to stop the liberation of neighboring Namibia. Every month throughout that period there were reports of deaths and losses from "the front." There was conscription of all white men at the time, and there was no hiding the body bags of young white men from the front. By 1990, ordinary white men and women had joined the "end conscription" movement, which aligned itself with antiapartheid activities, in their thousands. Those whose children were enlisted lived in fear. An estimated 2,500 white South Africans died in the border wars.

This was a deliberate move by Mandela. By 1990, not even the securocrats wanted to witness another Angola, where young white South African men had found themselves mired in an endless war they and their compatriots cared nothing about in a land they knew nothing about.

Finally, he asserted the supremacy of the civilian structures of the ANC over its army, Umkhonto we Sizwe. "Chris Hani was a soldier. He believed in iron discipline. He carried out instructions to the letter. He practiced what he preached." He told those who did not adhere to the message for peaceful protest that they would be acting contrary to the tenets of the man they claimed to be avenging, appropriating Hani for his strategy to ensure that a hard democratic win would come out of the assassination. But he was also telling the truth. As the trade unionist Mbhazima Sam Shilowa recalled, "Hani had been calling for peace when he died. So we just extend his message."

"Any lack of discipline," Mandela continued in this vein, "is trampling on the values that Chris Hani stood for. Those who commit such acts serve only the interests of the assassins, and desecrate his memory." He reminded South Africans of the purpose of struggle and of who and what Hani was: "Let us honor this soldier for peace in a fitting manner. Let us rededicate ourselves to bringing about the democracy he fought for all his life; democracy that will bring real, tangible changes in the lives of the working people, the poor, the jobless, the landless. Chris Hani is irreplaceable in the heart of our nation and people."

He went on to announce the funeral date, April 19, and concluded by underlining the legitimacy of people's anger and tears, saying "we are a nation in mourning." Chris Hani, in Mandela's speech, was not a victim but a brave soldier of the struggle who had given his life in battle. Hani, Mandela said, "has made the supreme sacrifice. The greatest tribute we can pay to his life's work is to ensure we win that freedom for all our people."

8:15 p.m.
Johannesburg

Carl Niehaus was in tears again. The broadcast had just been concluded and he was digesting the impact of the speech, sitting in Johan Pretorius's chair.

Then the phone rang.

Should he answer it? It was not his office, yet he thought he should in case it was one of his comrades who had gone along with Pretorius to the studio. It wasn't.

It was an Afrikaner woman. Without asking who she was talking to, she said: *"Het die ANC nou oorgeneem daar by julle?"* (Has the ANC taken over there?)

Before Niehaus could answer she continued, anger in her voice: *"Ek is naar om te moet luister na hierdie blêrrie ou Mandela!"* (I am nauseated by having to listen to this bloody old Mandela!)

Niehaus was so shocked he did not answer immediately. She hesitated and asked: *"Met wie praat ek nou!?"* (Who am I speaking to now?)

Niehaus recovered his voice. The moment was too delicious to pass up, so he responded quickly.

"Met Carl Niehaus van die ANC." (Carl Niehaus of the ANC.)

As he was to write years later, there was a long, shocked silence and then she exclaimed: *"O Here God!"* (O Lord God!) The phone went dead.

The speech was broadcast two more times that evening on the main channels of the SABC and on all public radio stations over the next few days.

For Niehaus, it was time to go home. He was not to know until the next day that after the ANC delegation left, Pretorius cynically cut Mandela's speech, showing only some parts of it on the 8 p.m. news on the English-Afrikaans channel historically designated for whites. Only later in the evening was the speech repeated in full.

Evening
Transkei

As Niehaus headed home that evening, Holomisa finished watching Mandela's address to the nation. He had, just before Mandela went on television, also received news of the killing of the Weakley brothers and reports of violence across the region.

He decided to act. He announced that Transkei police would be deployed in large numbers at all holiday resorts. He noted that hundreds of South African and foreign tourists were in resorts in the Transkei during the Easter period and his government was considering keeping major police deployments there permanently.

But he was too late. De Klerk was about to take drastic action on what he saw as an arrogant and irresponsible Transkei.

WEDNESDAY
April 14, 1993

So foul and fair a day I have not seen.
  Macbeth, Act 1, Scene 3

9 a.m.
Boksburg

Retha Harmse did not go to work on Wednesday morning. It was the day of mourning announced by the ANC and virtually no worker, Black or white, was going into work. The cosmetics factory where she worked was shut for the day, as were many others across the country.

Harmse was afraid for her safety and that of her family. She had had a torrid few days. On Sunday she had been taken in by the police and had to identify Waluś in a lineup. She had thought the suspects would be behind glass as she had seen in the movies, but this had turned out to be different. There were ten white men, standing in a line, and she stood just a few steps away from them. She was panic-stricken, trying to hide behind her sunglasses.

The men all looked straight at her. Her legs quivered. "It was so creepy," she said later.

Yet she could not positively identify the man who shot Hani.

On Tuesday, when she arrived at work, she was swamped by her colleagues. She couldn't get any work done. Everyone had one question: "What happened?"

Many of South Africa's workplaces had been desegregated in the late

1980s, but races did not mingle much. Yet that day one of her Black colleagues stopped her and blurted out: "You're my hero!"

Yet she was afraid. The phone calls had continued, and her picture had been on the front pages of the biggest newspapers in the country—the *Sunday Times* and the *Rapport*. Too many people recognized her.

She had cut her long hair on Tuesday after work. She now sported a baseball cap, pulled down over her new short hairdo, and her blue eyes were hidden behind dark aviators.

That morning she had helped Daan put up a FOR SALE sign in front of their house.

9 a.m.
Cape Town

Across the country, those who wanted to commemorate their dead hero started moving early in the morning. In and around Cape Town, hundreds of minibus taxis and buses left the townships and shack settlements that straddle the N2 and the N1, the main road arteries into the city, and joined the virtually empty motorways toward the center of Cape Town's business district. In Wellington, seventy-two kilometers outside the city, some 2,000 protesters hopped onto a train headed into the city. It was carrying at least a thousand passengers more than it should ordinarily load. Its doors were open. People clung to the sides and many hung out the windows and sat between coaches.

The people inside were singing and lustily partaking of the revolutionary *toyi-toyi* dance. It wasn't an appropriate song and dance for the train. At its most energetic, the *toyi-toyi* is something of a push and pull of the body accompanied by a call-and-response in the lyrics that are often made up on the spot. To illustrate, the song leader would chant:

"Kill the Boer!"

(All participants would be hopping on one leg, responding *"Hayi! Hayi!"*)

"The farmer!"

(Change to other leg, chanting again *"Hayi! Hayi!"*)

The problem was that when the dance called for a pull, participants hopped up and down on one leg, leaning in to one side, and the train leaned to the one side of the tracks. When the crowd pushed, it leaned in the opposite direction.

By the time the train reached Brackenfell station, halfway through its journey, it was literally lifting up and down with the dancing. "The whole train was heaving forward and backwards in unison with the passengers' movement," an eyewitness, Pieter Swart, who was sitting on his front porch near the train tracks when the train pulled into Brackenfell station, told the Afrikaans daily newspaper *Beeld*.

Then, as the train pulled into the station, there was a massive bang and blast and the train "literally sprung from the one track to the other," said Swart. The last coach broke off from the train and the three before it overturned. Screaming passengers ran in all directions.

It was just the beginning of South Africa's Day of Anger.

9 a.m.
Cape Town

As the movement to churches, stadiums, and other venues to observe Hani's Day of Mourning began, Andries Treurnicht, the seventy-two-year-old leader of the Conservative Party—and the man whose words inspired Waluś and his accomplice Clive Derby-Lewis—was struck down by a heart attack. He was taken to a private Cape Town hospital, where doctors advised him to cancel his commitments for four to eight weeks.

Treurnicht was a giant of the extreme right in South Africa who had said of Mandela in 1991: "He wants white capitulation. He wants Black majority rule! But I tell you, Mr. Mandela, we have a love of what is ours, and we shall protect it."

Three months after Mandela's release from prison, on May 26, 1990, Treurnicht had stood under a deep blue sky, as some 60,000 white people—grandmothers, babies, gun-toting men, and school-age children—congregated at South Africa's shrine to Afrikaner nationalism, the Voortrekker Monument in Pretoria, to listen to their leader. It was a gathering of people who had witnessed, over the previous five months, the upending of their closely held certainties during the previous forty-five years of apartheid rule. Mandela was free after twenty-seven years in jail. The ANC and the SA Communist Party were unbanned and their leaders were returning from exile and participating in peace talks. Petty segregationist laws that kept the races apart were struck aside.

Derby-Lewis and Waluś were in the crowd, enraptured, as Treurnicht spoke in the sonorous, hypnotic pastor's voice he had honed over decades at the pulpit. "You either rule or you are ruled. You are either politically free or you are in chains," Treurnicht declared.

Waving posters in Afrikaans proclaiming, "Stay White" and "The struggle for a free state has begun," his audience listened as Treurnicht declared: "The ANC hates the Boer people and the white nation . . . They demand our land. They reject our right to exist. But the government still sees its way clear to reach a negotiated consensus agreement with them.

"We shall not accept the threatened destruction of our nation's freedom but will fight to restore that which has already been unjustly given away."

The son of a farmer and one of nine children, Treurnicht studied theology and obtained a doctorate in political philosophy from the University of Cape Town before carving out a career as a clergyman in the Dutch Reformed Church. It was only in his late forties that he joined the National Party, rising through the ranks swiftly as an ideologue of the policy of apartheid. He was the deputy minister of education who, in 1976, introduced laws forcing Black children to be taught in Afrikaans, sparking the Soweto student uprisings that left 176 killed.

He edited the official journal of the most powerful of the three Dutch Reformed churches and wrote two Afrikaans books. In the *Credo van 'n Afrikaner* (*Creed of an Afrikaner*) he declared: "We wish to remain a white people with self-determination in our own territory."

His nickname was "Dr. No," because of his opposition to any piece of reform to the apartheid system. The "No" cry that Treurnicht used in speeches across the country was the operative word at the Voortrekker Monument rally that day. The festive gathering was asked by one speaker whether they wanted De Klerk to negotiate on their behalf.

"No, no, no, no!" they shouted back.

Treurnicht said moves toward majority rule "will just have to be stopped."

At that point he stopped and announced: "Our third freedom struggle has begun."

Waluś was later to say that he interpreted Treurnicht's labeling of the third freedom struggle as a call to arms. After all, he said, "I know from the history of the Boer that the first two freedom struggles were struggles with the use of arms."

Ironically, as Waluś listened to Treurnicht that day in May 1990, the Mandela who was being vilified onstage was speaking twelve kilometers away, in the Black township of Atteridgeville.

"Today, at this moment, in fact, Andries Treurnicht, that prophet of doom, is meeting over that hill . . . in order to oppose the effort made by the ANC and the government to bring peace into this country.

"We say to Treurnicht, 'We have defeated greater men than himself.' He will be defeated."

Back among the right-wingers, Derby-Lewis, too, heard a message from Treurnicht that allegedly compelled him to take up arms. He wrote years later: "As the previous two 'freedom struggles' were in the form of war against the British . . . both concerning the retention of political power, I naturally assumed, as did many judging by the numerous acts of sabotage carried out from then on, it was a declaration of a war to ensure the retention of political power."

Now, as the investigation into Hani's murder drew closer and closer to Derby-Lewis, Treurnicht was struck down. The Conservative Party announced that Treurnicht's deputy, Dr. Ferdi Hartzenberg, had taken over the running of the party. Gaye Derby-Lewis had, earlier in the year, given Hartzenberg the list she had compiled and later found in Waluś's flat. In the aftermath of the Hani murder Hartzenberg had announced that the party would raise money for Hani's killers' legal defense. It was a curious announcement for a party that did not know, that early on, that its member of Parliament and its chief English-speaking propagandist, Gaye, were implicated in the murder.

10 a.m.
Cape Town

The day started off peacefully enough in Cape Town. Then people kept on arriving. And more arrived. None of the key places of commemoration—Desmond Tutu's St. George's Cathedral, the city's pedestrianized Grand Parade, the city hall—had prepared for the extraordinarily huge numbers of people who arrived that morning.

"It has no beginning and no end, this crowd," wrote the antiapartheid *Weekly Mail* newspaper's reporter as the crowds swelled.

Tutu's famous church was overwhelmed by crowds. Inside, Tutu broke down in tears as he spoke of Hani. More people poured in. The doors were closed. The cathedral could not take more. He announced that mourners should go to the Grand Parade.

The situation was becoming dangerous. Police and ANC marshals were overwhelmed. It wasn't just in the city center. In the townships, burning barricades closed off major roads to prevent workers from going to their places of employment. As the morning proceeded, scenes of chaos increased. At the OK Bazaars, a popular department store, four police officers were pinned to the glass doors, fighting off a crowd intent on looting.

"You can't kill a leader of the people and expect nothing to happen," a young man told Gaye Davis, a reporter with the *Weekly Mail*, as shop windows splintered and crashed. Through the tear gas and the police helicopter beating overhead, Davis saw a woman being led away.

"Kill us," she shouted. "Kill us, we are already dead!"

At another point, police retreated from an angry crowd chanting: "No more peace, no more peace!"

In all these skirmishes, ANC marshals tried to stop looters and prevent mayhem. Everywhere, they were ignored and even threatened or attacked. At a KFC, ANC marshals formed a line in front of the store and entreated a crowd not to loot. They were booed and jeered. Soda cans, bottles, and even bricks pulled up from the pedestrian paving along the streets were thrown at them. The front glass of the franchise store shattered. The looters applauded.

"I can't keep them back anymore, they tried to fuck me up—these people are refusing to listen. Where is the leadership?" a marshal said. The leadership could not stop the mayhem. ANC National Executive Committee member Trevor Manuel tried, but he was punched in the face and beaten back when he implored looters to act "in a disciplined fashion." His comrade Joe Slovo and another popular Western Cape leader, Allan Boesak—a beloved cleric whose oratory displayed hints of Martin Luther King Jr.—appeared in front of the crowds on the Grand Parade. Their entreaties were ignored. The rioting intensified.

In those furious hours, dozens of stores were looted, a Black youth was shot dead, a peace monitor was stabbed, and a policeman was shot and wounded.

It started in the morning and did not let up until sunset. If anything illustrated the need for police, the ANC, and peace structures to work together, then it was Cape Town on that day. There had been no coordination, no preparation, and the sort of mayhem that Waluś and his co-conspirators wanted to trigger had been let loose.

11 a.m.
Soweto, Johannesburg

The previous day Mandela had been chided by his chief of staff, Barbara Masekela, for wearing a summer suit on a cold morning. His socks, she tut-tutted, were inside out. On this morning he was immaculately turned out in a "presidential" charcoal suit. By the time his motorcade arrived at Soweto's Jabulani Amphitheatre, a venue built for crowds of no more than

10,000, more than 25,000 people were gathered outside, pushing to go in, and another 20,000 were packed inside.

It was an angry crowd that wanted to give vent to its sorrow and anger, that wanted to be emotional for just a little while. Angry chanting rose and militant placards dotted the amphitheater. One read: "De Klerk Must Be Assassinated for Hani's Death."

Mandela would surely have wanted his political ally, Chris Hani, a master of these crowds, to be there.

Mandela was welcomed with a "thunderous, orchestrated roar," but the situation was clearly volatile. The organizers, realizing just how dangerous the packed stadium was, cut the program short and rushed Mandela to the microphone. The crowd pushed forward to get a better view, pushing journalists into Mandela, creating a messy huddle.

Mandela plowed into his speech. The sound system was poor.

The crowd booed and jeered when Mandela said he had received messages of sympathy from De Klerk's National Party. Realizing what a mistake this was, Mandela knuckled down with an unhelpful rejoinder: "We have to work with people we don't like. We don't like the National Party but I'm prepared to work with De Klerk to build a new South Africa."

Halfway through Mandela's speech, a huge roar rose from the entrance to the stadium. It heralded the arrival of Clarence Makwetu, president of the uncompromising Pan Africanist Congress (PAC). The PAC's armed wing had recently claimed credit for a spate of attacks on civilian whites and styled itself as the true representative of African nationalism.

The cheers for Makwetu were huge, and so Mandela paused, looked around, and invited him to come up and address the crowd. The PAC leader was a notoriously uninspiring speaker, his monotonous speeches capable of putting even his most ardent fans to sleep, but he silently accepted the invitation. He ascended the stage, said a mere twelve words, and stepped down. His single sentence drove the crowd wild.

"We have come to a time when leaders run out of words," he said.

The crowd ululated and set off firecrackers in response.

Mandela continued, repeating the message he had given in his address the night before, calling on the crowd to exhibit "the calm and dignity" expected of "a government in waiting."

Even though he was under pressure to say what his audience wanted to hear, he stuck to principle.

"I understand your anger," Mandela said. "There is no party that has been more responsible for your pain than the National Party . . .

"The African National Congress is a government in waiting, and we want you to remember that as members of the government in waiting, you have the responsibility to behave orderly and with dignity. We don't want to think of the past. We want to think of the present and the future."

Fearing that things could get out of hand with the massive crowd packed into the small amphitheater, Mandela was hustled out to his car around midday.

2 p.m.
Soweto

Tokyo Sexwale was at Jabulani alongside Carl Niehaus, the ANC spokesman who had spoken alongside him the morning before at Waluś's court appearance. Flanked by the ANC's Soweto executives, they now led the thousands of people from the stadium on a three-kilometer march toward the Protea Police Station, the largest in Soweto, to hand over a memorandum of grievances and demands. It was at the station that things fell apart.

An ANC local leader and trade unionist, Sam Tambani, was one of those leading the march. On arrival at the police station, he joined other leaders inside the charge office where they met with a Brigadier Strauss. They talked Strauss and the other policemen present through their list of demands—a rehash of the ANC's national demands for an election date and a transitional authority from apartheid to democracy, plus local demands for police to act against spiraling political violence. Tambani and his colleagues entreated police to undertake and ensure that they would not act impulsively or irrationally and would allow the crowd to head home in an orderly manner.

The delegation walked out of the police building.

Then, totally unprovoked and without any warning, about ten policemen behind a secure position inside the station started firing on the crowd. According to video footage shown on SABC television the next day, the police fired for ten minutes. Even as the crowd fled, police kept on firing, using live ammunition.

Tambani and three other Soweto ANC branch leaders were killed in a hail of bullets that afternoon. They were all shot in the back. More than 250 people lay on the ground, injured, when the shooting stopped.

Niehaus, who was on the scene and saw it all, angrily described the shootings as "unprovoked police brutality."

"There can be no other conclusion than that they were shooting with the aim to kill," he said. The police spokesman, Captain Eugene Henning, later claimed officers had opened fire "to disperse the crowd to protect their [police] lives and property" after protesters attacked the station with bottles and stones. He denied that the police were using bullets but failed to explain the deaths—or why the dead were all shot in the back, as were many of the injured.

Yet the most shocking defense of the police action came from the man who had incensed the ANC on Saturday, when he claimed that Hani's assassination seemed to be the work of a man operating on his own. Deputy Law and Order minister Gert Myburgh insisted that the police had been surrounded, that one officer had been in imminent peril, and that the crowd had fired first. All these points were contradicted by tens of reporters who were present, as well as television tapes of the incident.

To this day, not a single policeman has faced any kind of censure for these shootings. The incident underlined that if the ANC had lost control of its young militants, the government had lost control of parts of the police and the security forces.

The American journalist Patti Waldmeir was at the police station that day and wrote that—as one of three whites in her group of journalists—she could not believe that they would escape unharmed. "But the marchers steadfastly refused to indulge the racist anger which would have been so much more rational than tolerance. One ANC marshal, seeing my frightened face, even sought to reassure me. 'This is Africa. It's our land. You don't worry!' he told me with a broad smile. The ANC's long tradition of nonracialism, its forgiveness and its compassion, triumphed. South Africa was surviving yet another crisis."

2 p.m.
Cape Town

Meanwhile Muhammad Ali continued to make his way through South Africa. The marches and protests seemed to energize the former boxer, now slowed down by Parkinson's disease. Ali wanted to jump into the heart of the action wherever he could, even against the advice of his hosts.

The township of Mitchells Plain, about twenty-seven kilometers outside Cape Town, was a stronghold of the antiapartheid movement and a center of organization for the ANC. Like most of South Africa's urban townships, Mitchells Plain was built by the apartheid government in the 1970s to house "colored" or mixed-race South Africans who were forcibly removed from areas designated as "whites only" under the Group Areas Act. The ANC had drawn a huge contingent of MK soldiers from the township, and the ANC Youth League was very popular there.

Muhammad Ali probably found the place virtually empty when he visited on that Wednesday. The former heavyweight champion was in South Africa to support the development of boxing and sport in general, invited by a Muslim organization, and he had glad-handed his way through Johannesburg, Durban, and finally Cape Town. His tour through the townships of Cape Town was, however, on the biggest mourning day in South Africa. Many of the townships' residents would have stayed at home in protest against Hani's assassination or would be attending the memorials in town.

Ali's bus had returned from Mitchells Plain township early and was trundling into the city when police flagged it down and advised him against going any farther. The city looked apocalyptic. Smoke was billowing into the sky from torched and looted shops.

"Escort us to the city hall area, to the commemoration," Ali bellowed. The police refused. "Too dangerous," they said.

The former heavyweight turned around to the people in the bus: "Choose: you can come with me or go back to the hotel. I'm going on."

Ali, some journalists, and members of his entourage forged on into the burning city. The bus moved gingerly through the thousands of people on the streets until it reached the city hall. The chant that had followed Ali since his arrival in South Africa accompanied the bus all the way: "Ali! Ali! Ali!"

Then the mass of people around the bus became too knotted. The bus could not go any farther. Ali got out of the bus and pushed through the crowd. He headed for the back door of the hall. Ali, wrote journalist Jack Blades, "head and shoulders above the crowd, moved like an irresistible force."

The champion gave his huge smile and said to Blades: "Unbelievable! I've never had such a welcome, even in China!"

It was mayhem. Fights were erupting between angry youths and police as the entourage made its way into the hall. Gunshots rang outside as ANC marshals tried and failed to bring order to a situation that had spilled out of their control.

At one point, Ali was on a balcony of the city hall, watching the clashes between looters, angry youths, ANC marshals, peace monitors, and police, when a canister landed on the ground just below him and he was engulfed in a cloud of tear gas. He retreated into the hall, choking, but was soon back on the balcony watching the action as it unfolded.

2 p.m.
Umtata, Transkei

As the mayhem engulfed the major centers of Port Elizabeth, Durban, Johannesburg, and Cape Town, crowds converged on the small town of Umtata in the Eastern Cape—the capital city of Holomisa's

Transkei—arriving from nearby townships and villages in buses to march to the South African embassy.

Tensions were high by the time the crowd reached the embassy compound. The building itself was a basic affair: a squat, square white building surrounded by a large garden, a car park, and two barrier fences—one around the embassy and a second around the perimeter of the whole compound. The *toyi-toyi*ing crowd pushed against the perimeter fence, calling for Ambassador Horace van Rensburg to appear to receive their memorandum with demands for an election date and a transitional government. The man did not appear. The crowd got angry, demanding that Van Rensburg himself receive the memorandum.

Van Rensburg was later quoted as complaining that the Transkei authorities had not lifted a finger to protect the embassy, while Holomisa is adamant that Van Rensburg's failure to show empathy and appear to receive the memorandum was what inflamed emotions. In any case, the crowd was soon pushing against the fence.

Eventually, a section of the outer fence caved in. Some of the crowd spilled onto the embassy grounds, pelting cars with stones and pushing to breach the barricades of logs and rocks put up by the police and embassy officials as a second-tier defense. ANC marshals tried to stop them. They were overwhelmed.

The journalists George Galanakis, who is white, and Mkhululi Booi, who is Black, were caught in the crowd.

"*Mlungu!*" someone in the crowd shouted. *Mlungu* means "white person" in the Xhosa language used throughout the Eastern Cape.

"A De Klerk!" screamed another. All eyes turned on the two. The angry mob turned and surged toward the pair, while marshals and ANC officials tried to hold them off. The ANC's spokesman in the region, Nat Serache, who was one of the officials escorting the journalists from the scene, was pushed aside as the crowd tried to get at the two men. With Serache unable to protect them, the crowd rushed in and started pelting them with stones.

Gunshots were ringing out from the crowd of marchers and from the police and embassy security.

"Run, run!" a marshal shouted at the two journalists and the ANC officials trying to protect them. The reporters and the officials ran back toward the embassy building, jumping across the barricades of logs and rocks at the gates and running for cover in the parking lot as a hail of stones followed them.

Marshals managed to stop the mob at the embassy's second entrance while the reporters stood with nowhere else to run, trapped in a no-man's-land between the crowd and police locked behind the embassy's second fence. Finally, the police and ANC marshals managed to escort the two journalists out of the area.

The police continued running battles with sections of the protesters throughout the day. Later, personnel at the embassy were escorted home and the government released a statement saying spouses and children had left the area as a precautionary measure. The battered embassy was a sorry sight: smashed windows, bullet holes in the walls, uprooted fence poles, and a trampled garden.

2 p.m.
Johannesburg

Nelson Mandela was hungry. When the rally in Soweto broke up, Mandela did not join the march to the Protea Police Station. He wanted to have lunch. His motorcade drove around Johannesburg looking for a restaurant, but most were closed due to the general strike. They stopped at a restaurant that served south Indian cuisine, which Mandela loved, but that, too, was shuttered. The city center was empty, office blocks and retail shops closed, and their doors protected by burglar bars.

The entourage ended up at the posh Carlton Hotel in the Johannesburg city center, formerly a haunt of the country's most powerful businesspeople, and Mandela took Stengel to the Three Ships, the grandest of the hotel's three restaurants.

It was an eerie, slightly disjointed day—and lunch. The Three Ships was nearly empty—only two tables of businessmen were eating. The young man and the leader of the ANC sat in a private room meant for about eighteen people. Outside the Carlton's rarefied corridors, the country was erupting in violence. But Mandela seemed calm.

"There was, I must confess, a little sense of Nero fiddling while Rome burned," Stengel wrote in his diary that evening.

Was he right? Or was Mandela confident that the pressure following Hani's murder was being released, and that the day's events, terrible as they were, were a much better way of grieving and mourning than unchanneled anger and rioting? Except for the radio, the only source of news the two men had was a pager, a small wireless telecommunications device ubiquitous among journalists, businesspeople, and activists and usually attached to the belt. It was used primarily to send urgent messages for the carrier to call the office back, but in the South Africa of the early 1990s it had an added service—it carried news alerts provided by the South African Press Association (SAPA). On a busy news day one had to turn it to silent—reports of shootings, marches, deaths, and attacks would drop every few minutes.

Mandela was kept abreast of the many reports of clashes with the police by his security detail. Yet he remained calm, unhurried. Why? I venture that Mandela knew that when you ask hundreds of thousands out onto the streets after a traumatic event like Hani's murder, there would be clashes and situations the party could not control. The previous night, in his address to the nation, he had been very clear about it: "We pay tribute to all our people for the courage and restraint they have shown in the face of such extreme provocation. We are sure this same indomitable spirit will carry us through the difficult days ahead."

These were the difficult days he had spoken about.

Now, Mandela could have thrown himself into the melee—rushed from one hot spot to another putting out fires—but he chose to go about his day in a placid fashion, knowing that the day's events were part of the plan to give "the masses" an outlet to mourn and display their anger.

Virtually everyone interviewed for this book agrees that Mandela had an almost single-minded vision—his eye was on the greater goal: elections and freedom for South Africans. With that in mind, he understood that the week would be chaotic. Like his time in prison, it was a bucking horse to be ridden, a ship in stormy waters.

2 p.m.
Near Dawn Park

In Boksburg, the town near Hani's home where Waluś was arrested, Peter Mokaba was back trying to talk down not just his angry supporters but provocative white extremists too. He was leading a march, on foot, that started early in the day, traveling from Katlehong township to Vosloorus, over eight kilometers. Thousands joined along the way. By the time the crowd reached the Boksburg Civic Centre it had swelled to 20,000. Along the way armed members of the AWB held up guns and taunted the marchers, chanting: "AWB! AWB! AWB!"

Groups of ANC youths chanted their own slogan back: "ANC! ANC! ANC!"

Intermittent shots were fired, but the two groups did not engage. The windows of several cars and shops were smashed. Peter Harris's peace monitors and ANC marshals kept a group of right-wingers and ANC youths apart. Traffic officer Dorne Brits, sitting in his patrol car and handling his service pistol, accidentally shot himself in the leg.

The walls of the civic center carried posters declaring: "We demand joint control of the security services!" A few youths sported T-shirts with the slogan: "You can't die alone."

The crowd was incensed by the right-wingers. Mokaba and his senior colleague, Thabo Mbeki, had to beg them not to engage.

Mbeki told the crowd: "The time has come that Nelson Mandela should be president of this country. The only way that can happen is if we act in unison in a disciplined fashion."

Mokaba entreated: "It is the youth league which is expected to control our militants. That task falls on our shoulders." He vowed that the youth league's actions would be "militant but disciplined." "We will not hesitate to act against those who go against this," he declared.

In a way, Mokaba was doing the dance Mandela had himself been doing for three years with ANC members. Mandela would tell supporters: "Now is the time to intensify the struggle on all fronts." Then he would tell them to act with discipline.

The message was more urgent now. The "difficult days ahead" Mandela had spoken of were here.

2 p.m.
Benoni Police Station

Janusz Waluś had refused to cooperate with the police for three days. The police commissioner, General Johan van der Merwe, was under huge pressure from De Klerk to crack the case. The ANC's Tokyo Sexwale had told a press conference the previous day that the police were handling Waluś with too much deference and that was why the suspect was "not giving his cooperation." Sexwale called for a full investigation of the assassination by the international community.

The SA Police weren't in the habit of handling suspects gently. The Security Branch had, since the 1960s, sent all its members on courses to receive special training in torture techniques, which they had used on many of the detainees who came through their hands. Sleep deprivation was the basis of their interrogation methods, keeping prisoners awake for days on end until they broke or signed whatever piece of paper was put in front of them. Electric shocks were another common tactic. As apartheid thawed, renowned pathologist Dr. Jonathan Gluckman released "more than 200 files of post-mortems he had performed on Blacks that died during detention" and showed that 90 percent of those he had examined were killed by police.

Van der Merwe needed Waluś to start talking. So he called a man he could trust, a man who got results: Colonel Adriaan van Niekerk of the

Security Branch. In 1988, Van Niekerk had himself killed a well-known ANC activist while torturing him on the notorious tenth floor of John Vorster Square, the security police head offices in Johannesburg known for "mysterious" deaths in detention. The first man he called for help was Van der Merwe, who helped him cover up the whole thing.

Now, Van Niekerk in turn called for his star torturer, Captain Nicolaas Johannes Deetlefs. Deetlefs was forty-two years old and sported the type of bushy handlebar mustache favored by many security policemen at the time. The police spokesman and journalist-spy Craig Kotze had one so big he was nicknamed "the Moustache."

The call to Van Niekerk and to Deetlefs marked a departure in the case. Mike Holmes and his colleagues were with the Detective Branch, solving murders, robberies, and other "straight" crimes. Van Niekerk and Deetlefs were political. They were with the Security Branch—they hunted down ANC activists, tortured them, extracted information, and even killed them. They were not nice people.

Deetlefs was a particularly nasty piece of work. Political activists detained throughout the 1980s—including Carl Niehaus—knew him well. Niehaus had been recruited into the banned ANC's underground structures by his girlfriend, Johanna "Jansie" Lourens. After both were arrested for their plan to blow up the gasworks in Johannesburg, Niehaus recalled how Deetlefs once woke him in the middle of the night, took him up to the tenth floor, and, after cursing and hitting him, produced a tape recorder from his cupboard. Without saying a word, he switched it on. Jansie's tearful voice was singing "Die Stem van Suid-Afrika," the apartheid national anthem. Then he grinned at Niehaus: "I think it's time you started talking."

Niehaus was comparatively lucky. Deetlefs was known to begin his torture session by saying: "I am going to do something to you which, if you survive, is going to convince me you are not human."

One of Deetlefs's most notorious cases was that of twenty-eight-year-old Dr. Neil Aggett, a young white antiapartheid doctor. Deetlefs was part of a group that tortured him for six hours. Then Aggett was mysteriously found hanging in his cell. Deetlefs has denied torturing the activists despite their overwhelming independent testimony.

It was a perverse twist of history, therefore, that Deetlefs was called in to intervene in the Waluś case. He and Van Niekerk had been hating and fighting what they called "terrorism" all their lives. Now they were hunting the murderers of a man the government they served had long considered a terrorist. Or were they? Over the next four days they took over the case.

2 p.m.
Union Buildings, Pretoria

It was as high-powered a meeting of the National Party government as you could get. There were seven cabinet ministers in the room, one deputy minister, the chief of the army, the commissioner of police, the former head of the National Intelligence Service, and the current deputy head of the spy service. With them were eight of the top, supposedly nonpolitical, career civil servants who headed up various security departments.

Every document in front of the men—there were no women among the twenty-one—was stamped with the words "TOP SECRET."

As Mandela tucked into his lunch at the Three Ships in Johannesburg, a frantic De Klerk had called an emergency meeting of the notorious State Security Council (SSC). The SSC had been the heart of the security apparatus during the last two decades of apartheid. Launched in 1972 to "advise the government on the country's national policy and strategy concerning security, its implementation and determining security priorities," the body brought together the country's top securocrats into one room. It had gained prominence and notoriety in the 1980s when three things started happening: the student activists of 1976 started returning to SA and setting off bombs; the international community started rallying around the Mandela mystique and pushed Pretoria for change; and inside South Africa activists started agitating harder for change. When hard-liner P. W. Botha came to power in 1978, he used the SSC to retaliate brutally, turning SA into a violent security state. He unleashed death squads across the world to assassinate apartheid's enemies, deployed troops in townships to police schoolchildren and enforce apartheid laws, launched international propaganda campaigns, and infiltrated spies into antiapartheid organizations as far afield as London and Paris.

The SSC was accountable to no one. There was no oversight of any kind over it. It was a law unto itself.

In the room were men—including De Klerk and the minister of prisons, Adriaan Vlok—who had been party to SSC discussions and agreements to "shorten the list of politically sensitive individuals by means other than detention." This was a euphemism to assassinate activists. De Klerk had, for example, supported a decision by the SSC to "remove" Matthew Goniwe, an activist. Fifteen months later Goniwe and three other men were stopped at a roadblock, strangled with telephone wire, stabbed, and shot to death. Their hands were cut off. Their faces were burned so they couldn't be identified. All the men in the room, including De Klerk, denied that they knew anything about the murders.

By 1993, as the twenty-one men met inside the imposing Sir Herbert Baker–designed administrative seat of the government called the Union Buildings, the SSC was no longer the all-powerful body it once was. De Klerk had dismantled the "state security management system," bypassing parliamentary oversight.

Despite this, the SSC was still the most lethal security structure of the state. Why did De Klerk make this the first major structure he would turn to in the week of Hani's murder? The move was curious because the SSC's role was historically not the making of peace, which was needed now, but the waging of war.

It still had the exclusive membership of its worst days: special invitees only. There was Adriaan Vlok—the only man in the room Mandela had found too repulsive to deal with and had flatly refused to have in the negotiations. Vlok was the minister of law and order between 1986 and 1991, when the apartheid security apparatus was poisoning, kidnapping, torturing, detaining, bombing, and killing political opponents in their thousands. He oversaw a vast network of killers while at the same time brutally enforcing a state of emergency that incarcerated thousands of people without trial. When the ANC pushed for Vlok's removal, De Klerk had instead shifted him to the prisons portfolio, thus keeping him within the security cluster and as a member of the SSC.

Vlok was, ironically, later to be the only member of apartheid's leaders to approach one of his victims and ask for forgiveness. In 2006, he walked into a room not far from where he was sitting right now in the Union Buildings to meet a minister of religion called Frank Chikane. In 1989, Vlok had had Chikane's underwear laced with poison. It nearly killed him, and he had to be flown to the US for special treatment. In that 2006 meeting, Vlok, who had found God, approached Chikane and asked for forgiveness. He had shocked Chikane by producing a dish and bottle of water from his bag and asking to wash his feet, a Christian ritual that reflects cleansing and forgiveness.

De Klerk could heave a sigh of relief that Vlok's replacement in the law and order portfolio, Hernus Kriel, was on an official visit to Europe and unable to attend the meeting, though he was flying back to deal with the crisis. The hard-smoking, hard-drinking Kriel was one of the key members of a group known as "the Antis" in the cabinet because they opposed most of the agreements that heralded reforms to apartheid. Kriel was a constant critic of De Klerk. He felt the government had caved into ANC demands too easily without extracting enough in return. "We had no plan, no strategy, no bottom line . . . no clarity on the goal at which we wanted to arrive," he was to tell an interviewer. He looked down on De Klerk, believing his leadership during the negotiations to be disastrously weak. He was "constantly seeking a compromise," Kriel would say later, and was "unable to draw a line." Described as "cunning, devious, ruthless and charming," he and Vlok tended to push to crack down on the ANC on any issue that came up. De Klerk cunningly kept them onside to keep his party's conservative wing happy.

On that day, De Klerk was surrounded by Pik Botha, the flamboyant, hard-drinking foreign minister who had spent the previous sixteen years defending apartheid across the world while causing trouble for his boss, P. W. Botha (no relation), because in large measure his fidelity to apartheid would—intentionally or not—sometimes slip, particularly on the international stage.

Considered a *verligte* (liberal), Botha could be relied on to push for negotiations to continue and for further concessions to be made. In 1986, Pik Botha told a press conference that it would be possible for South Africa to be ruled by a Black president provided there were guarantees for minority rights. He was pilloried by outraged whites. President Botha nearly fired him.

Then there were the rest of the cabinet members. Some were in support of the changes led by De Klerk and others were against them.

"Kobie" Coetsee, the former prisons minister, now in charge of justice and defense, had started the negotiations ball rolling all those years ago with his "chance" meeting in the hospital with Mandela. He openly said he was prepared for a future with an ANC in power.

Dr. Tertius Delport, the minister of local government, had become an MP only six years before in 1987. Danie Schutte, the minister of home affairs, would later serve in the postdemocracy Parliament but would be described as looking "out of place—in the new, non-racial environment— like the paintings from the apartheid era staring down from the parliamentary walls." So uncomfortable, in fact, that he formed a new political party, National Action, in 2002 to cater to "the needs of Afrikaners."

Gert Myburgh, the deputy minister of law and order, was like his boss, Hernus Kriel: a huge critic of the ANC's mass action. Then there was Niël Barnard, now an adviser to Roelf Meyer, and the chief of the South African Defence Force, General Andreas "Kat" Liebenberg, a hard-liner. A veteran of South Africa's wars and incursions into the country's neighbors, where thousands had been killed everywhere from Zambia to Angola, he was a man of war.

There were only two items on the agenda: the assassination of Chris Hani and what to do about the troublesome Mandela darling, Bantu Holomisa, in the Transkei. Holomisa had been a bugbear for De Klerk for years because he accommodated not just the ANC's cadres and leaders such as Chris Hani, who had suspended the armed struggle, but also the liberation armies of the Azanian People's Organisation and the Pan Africanist Congress. The PAC's army, APLA, had specifically targeted whites.

De Klerk and his cabinet believed that these attacks were launched from Holomisa's area, where the militant APLA commander Sabelo Phama had reportedly been spotted just days before.

Vlok, Myburgh, and other hard-liners would have wanted De Klerk to send in the army and remove Holomisa from power. Pretoria had intervened before in its toy states. In February 1988, the cantankerous and brutal Lucas Mangope, the president of the Tswana homeland of Bophuthatswana, was overthrown by members of his Bophuthatswana Defence Force after allegations of corruption. South Africa had sent in its troops, swiftly put down the mutiny, and installed its favored puppet, Mangope, back in power.

The SSC meeting felt that it could not exactly invade the Transkei at such a sensitive stage, so they did the second best thing men of war could do. De Klerk ordered that the South African army be positioned at the border with the Transkei so that it could be ready to enter the territory at the shortest possible notice. Among the triggers for an invasion would be the "large-scale murder of South African citizens" or the burning of the South African embassy building. This was code: attacks on whites would lead to the SA army taking over Holomisa's administration.

The meeting instructed personnel at the Transkei embassy to leave the region temporarily and issued an alert to all tourists to cancel visits to the region. Then the men agreed that the next meeting of the SSC should discuss the issuing of weapons to the Transkei embassy staff. The ministers of foreign affairs and defense were ordered to deal with Holomisa's "arrogant utterances and diplomatic note," sent two days before, after Holomisa had reiterated his suspicion of state involvement in the slaying of Hani.

The meeting decided that emergency regulations would apply in nineteen magisterial districts around Johannesburg, including Boksburg, the scene of Hani's assassination. These restrictions meant curfews would be put in place and the army deployed to oversee these neighborhoods. This was a regression to the tactics that had not worked in the period 1985 to 1991, when government banned all political meetings—and activists responded by gathering in the thousands. The restrictions, in this instance, would render every meeting to commemorate Hani—including his funeral—illegal, surely a regulation that would immediately trigger the very unrest the SSC claimed they sought to quell.

De Klerk's ministers were panicked. None of the decisions that the SSC made that day differed much from what security councils of the past would have done. The acting minister of law and order, Dr. Tertius Delport, said future marches would have to adhere to strict legal requirements (being held within a restricted time frame, authorized by a magistrate, and restricted to a small number of attendees—all impractical in the context of the time): "South Africa simply cannot afford the recurrence of such radical outbursts, criminality and hooliganism—we have to ensure that all protest marches remain peaceful and orderly."

De Klerk got the meeting to agree that the ANC should be involved in efforts to bring about peace and calm and that it should accept joint responsibility for these efforts and their consequences. To this end, the meeting called for a reconvening of the National Peace Committee—the multiparty organization set up to ensure peace at political events—to take place as soon as possible.

Coetsee, the justice minister, had been told by the attorney general for the Johannesburg area that the police had no credibility and that he should accede to the ANC's demand for outside help in the investigation of Hani's death. Such an addition "may allay fears of any cover-up" by the police or the government, the attorney general had said. The ANC had made a similar demand in the days since its National Executive Committee meeting on Sunday. Myburgh, the law and order deputy minister, was against such a decision, saying the police were capable of solving the crime on their own. Coetsee had already liaised with the United Kingdom's Scotland Yard and Germany's police, and they had offered two top detectives.

The ANC's Mathews Phosa had approved the overture. De Klerk ordered that it should be implemented immediately.

De Klerk ordered that an urgent meeting be arranged between him and Mandela to "forge a common approach to violence and lawlessness." This, of course, would have been anathema to Mandela, who did not see the unfolding events as lawlessness but as people venting legitimate anger.

Then something extraordinary happened.

In the process of writing this book I have spoken to four of the twenty-one men in that room: President F. W. de Klerk, Dave Steward, Roelf Meyer, and (over email) Niël Barnard. All of them said it was a long time ago and they cannot recall the events of that day—or much of the week. None of them kept a diary, except for Steward, whose writings were sparse and skipped some days. None of them recall the debates in the SSC meeting.

We also know that at least nine of the men in the room sat in the same cabinet that would, in the run-up to the first democratic elections in 1994, issue secret orders for the destruction of records, effectively wiping the record on apartheid clean. At least forty tons of apartheid government files are estimated to have been destroyed by the National Intelligence Service (NIS) in 1993, Professor Charles Villa-Vicencio, director of research at the Truth and Reconciliation Commission, said in 1998.

And so we have no knowledge of who said what in that and many other meetings in the dying days of apartheid. Yet some of the men in that room kept a few documents from that time. One of those documents is a very brief summary of the decisions of the meeting. Titled "Top Secret," written entirely in Afrikaans, it gives us a few brief lines about the decisions made by that meeting—decisions among the most consequential in the history of South Africa's democratic transition. They signal the government's accession to the ANC's demands—and the rapid fall of apartheid from that day onward until a democratic and free election was held exactly one year later.

In the four days after Hani's murder, the ANC had been very clear about its demands: an election date and a transitional executive committee had to be agreed on immediately. Although the matter was not officially on the agenda of the SSC, the future of the negotiations and the demands of the ANC were introduced. We don't know who introduced the discussion given the terseness of the minutes, but we know from the document that the meeting decided to inform the ANC that it was prepared to agree to an election immediately—but it could not unilaterally set a date without input from other parties.

There was still no date for the election, but the SSC acknowledged that it wanted to give the ANC one. And while setting a specific date was technically one for all negotiating parties—not just the ANC and the government—to decide, given that the ANC and the government had over the past nine months been meeting in bilateral talks and steering the negotiations without any other parties, this was a moot point. As many of the negotiators were to put it, once the ANC and the National Party agreed to something, then it was a done deal.

The meeting's other big decision was to mandate Roelf Meyer to inform the ANC that the government "supported the rapid conclusion of an agreement on the Transitional Executive Council—the multiparty body which, in terms of the agreements we had reached, would be established to ensure fair play in the run-up to the elections." De Klerk said such a body "would give the parties in the multiparty negotiating forum a limited form of power sharing with the government."

The TEC was the ANC's idea, put forward to wrest power away from the National Party in the immediate period before the elections. Its job would be to ensure a climate for free political activity for all participants in the run-up to the elections. It would have power over the portfolios that had been essential to the maintenance of apartheid: law and order, stability and security, defense, intelligence, foreign affairs, status of women, finance, regional and local government, and traditional authorities.

The decision to accede to a TEC was extraordinary. The ANC had demanded such a council for years, but De Klerk had always proposed one that came with a veto for whites. In April 1992, he had offered to bring Black leaders into such a transitional body and proposed that his presidency be replaced with an executive council. Instead of a simple democracy, however, he suggested that the presidency of such an interim structure would rotate for a six-month period between designated leaders, and council members would make the executive decisions by consensus. If one of these leaders did not agree to a proposal, it would automatically be rejected, giving a small party among the five the right to overrule the party most likely to win the election. Mandela called it a "loser-take-all solution"—the smallest or most recalcitrant minority held the greatest power.

This was different, though. De Klerk and the SSC had just agreed to what the academic Padraig O'Malley said was "the first grip on state power for the extra-parliamentary liberation movements of South Africa . . . the first abdication of some of their areas of authority."

The government would no longer be, as the ANC had argued for years, "both referee and player in the elections." From its experience, the ANC believed the National Party used the public broadcaster, the security services, the judiciary, and other state institutions for party political purposes. Now, at least, these institutions would be in multiparty hands.

Crucially, the accession to a TEC also meant the government would no longer have sole control of the armed forces. Nelson Mandela and the organizations that had been branded terrorists for decades would be jointly in charge of the army, the navy, the police, and the entire security establishment. The most hard-line government leader in the cabinet, Minister of Law and Order Hernus Kriel, would be apoplectic when he heard about the overture on his return. Just two weeks prior to the assassination of Hani, he had accused the ANC army, the MK, of being "nothing but criminals."

Now Hani's assassination had opened the door for the ANC to have joint control and, in time, take over the government.

Hani was not there to see it, but, without any fanfare, the era of apartheid was over.

8 p.m.
Pretoria

De Klerk was seething. The riotous events across the country meant Mandela had "lost control" of his supporters. Despite the concessions at the SSC meeting earlier in the day, which had not yet been communicated to the ANC, De Klerk still wanted to be seen as the man in charge. That evening, he said, "was my turn to reassure my supporters and all South Africans who, in the wake of the serious riots throughout the country, were deeply concerned about the future."

So he, too, made a televised address to the nation. De Klerk had given a television interview on Sunday, but this was the first time since the Hani assassination that he was addressing the nation directly, without the mediation of an interviewer, as president. For such a historic appearance after he had given ground to Mandela, De Klerk made a fatal mistake in a country that—among Blacks and whites, Afrikaners and Zulus, across the age spectrum—values respect for humanity (usually referred to as *ubuntu* in the Nguni languages) and a sensitivity to the dead. He did not sympathize with the Hani family and those who loved the slain leader.

He started his speech with the violent events of the day rather than what many Blacks would consider the main tragedy, the killing of Hani. "April 14 was a dark day for our country and all its people," he said. "Despite all the precautions and despite the attempts of a wide spectrum of political and church leaders to ensure responsible behavior, violence broke loose in several places." While this wasn't untrue, De Klerk would have gained himself some points by first acknowledging just how dark a day April 10, the day of Hani's murder, was too. But he did not. Instead, he doubled down:

"What happened in South Africa today cannot be tolerated in any civilized country," he declared. That assessment was deeply antagonistic, with its racist undertone that anger at Hani's murder was "uncivilized." De Klerk also failed to acknowledge his administration's own failure to prevent Hani's murder, to say nothing of the widespread political violence his security forces had unleashed over the previous years—actions that could likewise not be tolerated in any civilized country.

De Klerk could not resist taking a jab at Mandela being booed at Jabulani Amphitheatre in Soweto earlier that day: "It was shocking," he said, "to see political leaders being rejected by some of their supporters."

He declared that it had been "decided to immediately take a number of additional steps to prevent further violence" and said an urgent meeting between himself and Mandela was being organized. He announced that police and other security forces involved with upholding law and order would be boosted with another 3,000 men. Thousands more could be called up within a few hours, and the government was ready to ensure that marches take place within the law. Faced with massive, unprecedented unrest, De Klerk was responding with suppressive force in a manner similar to his predecessor P. W. Botha.

It hadn't worked before. This time the stakes were higher—the more clashes there were between the security forces and angry Black protesters, the more cover there was for securocrats to try and oust De Klerk and take over. De Klerk may have decided to hold multiracial elections, but he was giving the rightists an opening to reverse that crucial step forward.

9 p.m.
South Africa

Between 90 and 100 percent of employees hadn't turned up for work in the economic heartland around Johannesburg. Business groups said most of South Africa's six million Black workers skipped work.

The collective memory of the period is that after Mandela's "white woman" speech, violence died down and there was peace in the land. Virtually all the main players in this story remember calm descending after Mandela's televised appearance, but, moving as the speech was, it was no magic wand. In fact, the violence worsened in the days after. In cities and towns across the country, but mainly in and around Johannesburg and Pretoria, Cape Town, and the Eastern Cape and Transkei, the scenes were the same. The day after the majestic speech was the most chaotic since the Hani assassination.

Throughout the day the white-bibbed National Peace Accord monitors were run ragged, keeping police and protesters apart, talking down heated situations. Most of the demonstrators "were peaceful, disciplined and listening to those in charge," Desmond Tutu said, insisting, that "we mustn't let the lunatic fringe detract from the fact that many people of all races came to mourn."

The ANC secretary-general, Cyril Ramaphosa, said the protests had been a success despite "the actions of quite a number of unruly people," when "the grief that they were feeling got the better of them."

"The casualties have not been too numerous that one can say the whole event was disastrous," he added.

Yet the toll was high. By nightfall at least seventeen people were dead and more than five hundred were injured in a day that saw nearly a thousand separate gatherings, marches, and protests take place across the country. Mandela, Ramaphosa, and the ANC were adamant that the protests were the result of, as Ramaphosa would call it, "an unprecedented show of feeling." But how long before that feeling would subside? If his twenty-seven years in prison had taught Mandela anything, it was that the events of a single day such as that Wednesday should not define the arc of an entire struggle. Wednesday, as he had predicted, was difficult. Masekela, Mandela's chief of staff, said the key thing to understand about Mandela is that he operated in that period with a very clear, almost obsessive objective in mind: elections and freedom for South Africans. Nothing would divert him from that goal. The objective that week was to get to Hani's funeral and then return to the talks table to fulfill the bigger mission. No amount of violence fanned by extremists would stand in his way.

That evening Ramaphosa and Meyer agreed to meet the next morning. The channel was open. Would it keep the peace?

Midnight
Johannesburg and Pretoria

Why, with the widespread violence of that day, did De Klerk not call off talks? Why, after the murder of Hani, didn't Mandela do the same?

Even with the securocrat measures and aggressive language used by De Klerk in his television address, the State Security Council notes record that the meeting reflected "that there is only one solution for the current instability, namely the route of negotiations."

There was a growing appreciation for something Thabo Mbeki had said the year before, when the entire ANC leadership, except for him, had agreed with the walkout after the Boipatong Massacre. It was the most passionately Mbeki had ever argued any position. A return to talks was inevitable, he said. "If you stop these negotiations now," he said, "we'll have to come back to them later."

Mbeki had been the key ANC emissary in meetings dating back to the early 1980s with Afrikaner intellectuals, clergy, businesspeople, and spies. In August 1988, at Wilton Park in the English countryside, he gathered with some of these to debate numerous issues bedeviling the country and the impasse it was in. At some point between August 19 and August 24, 1988, they got to a point where they knew that talking was the only solution.

"The idea of negotiations as the only option was a position that had developed over time," wrote the Afrikaner professor Willie Esterhuyse, one of the attendees, later. "Can any government govern a ruined economy? Can a war be waged against poverty if the civil war reduced everything to ashes?"

The two sides had no option. If they did not see the talks through, they would govern, one way or the other, a ruin.

The antiapartheid activist Jay Naidoo, head of the nation's largest trade union coalition, reflecting on why negotiations were necessary on both sides, said: "The apartheid regime could not defeat us and we could not defeat them. We were at a stalemate. The alternative was a scorched earth."

Mathews Phosa had spent the previous three years talking to the apartheid government as one of the ANC's top five negotiators. At one of the meetings with the government side he had been talking to Mike Louw, who later became head of the National Intelligence Service. Louw had told him that neither side had the stomach to go back to the engagements of the 1980s: "War has taken the worst out of us."

They had to keep talking. There was no alternative. The next few days would be crucial.

THURSDAY
April 15, 1993

You should not have believed me,
For virtue cannot so inoculate our old stock
But we shall relish of it.
I loved you not.
　　　　Hamlet, Act 3, Scene 1

8 a.m.
Benoni Police Station

Deetlefs and his sidekick, Warrant Officer Andre Beetge, were friendly toward Waluś. When they arrived on the morning of the fifteenth, they told Waluś they were taking him back to his flat in Pretoria. They traveled in two cars. Once there, Deetlefs took pictures and asked questions, and then they visited a firm where Waluś had worked in a suburb of the city called Despatch.

They were back in the cells in Benoni shortly before 4 p.m. Waluś went to sleep. Deetlefs went off, he told Waluś, "to think."

When Deetlefs returned to Waluś's cell at 6:40 p.m., he and Beetge asked Waluś about the assassination. Waluś requested having a lawyer present.

Deetlefs didn't mind having Waluś's lawyer there, he said. But that would not be necessary. He (Deetlefs) was just there for a chat, nothing formal. He questioned Waluś about his family, in a friendly, chatty way, like they were colleagues who were getting to know each other.

Deetlefs had picked up a photograph album in Waluś's apartment, and he inquired about the various family and friends in it. The taciturn Beetge just took notes.

"You are wasting time with the notes," Waluś told Beetge. "I am not going to sign anything."

Deetlefs laughed with Waluś, sharing a joke at the expense of the studious Beetge.

"Don't worry. Those are private notes. They have nothing to do with the court case," Deetlefs said.

The questions continued. They had spoken a bit about Mike Holmes, the investigating officer. Deetlefs explained to Waluś why he and Beetge were there: "You know we are from the Security Branch? The murder is really a side issue for us. Our tasks are absolutely different from those of the regular police. We are only here for security issues."

The Security Branch was the intelligence-gathering, torture, and kill squad of the apartheid government. In the three decades up to 1993, it had secretly arrested, detained, tortured, disappeared, and killed thousands of antiapartheid activists.

They kept on talking. Hour after hour. The night got old. Midnight came and went. This was nothing like what an interrogation would be like in Poland, Waluś thought to himself. There would be torture there. There would be tears and blood. This? This seemed to him to be a "friendly chat."

I don't feel threatened, he thought. *I have no fear.* Whenever he asked for the toilet he would immediately be given time to go. When he asked for a drink he was given one.

He relaxed.

"I can't tell you how glad I am that Hani is dead," said Deetlefs as the night wore on.

Waluś listened.

"You know, in the Security Branch we are always fighting with the ANC. I have looked at everything the ANC is doing . . . It's good. It's good that Hani is dead. I am not the only one. Many other policemen who are engaged in the fighting against the ANC feel the same way," he told Waluś.

Deetlefs said he felt thirsty. He ordered a beer. He offered one to Waluś. Waluś accepted so he passed his glass on to him. Then he asked Beetge to bring him a brandy and Coke, a drink well known to be a favorite among South African cops. They drank. Deetlefs continued talking. More drinks were served.

Deetlefs dropped names. He told Waluś a story about how he had fought against the terrorists and the communists. He told him about the time when he had made Jansie Lourens, now Carl Niehaus's wife, sing the apartheid national anthem, even though she was an antiapartheid fighter who probably loathed it. The three men laughed about it.

Deetlefs made jokes deriding the police sergeant, Mike Holmes, from the detective team.

"You know what Holmes is obsessed with? He is obsessed with the can of cool drink [soda] that was found at the murder scene."

Holmes had been trying to work out if Waluś had an accomplice. Waluś claimed he had bought the can of soda himself, but Holmes did not believe that he would have just left a piece of incriminating evidence at the crime scene.

Others had spoken of cigarette stubs at the scene as well. There had also been talk of a second car, white, with some witnesses claiming they saw it leave Hani's home. The ANC's Mathews Phosa had already badgered the investigative team about it. Holmes was tying up the loose ends, following up these leads. Deetlefs continued to joke, to belittle Holmes and his investigation.

"You know what's the biggest problem with this case for Holmes? What he wants to solve? Not why the can was there, but this: Was it really Coke, or Fanta?"

The beer was going down well. Waluś laughed along.

Deetlefs dropped another name: General Tienie Groenewald, the former chief of military intelligence in the mid-1980s under President P. W. Botha. He was legendary in right-wing and military circles, particularly for the brutality with which his tasks—orchestrating covert schemes to assist rebels in Angola and Mozambique—were executed.

Groenewald and Waluś were friends. The two had met when Groenewald had visited the QwaQwa area where Waluś and his father ran their glass-making factory. He was fascinated by this Polish man who loved Afrikaans and the Afrikaner and espoused a hatred for communism. They had conversed for forty-five minutes that first day.

Deetlefs told Waluś he was one of Groenewald's men from military intelligence. He knew that such a detail would impress Waluś. "General Groenewald is already prepared for the fight against the ANC and the government," he said.

It was well known in right-wing echelons that Groenewald fervently believed that the ANC and the De Klerk government were planning to form what he called a "typical South American junta." Groenewald told journalists that such a development would lead to violent reactions by the Afrikaner community and a state of emergency would be declared. Martial law would be introduced. "And this is when at least 5,000 people would be locked up without trial, not because they're necessarily planning something, but because they have the capability or they are a potential threat." Groenewald claimed to have seen a list of the targeted detainees and boasted that there were "actually 5,590" people listed on it.

The right-wingers also believed stories planted by SA's military intelligence that Hani had an army of 10,000 troops at the ready if the vote, whenever it happened, did not swing in favor of the ANC.

The drinking and chatting went on. Deetlefs talked about his enthusiasm for fighting communists. He told Waluś about beating up Niehaus. Then he became conspiratorial.

"Holmes and his people have been looking into the calls made to your apartment and the ones you made from there," Deetlefs said. "They are checking the names right now . . . They will probably know the names tonight or by early morning. You know those guys, they don't sleep. They will probably make an arrest in the next few hours, maybe this morning."

Waluś's emotions were mixed. Later, he would say he may have been given drugs. The apartheid security network was full of stories about the use of chemical weapons developed by the chemical and biological warfare program. It was alleged to have developed a sterility vaccine to use on Black South Africans, employed toxic and chemical poison weapons for political assassinations, and in the late 1970s provided anthrax and cholera to Rhodesian troops for use against guerrilla rebels in their war to overthrow Rhodesia's white minority rule. The so-called truth serum, sodium thiopental, was often spoken about in hushed tones in such circumstances. The drug, which was used as recently as the 1960s in the US, allegedly weakens the resolve of a subject.

Beetge was quiet, still taking notes. Deetlefs told Waluś that his special role within the right-wing matrix was to spring people from jail, to keep them free from the police.

"We are running out of time," Deetlefs said. "Holmes and his people will have identified the people you were working with soon, maybe by this morning. We need to warn them quickly."

Waluś was still not biting. Deetlefs told him a few more stories, elicited some more laughs. Sipped from his brandy and Coke.

"It would be very inconvenient if someone from the senior ranks of the right wing was to be arrested right now. We are just not at the right point to have such destabilization. Not everything is fixed to the last point when it comes to the armed struggle we are going to have against the ANC and the De Klerk government's 'junta,'" he told Waluś.

"Time plays a big role. You have to tell me now who you are working with so I can warn your contact. I won't be able to find out from Holmes. He is one of De Klerk's guys. Only you can save this person—if you give me the name and I warn him in time. But we don't have time," he said.

Waluś believed him. With the stories Deetlefs told him about General Groenewald, the way he had tortured Afrikaner "traitors" such as Carl Niehaus and made Jansie Lourens sing "Die Stem," how could he not trust him?

His coconspirator was a major figure in conservative circles. He was surely needed in the coming insurrection. So Waluś gave up the name of the man who had given him the gun and ammunition.

"Clive Derby-Lewis," Waluś said. "I worked with Clive Derby-Lewis."

8 a.m.

Boksburg

Throughout that week the spotlight was on the ANC's impatient young supporters, its militant leaders, and their reaction to Hani's murder. Yet it was very clear in the days after Hani's assassination that the right wing was galvanized. Members of the AWB that Waluś belonged to had fired guns at Black township residents from pickup trucks, scattering and taunting them: "Your king is dead." The SABC reported that after AWB leader Eugène Terre'Blanche had said he would have killed Hani himself in a combat situation, extremist "leaders warmly and publicly congratulated Hani's accused assassin, hailed his 'bravery,' and dubbed him a true 'volks en oorlog-held' (national war hero)."

The leader of the Pretoria-based World Apartheid Movement, Koos Vermeulen, boasted that the fund he had set up for Waluś's legal defense was receiving huge donations.

"Our post box is overfilling. We can't keep up with the response," Vermeulen said. Wim J. Booyse, head of a private political consulting firm in Pretoria, told the *Los Angeles Times* that the Hani killing had showed right-wing whites that killing antiapartheid leaders had the potential to spark Black anger which would, in turn, drive frightened whites into joining the extremist cause.

"They're going to continue to do these things to provoke the black militants . . . It really shows you how volatile this society is. And the right will thrive on this chaos."

The right wing wanted this chaos badly because it was desperate. After De Klerk had won the referendum the previous year, the right wing in SA knew that white supremacy in the country had run out of rope. It was organizing by exploiting fears of a Black government. Risk of racial conflagration was in fact heightened by news that the De Klerk government was inching toward agreement on an election date and a transitional executive committee.

The young trade unionist Sam Shilowa believes that the danger of the moment was not just that Blacks were angry with De Klerk and whites for the killing of Hani. Black anger put pressure on De Klerk, making him vulnerable to the ANC's demands. Paradoxically, it also made him vulnerable to the white right wing that could try to exploit his weakness by fueling white fears about a future in which Blacks held power. The job of Mandela and the ANC, therefore, was to corral and channel Black anger while keeping De Klerk in power and ensuring that the dawn of democracy was not derailed.

9 a.m.
Johannesburg

On the morning of Thursday, April 15, the trade union federation COSATU had called an urgent meeting of its central executive committee, along with delegates from the ANC and SACP. The meeting, described as "steamy" because of the colorful language used, analyzed the previous day's deaths, destruction of property, and reputational damage to the ANC. The consensus was that the organizations had underestimated people's anger at Hani's assassination. The mayhem in Cape Town, in particular, alarmed some. Cautious voices in the meeting said calm and restraint was now needed; perhaps mass action should not be the only way forward.

COSATU's leaders—the general secretary, Jay Naidoo, and his deputy, Sam Shilowa—had expected such sentiments. As Shilowa pointed out, the ANC was not a uniform body. The ANC's president and his deputy, Mandela and Walter Sisulu, had been in prison for nearly thirty years. Wise and measured, they were sometimes out of touch with the country. Other leaders had been in exile since the 1960s and had become detached from the country of their birth.

COSATU and the internal generation of leaders such as Ramaphosa knew one way of protest: you go out on the street, get arrested, then go back out on the street. They had seen mass action defeat apartheid from within the country. In COSATU's view, negotiators who were not backed by a mobilized workforce tended to sell their side out. "It was not a matter of negotiations or mass action," said Shilowa, one of the trade union leaders, recalling the debates in that meeting. "For us it was negotiations *and* mass action."

It was a point that Ronnie Kasrils, one of Hani's closest comrades in the SACP and the ANC army, put forward bluntly: "Marches are not a tap. You don't turn them on and off."

So they agreed with their young, militant members' instruction: go to the ANC meeting in the evening and tell Mandela that mass action must go on, with marches on Saturday and a total stayaway on the day of the funeral. They went further. Pressure the ANC to announce a month of new protests until the actual election date was announced to the public.

9 a.m.
Umtata

The South African army deployed troops at all roads leading into the Transkei. Roadblocks were set up and searches conducted. They were on a war footing.

9 a.m.
Johannesburg

Roelf Meyer and Cyril Ramaphosa met that morning. Meyer gave it to him straight: De Klerk wanted a meeting with Mandela. He was incensed by Wednesday's violence and believed that only a meeting between the two would resolve things. Ramaphosa said the ANC leadership had listened to De Klerk's address and were themselves incensed. They believed De Klerk was buckling under pressure from the conservatives who spoke only of damage to property and not the many Black lives being lost to political violence daily.

Ramaphosa expressed the ANC's "strong opposition to further unrest areas being declared" as had been done by the police commissioner, Johan van der Merwe, on Tuesday—and the new ones following the SSC meeting. This was akin to outlawing the ANC.

Chris Hani, a fierce opponent of the apartheid system, was chief of staff of the ANC's armed wing, Umkhonto we Sizwe, and a leader of the ANC's ally, the SACP. A 1992 poll found that he was the most popular political leader in the country after Nelson Mandela.

Mandela always asked Hani to accompany him to volatile areas where the younger man was idolized for his militant rhetoric. In this 1993 picture, Mandela and Hani arrive in Richmond, a township in the southeastern province of Natal known as the "Killing Field of Natal." Hani called for peace.

3

In 1991, the apartheid government and eighteen other organizations committed themselves to peaceful negotiations with the goal of transitioning the country to democracy. Here, Mandela speaks with F. W. de Klerk while Foreign Minister Pik Botha and Justice Minister Kobie Coetsee look on. In June 1992, the ANC walked out of these talks following the Boipatong Massacre, where forty-five people were killed while they slept.

The extreme right in South Africa was extensively organized. The neo-Nazi AWB is believed to have had some 127 military camps within the country where 5,700 people were trained. Many of these people were alarmed when democracy talks started back up again in April 1993. This packed meeting of several extremist groups took place a month later.

ANC provincial leader Tokyo Sexwale, ANC spokesperson Gill Marcus, and trade unionist Mbhazima Sam Shilowa held an impromptu press conference at the Hani home in Dawn Park a few hours after Chris Hani's assassination on April 10, 1993. "They killed a man of peace," said Sexwale, seen here (in a multicolored tracksuit) weeping on Marcus's shoulder.

6

Hani's house became a site of pilgrimage over the next nine days. Here, former world heavyweight boxing champion Muhammad Ali is seen paying his respects to Hani's daughter, Nomakhwezi, who witnessed her father's murder.

Hani's assassination set off thousands of impromptu protest marches across the country. Here (above and middle) crowds march through Johannesburg while (below) police watch protestors in the eastern coastal city of Durban in some of the many protests in the nine days following Hani's murder.

7

8

9

Schoolteacher Alistair Weakley, who participated in peace committees in his hometown of Grahamstown, would be one of the casualties of the violence. He is seen here in happier times fishing on the Wild Coast.

Mandela and De Klerk would stop speaking as tensions rose, but Cyril Ramaphosa and Roelf Meyer, the chief negotiators for the ANC and the government, had established a rapport that allowed for negotiations to continue despite raging violence. Ramaphosa used the days after Hani's assassination to extract long-desired concessions from the apartheid government.

ANC-supporting youth clashed with police and peacekeepers (above and right) outside the FNB Stadium in Soweto where more than a hundred thousand mourners had gathered for Hani's funeral on April 19, while (below) armed right-wingers guarded the houses of whites in Elspark, Boksburg, where Hani was buried later that day. Police would fire tear gas and live rounds, but widespread violence was avoided.

12

14

13

Mandela with Chris Hani's widow, Limpho, and daughter, Nomakhwezi, on April 15, 1994, at the unveiling of Hani's tombstone at Elspark cemetery. Two weeks later, Mandela would be elected president.

Mandela and De Klerk greet the crowd in front of the Union Buildings, the seat of the South African government in Pretoria, after Mandela's inauguration. De Klerk was appointed one of two deputy presidents alongside Thabo Mbeki.

Janusz Waluś and Clive Derby-Lewis would be the only two people convicted for their role in Hani's assassination. Here they are at the Truth and Reconciliation Commission hearings in Pretoria in 1997. The two men's application for amnesty was denied, as the Commission remained suspicious they weren't telling the whole truth.

18

A judge found that Gaye Derby-Lewis lied in her testimony about compiling a hit list but acquitted her of murder. Questions about who else may have been involved in the plot to assassinate Chris Hani remain to this day.

Meyer offered the "carrot" of a transitional executive committee even before a constitution was agreed on and without a veto power for whites.

Both men knew this was a great triumph for the ANC, but Ramaphosa replied only by saying the ANC was to hold a meeting that evening and would consider Meyer's message. Ramaphosa was cognizant of the fact that "in the end it is not in the interests of the democratic forces in this country for De Klerk to lose power." That would happen if the securocrats or even just the conservative wing of the National Party gained the upper hand and ousted him. He knew the ANC needed De Klerk as much as he needed the ANC—perhaps more.

9 p.m.
Plein Street, Johannesburg

Meetings of the ANC's National Executive Committee were usually held once a month and in later, more sedate years, once every quarter. The meeting this evening was the second in four days. It had gone on for far too long, but there was much to discuss. It was toward the end of the meeting that the real differences would bubble up.

Ramaphosa outlined Roelf Meyer's message: De Klerk wanted a "summit meeting" with Mandela to discuss the violence. Mandela had been talking about the escalating violence for three years and had been dismissed by De Klerk. Now Mandela was angry, saying De Klerk's "first instinct was to convene his State Security Council" following Hani's killing.

"These are the reflexes of a P. W. Botha [De Klerk's arch-conservative predecessor]. The crisis is political, it calls for political solutions, not a return to the reign of a clique of the securocrats," Mandela and those who agreed with him argued.

Mandela was disappointed with De Klerk. He believed that with his silence on the white right's violence in killing Hani, and the emphasis on "controlling" Black anger, De Klerk had responded to the crisis not as a national leader but rather as a white minority leader. The deployment of the 23,000 troops and police reservists drew anger.

The discussions circled back to the elephant in the room: many of the ANC's exile and prison leaders felt chastened by the events that had taken place on Wednesday, particularly in Cape Town where the ANC's own leaders and marshals had been overwhelmed by militant elements.

Perhaps, one ventured, it was time to stop the mass action and concentrate on the funeral and the negotiations. This was the first time that there was a moment of doubt in the ANC's National Executive Committee. Before this meeting the debate had been about taking drastic measures like walking out of the negotiations or, for the more militant, announcing that the suspension of the armed struggle was being reviewed. The marches and commemorations were seen as the bare minimum that could be done.

Now, some were saying, perhaps mass action did not work. Perhaps it was pushing De Klerk away.

The COSATU contingent, and the internal activists, were ready. Led by Naidoo and Shilowa, with Ramaphosa in quiet support, they repeated a trade union tactic: the ANC should not give up its most effective peaceful weapon, mass action, at such a crucial time. Ramaphosa, drawing on the tactics he had learned at the National Union of Mineworkers in the 1980s, said the ANC should hold fast and use the people on the streets to extract the greatest concessions it could from the National Party. Ramaphosa was to later explain his adopted strategy and tactics this way: "We pushed it to the precipice, to the point where everything could break down. Government could not risk the breakdown of negotiations. We knew by force of argument and what was at stake that we would come out victorious."

The assassination of Chris Hani, for him and those who supported him in the meeting, was an opportunity to extract maximum advantage from the government. "The objective had been there but it tended to be a bit fuzzy at times. After Chris Hani died we went for the kill," Ramaphosa said.

The government's concession on the unconditional establishment of the Transitional Executive Council should be a mere first step, the meeting members felt. The overture lacked detail and needed to specifically commit to the TEC having control over the security forces.

The ANC emerged from the meeting with an even tougher stance and clearer demands than when it went in. First, it announced that it would embark on mass mobilization—protest marches across the country on Saturday and Sunday, work stayaways on the day of Hani's funeral and designated days afterward, and pickets—for the months of April and May.

"Before the end of May, a date for a democratic election must be decided. Such a date cannot be postponed," the party's statement said.

De Klerk had threatened that there would be action taken against what he called ANC "radicals." Ramaphosa was not bothered by this. He responded: "We are radicals. We are a radical organization. Our radicalism stems from the radical demands of our people, and we are not apologizing to President De Klerk about it. However, we are working in a responsible manner to achieve our goals as peacefully as possible."

The ANC's stance was uncompromising on the two key demands. While Mbeki and others were mandated to work with the National Peace Accord structures to ensure that "unrest areas" were not declared in the Johannesburg heartland, the party also used the threat of its trade union muscle to declare to De Klerk that it would not take the threats of a security clampdown in a docile fashion. Jay Naidoo, the general secretary of COSATU, said: "If the government issues regulations meant to prevent the alliance's supporters from partaking in memorial services freely, we will ignore those regulations."

Naidoo said the ANC and COSATU wanted a conclusion to the talks and an election date. "The people's patience is not endless," he said.

FRIDAY

April 16, 1993

Heat not a furnace for your foe so hot
That it do singe yourself.
  Henry VIII, Act 1, Scene 1

Morning
Pretoria

The Mandela–De Klerk relationship was coming unstuck.

De Klerk's language over the week had moved from a calm assessment of the situation to condemnation of the ANC. He wrote that "the ANC had failed to exercise control over its followers" and that "once again the country had been plunged into crisis" by the ANC's demonstrations in commemoration of Hani.

Mandela, who had for years been badgering De Klerk to act decisively on political violence, was offended by this condescending tone. Indeed, the cause of the souring of the relationship between the two men over the previous three years was Mandela's contention that De Klerk just did not care enough for Black life to stop the endemic political violence in the country.

Yet if we stop here and strip the noise away, it is clear that the fight was unnecessary. The two sides no longer had differences. Following the SSC's agreement to a no-veto TEC, the two sides were agreed. All that was left was to work out the details. They just had to hold tight and get through the funeral on Monday.

Afternoon
Plein Street, Johannesburg

Mandela was exhausted. He had got home late from the National Executive Committee meeting the night before. He had gotten up early to sit
down with Stengel for their 5 a.m. meetings. The deadline for their book
was looming. And he had kept going all day.

"I'm tired, I can hardly keep my eyes open. Can you tell?" he said to
the writer when they met that afternoon for a second session. Mandela
had many of these kinds of days where he would be up at dawn and have
back-to-back meetings and engagements until late. He had a secret trick
for getting through these. Masekela told me that on such days Mandela
would ask to go off for a nap. In his bedroom, he would shut the curtains,
make sure it was absolutely dark, get between the sheets, and nod off for
twenty or thirty minutes until his bodyguards came in and woke him, re-
juvenated and sharp as an axe, at the exact time he had requested.

Not today. He needed to get on the phone to raise money for Hani's
funeral. Mandela was the ANC's most effective fundraiser, with his profile
attracting funds in a way no other leader could. In an eleven-day US tour
in 1990, he had raised $7 million. When in South Africa, Mandela raised
funds from publicly listed companies, often calling CEOs and chairmen of
the entities directly, and from foreign governments, particularly the Scan-
dinavian countries, and individual donors.

"Yes," Mandela was saying into the phone when Stengel walked in.
"We would like funds to help the ANC defray the costs of the funeral on
Monday . . . Well, that is up to you . . . I can tell you that we've received
thus far individual donations between R 10,000 and R 50,000 . . . I can tell
you the names of the other companies we are phoning, Anglovaal, SAB
[South African Breweries], etc. etc. . . . . [long pause] . . . Ah, that is very
good . . . No, you should not make the check out to me but to the ANC
Chris Hani Funeral Fund. That's right. Thank you very much."

Mandela had received a draft of the speech he had asked for from
Mac Maharaj, the comrade he had spent time with on Robben Island,

and the ANC's head of education, Raymond Suttner. He didn't like it. He was working on a new draft with the Department of Publicity led by Pallo Jordan.

It was six days after Hani's murder, and Mandela's preoccupation was with ensuring that the protests and commemorations were mounted relatively peacefully through to Monday. De Klerk's threat to declare certain parts of the Johannesburg area as "unrest areas," however, was a major concern, as it would automatically outlaw any political gatherings.

The country was shutting down in anticipation of the funeral. The annual Rand Easter Show, southern Africa's largest agricultural exhibition (stands ranged from livestock competitions to foreign countries bidding for tourists to the military and police burnishing their images) that had run since 1895, announced that it would close on Saturday, a day earlier than advertised. The Nasrec buildings, which housed the exhibition's eleven-day extravaganza, were next to the First National Bank (FNB) Stadium where Hani's body would lie in state on Sunday and from where the funeral procession on Monday would start.

Violence linked to, or sparked by, anger at Hani's murder was still rife across the country. At least eighteen people had been killed countrywide in the twenty-four hours to Thursday evening, according to police reports, twelve of them in the volatile province of KwaZulu-Natal. Several shootings—three fatal—were reported in the townships around Hani's home. In the Cape Peninsula, a limpet mine was found near a railway station. A man was burned to death in one of thirty shacks set alight in the Black township of Khayelitsha.

The funeral would be a big affair. The SABC announced that it would for the first time in its history carry live broadcasts of the memorial and burial services. Hani's funeral would be treated like a state funeral—only without the state participating or carrying the costs.

Ambassadors from numerous countries across the globe were preparing to attend the funeral. Mandela was fuming that the government would not be sending any official representatives. He had put himself in the path of ridicule at the Jabulani Amphitheatre—when he said the NP had sent messages of condolence—and yet there was nothing humane emanating from the National Party. The liberal SA ambassador to the US, Harry Schwarz, had to defend himself after he flew the flag in Washington, DC, at half-mast in honor of Hani.

Instead, the war talk was piling up.

The hawkish law and order minister, Hernus Kriel, was back from his overseas trip and was telling reporters that the ANC must bring its "radical elements" to heel "once and for all." Kriel said the police, assisted by the army, were on standby "with the most modern weapons and equipment" to deal with potential violence. He said nothing about the shooting of four young Black people in Vanderbijlpark, part of Hani's neighborhood, by a fifty-six-year-old white man—without any warning.

De Klerk and his government had gone full securocrat on Black South Africa. Yet there is nothing in any of the National Party government's utterances that week that reflects an understanding of the fact that the danger for the country, and the threat of the race war Mandela feared might happen, could actually come from the white right wing.

Thus Mandela's hope to avert a race war depended on the weekend's events and the funeral on Monday passing without triggering an adverse event between youth and the security forces that would in turn set off the racial clashes that Waluś and company wanted to initiate with their assassination of Hani. As the Hani funeral approached, the right wing was arming itself and preparing for confrontation.

Mandela could only hope that the efforts of people like Mbeki, Gungubele, Peter Harris at the Wits-Vaal Regional Peace Secretariat, the police, and others in building consensus between the police, ANC marshals, and national peace monitors would succeed.

Midday
Benoni Police Station

Waluś's first interrogation session with Deetlefs had lasted fourteen hours. He was returned to his cell at 5:20 a.m. on Friday, April 16. A few hours later he was shaken awake again and taken back through to the interrogation room. Beetge and Deetlefs were waiting for him.

Deetlefs was in a jovial mood.

"Don't you worry, Janusz. Everything is under control, everything is secure," he said, adding that Waluś would be taken to Pretoria Central Prison for his safety, as there was information that some members of the police in Benoni planned to kill him.

Deetlefs's jubilation was setting off alarm bells in Waluś's head. The shame began to spread through him. Had he been duped? The stories that Deetlefs had told him about torturing people such as Carl Niehaus and others were so authentic, so convincing, that he could not have been lying, Waluś told himself. He managed to convince himself of this, and slowly the feelings of doubt and shame that he had been naïve passed.

It wasn't until the following month, when Deetlefs took Waluś to his brother's farm, that suspicion set in for good. When Waluś pointed out to his interrogator the place where he had tested the pistol he used to kill Hani, Deetlefs did not throw away the spent cartridges lying around, as Waluś asked him to. Instead he collected them as evidence.

"It was then that I realized he had fooled me," Waluś said.

11 p.m.
Johannesburg

The delegates and leaders of the Wits-Vaal Regional Peace Secretariat had worked through the night on Thursday and all day on Friday. By Friday evening, as midnight ticked closer, they were exhausted, but elated. They believed they had a deal.

Thabo Mbeki, the ANC negotiator, and Peter Harris, the anti-apartheid lawyer and director of the secretariat, were meeting with General Koos Calitz, the police commissioner of the Pretoria-Witwatersrand-Vereeniging region. Away from the heat of politics, the three men and their colleagues had been trying to mediate a code of conduct to avert chaos at the marches on Saturday and disaster at the Hani funeral that would start with a night vigil on Sunday. They had three goals: keep mourners safe from the numerous far-rightists who were massing along the route from the stadium where the Hani service would be held to the cemetery; keep people and property safe from provocateurs and looters; keep police away from provoking marchers. Now, finally, they were ready to shake hands on it.

That handshake nearly didn't happen. Earlier, when Calitz had submitted his plan to his boss, Police Commissioner Johan van der Merwe, for approval, it was rejected. Zirk Gouws, the regional commander of the security police in Johannesburg and part of Koos Calitz's team, said, however, that Calitz was a "modern-day" police officer, unlike the hard-liners at the top of the police service at the time, and was adamant that it should go ahead.

"He had practical grassroots experience about practical policing realities in Johannesburg. He understood the massive potential for violence to erupt in the context of the Hani murder, the threat to the peace initiative in SA, and he took the responsibility to sign the agreement," said Gouws.

The key to the agreement was that the police would step back and would "under-police" the events of the next few days. This had huge political significance. It was in direct contradiction to the call to enforce "law and order," made by the minister Hernus Kriel. It was a step toward what the ANC had been calling for: community-based policing. If Mandela's address to the nation on Tuesday signaled the shift of political power, this agreement signaled even more of the same shift. The ANC's demand for joint control of the security forces had not yet materialized, but it was beginning to happen in practical terms.

Despite the saber-rattling from De Klerk and Kriel, the agreement committed them to not declare Johannesburg an "unrest area," a move that would have effectively limited Hani's funeral to family members only— or to being an active crime scene. The ANC, its allies COSATU and the SACP, and their affiliated bodies agreed to be held legally accountable for any criminal action on the part of their supporters. They also undertook, through the deployment of their marshals, to ensure the safety of individuals as well as of property.

The police acknowledged that they were often the oil that inflamed the fire and so committed themselves to maintaining a low profile. This meant that the ANC would provide marshals at each venue to ensure the strict control of supporters. The police were conceding that they had so little authority/legitimacy in the community that they could not handle ANC crowds, despite Hernus Kriel's crowing that they had the "most modern weapons and equipment." Only 1,000 policemen and 1,000 SA Defence Force soldiers—acting as backup for the marshals—would be deployed.

Three thousand ANC marshals were granted powers of arrest. The city's law firms were recruited to provide legal advice to the peace structures and to peace marshals (should it be needed over disputes about powers of arrest, police overzealousness, and basic evidence-gathering) stationed at the hot spots (the funeral stadium, the route to the cemetery, and at the whites-only cemetery where Hani would be buried). A twenty-four-hour "peace line" for citizens to call in flare-ups of violence was set up.

Mbeki emphasized the need for joint action.

"We are trying to protect the right to peaceful demonstration and the rights of ordinary citizens," he said. "It is an important pioneering agreement which could set a framework to enable us to deal with similar situations."

Among those who witnessed the signing of the agreement was Mondli Gungubele, who along with Gouws had the task of ensuring its implementation in the volatile East Rand. The secretariat's job was daunting: up to 250,000 people were expected to attend the events at the stadium and the cemetery. Between 150 and 200 peace monitors would be operating day and night.

Yet as the funeral day approached, Gungubele still prayed that the agreement would survive the pressure brought to bear by the thousands of mourners from across the country who would come to say farewell to their hero.

SATURDAY

April 17, 1993

Sometime am I
All wound with adders, who with cloven tongues
Do hiss me into madness.
> *The Tempest*, Act 2, Scene 2

11 a.m.
Boksburg

Muhammad Ali was back in Johannesburg. On Saturday morning, after his scheduled breakfast with the mayor of the city, the former boxer Les Dishy, Ali headed to Dawn Park to visit the Hani family. He was supposed to do a ticker-tape parade through the streets of Johannesburg, but he canceled it.

At the Hani home, Ali had a message of peace. The boxer had not lost the gift of gab, and he told the crowd outside the home a message that was politically very similar to what Mandela was saying that week. "I call on the young people of South Africa to exercise self-discipline during these difficult days," Ali said. "The cause of democracy is too important and your future is too precious to allow the actions of one man to interfere with your destiny."

From the Hani home Ali visited Oliver Tambo, Mandela's friend and president of the exiled ANC until 1991. Tambo had suffered a stroke in 1989, on the eve of the unbanning of the ANC. He was to suffer another stroke and die just a few days after Ali's visit, on April 24. But on this day, Tambo felt hopeful about the country's future. That morning the few marches that had been organized around Johannesburg seemed to be low-key and without incident, thanks perhaps to the agreements between the ANC, police, and peace secretariat. Tambo told Ali that the situation in South Africa would calm down after the funeral—and that the negotiation process should speed up after that.

2 p.m.
Pretoria

The calm that Tambo assured Ali would return did not seem imminent that weekend, however. The militant talk began to ratchet up again. ANC firebrand Winnie Mandela told a rally that the youth should "storm the streets and occupy them until the fascist regime is removed from power."

Peter Mokaba, the ANC Youth League leader, said young people should arm themselves, "legally or illegally," to "defend your revolution." It was militant doublespeak again but in reality he was following Mandela's call for restraint as he had demonstrated in rallies and marches throughout the week. To the listener, and to the many angry young people he led, it sounded like a call to arms.

It certainly did to those, like De Klerk's most hawkish minister Hernus Kriel, who wanted to read it that way. Kriel accused the ANC of making "political propaganda" out of Hani's death. Then he uttered a statement that seemed like a threat: "One thing that is terrible in this country is Black violence, but there is one thing that can be worse and that is white violence," said Kriel. "If leaders do not act decisively now, a racial war is not out of the question."

Was Kriel saying this to incite violence?

6 p.m.
Johannesburg

They came for Clive Derby-Lewis as the sun was setting, in a flurry of police cars that surrounded his home in the West Rand town of Krugersdorp.

There were twenty policemen, led by Mike Holmes and Colonel Ivor Human.

Human knocked on the front door. It opened, and Derby-Lewis stood in front of the two men.

"Hello, my name is Colonel Ivor Human. You are under arrest for the murder of Chris Hani and ..."

Human could not finish the sentence. Derby-Lewis went pale, keeled over, and lost consciousness. One of the policemen ran to the kitchen, got a jug of cold water, and poured it over his face. After a while Derby-Lewis, mustache twitching, came to.

The police searched every room in the house and removed documents and two computers. Six hours later they took Derby-Lewis to the Benoni Police Station, where Janusz Waluś was being held. It was 12:35 a.m. when they booked him into the cell. Within an hour they took him into an interrogation room where two computer technicians were working on his and Gaye's computers.

Derby-Lewis was in a bind. Early on, forensic tests had established that Hani was murdered by the Z-88 pistol from Derby-Lewis, found on Waluś. Blood that matched Hani's and cordite residue had been found on Waluś's clothes and shoes. The detective, Holmes, had established the gun trail from the South African Air Force armory and how it went to Cape Town for a silencer to be fitted and how it then came back to Derby-Lewis and then, ultimately, to Waluś.

Between 1:00 a.m. and 4:45 a.m. the techies downloaded all the files on the computers and stored them on hard disks for analysis.

At 8:15 a.m. Derby-Lewis was brought back to the interrogation room. Then he was returned to the cells at 11:50 a.m. This to-ing and fro-ing continued for twenty-four hours until he started telling stories.

The lies that Derby-Lewis and his associates told are many and varied. They lied and admitted their lies almost immediately to their interrogators. They lied and admitted to their lies in court later on at their trial in October 1993. Given a chance to walk free if they disclosed everything to the Truth and Reconciliation Commission in 1997, Clive Derby-Lewis and Janusz Waluś still did not convince the body—or pretty much anyone else in South Africa—that they were telling the truth. Three decades after Hani's murder, it is still difficult to unravel the truth because they have given so many different versions of what they did.

The lies started that Sunday, April 18, as Derby-Lewis began to "sing like a canary," in Holmes's words. The lies ranged from the mundane to the meaningful aspects of the case.

For example, both Gaye and Clive were later to claim that they were treated badly by the police. And yet after her transfer to Pretoria at the end of her interrogation, Gaye wrote an effusive "thank you" letter to the police and promised to visit them when the case was over. She was later to tell the police that they treated her so well she would like to join the force.

It is worth stopping here, dear reader, and rounding off the many curious tales spun by Waluś and the Derby-Lewises over the past thirty years about the assassination of Chris Hani. These stories were told in the Supreme Court (Witwatersrand Local Division) in October 1993, when the three were charged with murder in a sensational trial marked by racial acrimony. More stories appeared in the Appeal Court of South Africa when Waluś and Clive Derby-Lewis launched their appeal in November 1994. Then, over weeks of testimony, when Clive Derby-Lewis and Waluś applied for amnesty at the Truth and Reconciliation Commission in 1997.

In October 1993, the Rand Supreme Court burst into ululation, singing, and hugs from ANC supporters when an Afrikaner judge, Fritz Eloff, found Waluś and Clive Derby-Lewis guilty of murdering Chris Hani. At the time South Africa had no Black judges, and it does not use the jury system. Eloff sentenced the two men to death for murder, saying: "I want to send out a message loud and clear to those who contemplate the assassination of political leaders."

Gaye was acquitted of charges that she conspired with the pair by compiling the hit list. Judge Eloff said he found the reason she offered for compiling the alleged list to be "inconsistent" and "far-fetched." However, he acquitted her because her explanation may have been an "innocent attempt" to protect her husband.

Ironically, the two men's death sentences were commuted to life when the ANC came to power in 1994 and repealed the death penalty, meaning that the men would serve life sentences with the possibility of parole.

To help heal the wounds of apartheid, in 1995, South Africa set up a new body, headed by antiapartheid clerics Archbishop Desmond Tutu and Alex Boraine instead of judges, to find the truth about apartheid atrocities. Those who came forward and fully disclosed their political acts under apartheid were offered amnesty from prosecution and those who had been convicted would receive full pardons. In April 1999, the Amnesty Committee of the Truth and Reconciliation Commission (TRC) refused amnesty to Derby-Lewis and Waluś. It said both men failed to make a full disclosure and show political motivation in their acts.

One cannot blame the TRC for its decision. Full and meaningful disclosure from the two men is rare—and questions about their conduct are numerous. Here are some of the questions that still have to be answered for South Africans, and the Hani family and their friends and comrades, to perhaps consider whether disclosure has been truthful and meaningful enough.

Was Waluś alone on that day, just an amateur who got caught—or did he give himself up for capture to let bigger fish escape?

His actions were decidedly not those of a man who wanted to evade arrest. At the amnesty applications for both Waluś and Derby-Lewis at the TRC in 1997, Judge Bernard Ngoepe asked: "What worries me . . . was that [in] broad daylight [Waluś] goes to Mr. Hani's place, he shoots him, he walks away, gets into the car, drives away, the weapon is left in the car and he just normally joins the traffic as if nothing has happened. What assurance did he have, did he have some kind of assurance that, don't you worry, you can do it, even if I do it you can be covered somehow, don't you worry?"

Derby-Lewis and Waluś claimed that no one else knew about the

Hani murder plot. Yet the same set of people kept on cropping up again and again before and after the murder with surprising regularity.

Arthur Kemp, the "journalist" who admitted to fleshing out the hit list with addresses, was reportedly a former member of the SA Police and the Security Branch. He had insisted on handing the list to Gaye Derby-Lewis in person at the Rotunda bus station in Johannesburg, where she was departing for Cape Town on January 29, 1993. Edwin Clarke drove Gaye from her house in Krugersdorp to Rotunda that day to get the bus. The three met. The list of names was handed over. Kemp complained about working at the *Citizen* newspaper. The three parted.

Just a week later, on February 6, 1993, SAA flight 232 took off from Johannesburg en route to London. On board was Chris Hani and, unknown to Hani, Arthur Kemp. Was Kemp monitoring Hani? Clarke was again at the Derby-Lewis home on April 6, 1993, when Clive handed over the gun to Waluś. The three men claimed Clarke was doing "computer work" and was not involved in the conspiracy.

Waluś had also met Edwin Clarke at the Derby-Lewises' house several times, ostensibly over barbecues. In testimony to the Truth and Reconciliation Commission, Clarke said that if Derby-Lewis had approached him to kill Hani, "The answer is that I would seriously have considered it and quite possibly I would have said yes." Johannes Visser, who was well known in right-wing circles, later claimed that Clarke tried to provide about R 360,000 in stolen money for Derby-Lewis's defense. Clarke denied Visser's claims.

Gaye Derby-Lewis testified that after receiving the hit list from Arthur Kemp, she left it lying on the desk of Dr. Ferdi Hartzenberg, the deputy leader of the Conservative Party in South Africa between 1993 and 2004, to use it in parliamentary questions. He did not use it. According to Gaye, he gave it back to her, no questions asked. Gaye brought the list back home in March 1993 and left it lying on her filing table in the study of her Krugersdorp home. Her husband helped himself to it and gave it to Waluś, she claimed. Then, later, she admitted she lied at the trial, saying she was protecting her husband.

On that trip to Cape Town on January 29, 1993, Clive (who had flown earlier) had with him the gun he had acquired from Faan Venter. It was then fitted with a silencer in Cape Town. Yet these two purportedly never spoke about the items they had in their possession despite being, as the Hani family lawyer and Mandela friend from the 1950s George Bizos was to ask, "a loving couple."

The players in this saga seem to run into each other at key moments. Faan Venter, the gun provider, and his wife, Maureen, just so happened to be entertaining the Derby-Lewises at their home on Saturday, the tenth of April, at the exact time that the gun was being used to kill Chris Hani. Could they have been waiting for news of the kill? Why did the Venters' son feel the need to call them that day to deliver the news about the murder of Hani?

Venter said he delivered the gun to Lionel du Randt, another right-wing acquaintance, on March 10, a full month before the murder. The Du Randts said that was not true—it was in the second half of February. They knew this because they delivered it to the Derby-Lewises on their way to their daughter's birthday celebration on February 25. But Lionel du Randt's original police statement said he had received the gun on March 31. Then Du Randt changed his story and said yes in fact he had received the gun on March 10. Then he contradicted his wife and said his daughter's birthday was February 28.

Du Randt, under questioning from lawyer Gcina Malindi at the TRC during the Derby-Lewis/Waluś amnesty hearings, said it was of no concern to him that a gun was delivered to him at his house by Venter in a clandestine manner.

"Is it because you knew why it was delivered at your house and for what purpose?" Malindi asked.

"No, I didn't know anything," answered Du Randt.

He also said he'd handed Derby-Lewis the gun wrapped in a sweater, but there never was a sweater. The gun was still in its manufacturer's box, in a plastic bag. He claimed not to have seen the gun himself while it was in his possession, despite his son and wife saying they saw it; he told the TRC that his wife was a liar.

After Clive Derby-Lewis was arrested for his part in Hani's killing, the Du Randts visited Gaye Derby-Lewis to console her. According to Lionel du Randt, there were several such visits. Not once did he and his family inquire if the gun they had delivered was the one used to murder Hani. So the question can be legitimately asked: Were all these people who interacted on numerous occasions in the three months before Hani's murder a terror cell?

Police arrested Du Randt, Venter, and Kemp soon after the arrest of Clive Derby-Lewis. They released them days afterward. Du Randt, Venter, Kemp, and Clarke were not charged in the Hani case. Du Randt, Venter, and Kemp testified as witnesses for the prosecution in the case against Clive Derby-Lewis, Gaye Derby-Lewis, and Janusz Waluś in October 1993.

Was Waluś an angry, ordinary man or had he had military and sniper training—a trained killer? Did he have connections to the intelligence community?
On January 26, 1989, Waluś read an advertisement in the *Citizen* recruiting men for a "dangerous assignment, approximately six months in duration," at a salary of $5,000 per month with an outfit called the South African Institute for Maritime Research (SAIMR).

The SAIMR was a mercenary group. The UK's *Guardian* wrote about them in 2020, naming its commodore as Keith Maxwell, who "liked to dress up on special occasions in the garish costume of an 18th-century admiral, with a three-cornered hat, brass buttons and a cutlass."

"Beneath the bizarre trappings lurked a powerful mercenary outfit that members claim was entwined with the apartheid state and offered soldiers for hire across the continent," the newspaper said.

Why would Waluś apply for a position with a military outfit if he had no military training? If he did, where did he get it?

Waluś had long-standing contacts with South Africa's military intelligence agents. From 1985, he was in touch with Johan Fourie, who Waluś said had offered him money to be a source. Although Waluś claimed not to have taken the money, he stayed in touch with Fourie over the years. In fact, although he claimed he lost touch with Fourie in 1990, phone records showed he called Fourie on March 13, 1993. Why—and why lie about it?

The far-right former military intelligence chief General Tienie Groenewald was linked to the SAIMR. Groenewald had met Waluś in QwaQwa at the family's glass-cutting business, and they met again several times after that. Waluś also got to know Groenewald's brother Jan. What was a general doing with a down-at-heel glass manufacturer?

Gaye Derby-Lewis's first husband was an intelligence officer: Anton Graser.

One of Gaye's best friends was Craig Kotze, journalist-turned-apartheid-cop, who reportedly liked to drink at Truckers, the gay bar she had managed in Hillbrow. He was the police spokesman who rushed to say Hani's killer was a lone wolf just hours after the killing—without any proof whatsoever.

We already know that Waluś was a fit martial arts aficionado, a crack shot, and had often engaged in target practice at his brother Witold's farm outside Pretoria. He was a plausible triggerman, but he was certainly not the mastermind. Derby-Lewis was a fanatic, but his fainting and blushing does not mark him as a mastermind, either.

The big mystery of the case is that the arrest of Derby-Lewis and the court evidence was provided by Holmes and his team of detectives led by Colonel Ivor Human. But from Wednesday, April 14, the case was handled almost entirely by the Security Branch with Deetlefs as the point man. These murky characters, the journalist Evelyn Groenink points out, pointedly instructed Holmes and his team to stop investigating Waluś's links to Peter Jackson, the man who employed him and who owned the red Ford Laser. Groenink described Jackson as "a chemicals transporter with arms trade connections." Security police captain J. H. de Waal told Holmes's team "not to bother exploring [Jackson] or his arms trade and secret service contacts." De Waal issued several such written instructions.

Waluś carried an "agenda book" or diary. It disappeared from the police docket. In the copy that remained, the pages relating to the week leading up to the murder of Hani were missing. Witnesses who claimed there was a second car, and a second man, at the scene were dismissed or intimidated. One such witness, Dudu Kraii, was visited by police at 4 a.m.

Most curious of all was Holmes's defense of these lapses. He told Groenink: "We didn't need to look at all the evidence because the security police put everything we needed in a box for us to work with."

Was the Hani assassination an impulse killing, as Waluś would have us believe?

The narrow narrative told by Waluś and Derby-Lewis is that they planned and executed the murder in April 1993, but there are numerous indications that things had started rolling way earlier than that. In his testimony at the TRC, Waluś claimed that he had bought tape to mask the red Ford's registration that morning. He was lying. The masking tape was bought on March 2, as police established. Waluś had been planning it for more than a month.

Or was it three months? Gaye Derby-Lewis had telephoned Arthur Kemp in January and sent him the list of names that finally made up the hit list. Gaye gave three different reasons for compiling the list. First she said she was writing a story about the ostentatious lives of antiapartheid and communist leaders who purportedly lived in luxury while their supporters suffered. Then she claimed she aimed to write a book with the far-right pundit Aida Parker, formerly of the *Citizen*. Then Gaye said the list was for use by Conservative Party leader Ferdi Hartzenberg in Parliament to expose ANC leaders' lifestyles. If it was for Hartzenberg's use, why the addresses and security details? If it was for Parker's use, why the addresses and security details? If it was for her own use, why the descriptions of security features on, say, Mandela's house?

Tellingly, in 2016, Gaye boasted to Hani's daughter Lindiwe that *she* had found the Hanis' home address for the hit list. In her book *Being Chris Hani's Daughter*, Lindiwe writes that she was told by an amused Gaye how she had found the address "in the phone book" while working on a story about "Gucci socialists." Her story all along was that she had merely compiled the names while Kemp had researched the addresses.

Was there a wider conspiracy to assassinate Hani?

Weeks after her husband's murder in 1993, Limpho Hani called the police investigation "a waste of time and people's taxes." "Unless the think tank that planned Chris's killing is brought to trial, we shall continue to be in danger," she said at the time. Sexwale told a crowd at the beginning of the trial of Waluś and the Derby-Lewises: "In that court we have the killers, not the plotters. We may close the file on the killers, but the file on the plotters will remain open."

Conspiracy theories around Hani abound in SA. Little evidence is ever proffered. The result has been fear, suspicion, and loathing, particularly inside the ANC.

The rumors tend to resurface in times of ANC contestation for leadership and are used to besmirch rivals. How better to undermine a candidate than to imply they had a hand in the assassination of the country's most loved political son? In 2001, Steve Tshwete, the safety and security minister of then South African president Thabo Mbeki, alleged that Cyril Ramaphosa, Tokyo Sexwale, and Mathews Phosa were responsible for rumors circulating that Mbeki had a hand in Hani's murder. The three men vehemently denied the claims and, months later, Tshwete apologized and said the claims were without any foundation.

Fighting off corruption charges in 2019, former president Jacob Zuma told supporters that when he was head of the ANC intelligence wing during the struggle against apartheid, he came across information that suggested someone betrayed Hani by leaking information to the apartheid government. And yet, despite serving as president of the country for nine years, Zuma never revealed this information or ordered the reopening of the investigation into Hani's death.

There have been occasional pieces of evidence that may have intimated a wider conspiracy. In 1997, the *New Nation* newspaper revealed that a report in the hands of South Africa's National Intelligence Agency pointed to the involvement of apartheid-era police death squads based at the notorious Vlakplaas farm near Pretoria in the initial stages of a conspiracy to murder Hani. This was not as far-fetched a claim as it sounds. The following year (1998), Ferdi Barnard, a former apartheid-era government death squad member, was convicted for the assassination of the academic and antiapartheid activist David Webster in 1989. Barnard shot Webster with a shotgun, in front of his home, in a hit similar to the Hani assassination. But the full NIA report never came to light, and the ANC's own review of the investigation has never been released.

Of all the examinations into a wider conspiracy surrounding Hani's death, the most far-reaching is the work of Dutch journalist Evelyn Groenink, who believes Hani's murder was linked to those of the ANC Paris head, Dulcie September, who was shot in 1988, and the activist Anton Lubowski, shot in 1989. In an investigation spanning three decades, Groenink has found disquieting evidence for known arms dealers' attempts to insinuate themselves into the lives of Hani, September, and Lubowski. One of the first acts of the new South African government in the late 1990s was to acquire $4.8 billion worth of weaponry it had no use for; Hani was, at the time of his death, already at variance with some of his comrades about future arms procurement. And yet despite this possible motive, there has not been any official attempt to reopen the Hani case.

Jeremy Cronin, a long-standing South African Communist Party leader, had campaigned for nearly thirty years for the continued incarceration of Waluś, whose life imprisonment always meant that he was eligible for parole if he met a variety of requirements, including good behavior. Cronin had argued that the assassin must disclose the full truth before he can be released. He has drawn attention to the intense character assassination of Hani in the year before his murder, including the planting of false stories of Hani starting a violent breakaway army from the ANC and senior politicians such as Minister of Justice Kobie Coetsee, who warned:

"The ANC would be well advised to sever its links with the Communist Party, and especially one Mr. Hani." Cronin asked: To what end was this vilification of Hani? He also asked whether some elements of the government were laying the groundwork for a muted public outcry when one of its own men did kill Hani.

"You can choose to believe Hani's murder was just the work of a lone Polish immigrant and a bumbling, Dad's Army Derby-Lewis. But you don't have to be a conspiracy enthusiast to think otherwise," says Cronin.

Hani's daughter Lindiwe has visited Waluś in prison and the Derby-Lewis couple at home, looked them in the eye, and asked them for the truth about the assassination plot. She didn't get it. They insisted they acted alone. Unless South Africa's democratic leaders reopen the case, simply by following up on some of the glaring contradictions revealed by the Truth and Reconciliation Commission hearings into the murder, we will never get to the truth.

In its final report the TRC said: "Both Derby-Lewis and Waluś had strong ties with Mr. Koos Vermeulen, leader and founder of both the World Preservatist Movement (WPB) and the World Apartheid Movement (WAB). Both were and are suspected to have been South African Police fronts . . . Waluś himself operated as a National Intelligence Service source. The weapon used in the killing was stolen from the Pretoria SAAF air base by Piet 'Skiet' Rudolph . . . in April 1991. The commission was unable to find evidence that the two murderers convicted of the killing of Chris Hani took orders from international groups, security forces or from higher up in the right-wing echelons."

This conclusion of the TRC has not stopped a veritable industry of persistent reports of a wider conspiracy involving apartheid military intelligence operatives—and ANC leaders. Over the years, shadowy intelligence operatives have leaked stories, spread rumors, and insinuated a wider conspiracy. None of it has come to much.

What we do know for sure, however, is this: Clive Derby-Lewis and

Janusz Waluś, assisted by about seven minions (who have all vehemently denied active involvement in a conspiracy), almost all of whom had links to South African intelligence and military intelligence agencies and leaders, killed Chris Hani. We know their stories don't make sense. But none of these primary players in this saga have spoken about whether a Third Force controlled their actions. South Africa still waits for the truth.

SUNDAY
April 18, 1993

Lay her I' th' earth,
And from her fair and unpolluted flesh
May violets spring! I tell thee, churlish priest,
A ministering angel shall my sister be
When thou liest howling.
Hamlet, Act 5, Scene 1

1–8 p.m.
FNB Stadium, Johannesburg

Many were later to say that Chris Hani's was the first state funeral of the new South Africa. In many respects it was. The public broadcaster had undertaken to air most of it live, the first time such an honor was extended to a Black person and an antiapartheid leader. Buses were packed with chanting mourners from all corners of the country that weekend, all headed to the 90,000-seater FNB Stadium in Soweto. For many who had traveled fifteen hours by bus from South Africa's southernmost province, the Cape, the pilgrimage would take up to three days.

The official funeral program lasted for twenty-four hours, starting on Sunday the eighteenth at 1 p.m., when the hearse carrying Hani's body entered the stadium. The entire stadium stood up in absolute silence. Hats were held to the chest. The silence was so forceful, so complete, it was "unbearable."

MK cadres in olive-green fatigues carried the coffin to the middle of the soccer field, where a yellow-and-gold marquee had been set up. An MK soldier carried a white satin cushion on which lay Hani's MK camouflage cap.

Hani's three daughters, Lindiwe (eleven), Neo (twenty), and Nomakhwezi (fourteen), walked behind the MK cadres, their faces composed. While MK combatants standing at attention nearby cried openly, tears streaming down their faces, the three Hani children shed no tears. Nomakhwezi, in a white blouse, navy jacket, and tartan skirt, averted her eyes from the open coffin. She stood at the foot of the coffin while political and church leaders filed past, paying their respects. Next to her stood the ANC secretary-general, Cyril Ramaphosa. He stood by her until she went to sit.

Immediately behind the children was their mother, Limpho, and Hani's parents, Gilbert and Nomayise.

The stadium was festooned with the red flags of the Congress of SA Trade Unions and the Communist Party and the black, green, and gold of the ANC. Dressed in fatigues, ANC T-shirts, and other party paraphernalia, the thousands of supporters—reported to be between 75,000 and 80,000 by sunset—continued to file past Hani's coffin while a police helicopter circled above.

Holomisa had flown the Transkei Defence Force brass band in for the ceremony and they played a plaintive, sad melody as the viewing proceeded.

Mandela's cavalcade entered the stadium at 6:15 p.m. The emcee introduced him as the next president of South Africa. Mandela received the biggest round of applause of the day, rivaled only by that which greeted the KwaZulu-Natal militant Harry Gwala. The crowd was already in a fervor of chanting and dancing the *toyi-toyi*. They stamped their feet in the stands. The stadium shook. Mandela walked to where Hani's body lay, dressed in camouflage. About seventy MK cadres, in green army fatigues, stood to attention.

At around 6:55 p.m., an interdenominational church service got underway for the communist leader. The Catholic bishop of Johannesburg, Reginald Orsmond, told reporters that Hani "certainly never gave up his Christian beliefs."

Winnie Mandela arrived to wild cheers. She was ushered to the stage, looking "sour and grumpy," according to one description, and sat next to Harry Gwala. Winnie was dressed in MK fatigues with an MK hat, designer Italian high heels, and a leather Hermès bag.

6 p.m.
Elspark suburb, Boksburg

The news out of the stadium was being followed by fearful whites too. For days in the run-up to the funeral one could see the hate and fear raging through the mainly white suburbs around Chris Hani's home. Hundreds of guns were bought by residents fearing attack. Many were not just afraid. They wanted, like Waluś and Derby-Lewis, to stay in the old South Africa that was crumbling all around them.

Until June 1991, the cemetery where Hani was to be buried was reserved for whites only. Now it was about to host a militant leader of the antiapartheid movement. The prospect drove the neighborhood into rage and fear. In Elspark, the suburb across the road from the cemetery, white residents sent women and children away for the day en masse. The men of the suburb stayed behind to "defend" their property.

They had called in the AWB to help them in their defense of the suburb. The AWB claimed to have more than 2,000 heavily armed members in the area. An AWB "general," Johan Thompson, said the organization was ready for battle.

"If we are all dead by the end of today there will be only one hundred Blacks left," he said, standing in front of a group of AWB members. They held their guns aloft and smiled for press photographers.

"Most people here are peace-loving people," said Brian Robinson, twenty-one, a local gun shop owner. "But sometimes it's hard, especially when you hear these people saying, 'Our next bullet's for you.'"

"We are worried about a savage horde coming to wreak havoc here," said Edmund Heine, a forty-five-year-old AWB member who was guarding one house near the cemetery with a shotgun across his lap and a pistol in his belt. "This is a purely defensive mission. But we will not hesitate to shoot."

Heine paid tribute to Janusz Waluś: "I take my hat off to the man. I see him as a hero."

Japie Marais, a rigger, had volunteered his house as the AWB headquarters for the day.

"No one can tell what will happen here today, so I brought the AWB here to protect my property and to protect myself. I like living here, but we have never seen anything like this.

"I have never seen such a large crowd of Black people. I think it is stupidity. But as long as they stay on their side, I will stay on mine," he said.

"Why did Chris Hani have to be buried here? Why couldn't he have been buried in his homeland? I say thanks to the AWB because they were the first that approached me offering protection."

Ken Finley, who claimed to be a "brigadier" in the AWB, was decked out in a Stetson-style hat and the all-khaki uniform of the AWB. He told a reporter: "We are not racists. We are not anti-Black. We just want a home to ourselves and to live in peace."

Fondling his gun, he complained that "there is no such thing as a white place anymore."

9 p.m.
Sebokeng township, Johannesburg

Outside the stadium, death was still stalking the land. In one of the most senseless acts of violence yet perpetrated in a South Africa replete with killing, unknown gunmen drove back and forth through the township of Sebokeng, south of where Hani lived, in two cars, shooting randomly at residents. The first assailants, driving a stolen Volkswagen, which was later found burned out in the township, killed eight people in four attacks that night. At the same time, in what seemed like a coordinated attack, nine other people were killed in three other attacks by assailants in a Toyota.

Two more bodies were discovered the day after, bringing the death toll to nineteen. Ten people were injured.

The stories of what happened that night are haunting. Alina Mapelo Magoda told the Truth and Reconciliation Commission that when she heard gunshots outside her house, she immediately turned off the lights. Shortly afterward a neighbor knocked at the door of her house. Her husband went outside and found the bodies of Magoda's daughter and her friend. They were dead. Three members of the Moshodi family had also been sitting in their front yard in Sebokeng when shots had rung out from one of the two killer cars. Edward Maseko, Maria Moshodi, and Paul Moshodi were all gunned down.

Edward was eight years old.

11 p.m.
FNB Stadium, Johannesburg

At 11 p.m., the body of Chris Hani was transported out of the stadium, followed by his family. Speeches and singing continued while the sound of gunfire echoed through the night.

By midnight the stadium was shaking with the force of the energetic gyrations of the thousands singing and dancing in the stands. It was so energetic a reporter noted "bits of plaster coming off the walls." An ANC official begged the crowd to calm down because the "stadium can collapse at any moment."

Peter Harris was in one of the stadium's private boxes where a joint operations center had been set up to monitor the situation and avert conflict where necessary. The peace monitors and ANC marshals were well versed in intervening in scuffles, but a stadium collapse?

Harris feared for the night ahead and the possibility of a right-wing attack. "I feel that it will take a miracle to survive this crisis," he later remembered of that night.

He did not know, yet, that some of the killers trying to stop the birth of a new South Africa were already doing their dirty work in Sebokeng.

Midnight
FNB Stadium, Johannesburg

Back inside the stadium at Hani's night vigil, the anger and emotion of the past week could be seen and felt. The firebrand Gwala stood up to speak and was in his usual militant spirit. He said that those who had caused and plotted Chris Hani's death "had signed their own death warrants." His words were met with massive cheers. Now, in the doublespeak of the ANC's leaders at the time, Gwala could very well have been meaning that apartheid had suffered its death knell, or that the actual murderers or conspirators would receive death sentences, but in that stadium his words could not have been understood that way by all of the angry young people listening. The militancy left enough ambiguity for it to be interpreted, coming from a militant leader who was engulfed in a small war in his home province of KwaZulu-Natal, as a call to arms.

"We are prepared to fight. We did not go for negotiations, we forced negotiations on the oppressor," Gwala said. Winnie Mandela, along with the entire stadium, stood up for Gwala and applauded. The speeches that night and over the next twenty-four hours would be in much the same vein, however. There would be militancy, then that would be tempered with a call for peace.

Holomisa had also arrived to massive cheers from the packed stadium. Like Gwala, Winnie Mandela, the youth leader Peter Mokaba, and a few others, he was a darling of the militant youth and could be relied on to deliver a rousing and warlike speech. What was interesting about their speeches is that they were militant and yet at the end they would call for "discipline" and adherence to the leaders' call for calm. So Holomisa also delivered his own militant message—but went further. "I say to the Umkhonto we Sizwe people at this stadium: Don't cry . . . You must carry your own guns with or without licenses, and defend your leaders from this day on," he said. Shots were fired into the air from among the crowd in response to his speech.

It is difficult not to draw a "hawks" versus "doves" divide when reflecting on these speeches by ANC leaders that night. Yet on an occasion like the funeral, there actually was no divide. Many of them were venting, pushing out their frustration and pain, and much of the speeches were an expression of that pain, mixed with a bit of politicking and the real message they wanted to convey: let's not jeopardize this when we are so close to ultimate victory.

MONDAY

April 19, 1993

Alack, my child is dead;
And with my child my joys are buried.
    Romeo and Juliet, Act 4, Scene 5

9 a.m.
FNB Stadium, Johannesburg

The day of the funeral matched the previous Wednesday for the biggest work stayaway ever undertaken by workers in the country. In the economic heartland, the PWV area around Johannesburg, 100 percent of the workforce heeded the call to stay home. Countrywide, more than 80 percent heeded the stayaway call.

The assassination had moved great parts of South Africa. Death row prisoners at the Pretoria Maximum Prison collected R 750 in a gesture of solidarity with the Hani family. The 290 prisoners, among them a Black government agent who had talked to the press to expose the administration's secret hit squads, said they condemned Hani's murder.

De Klerk's government was not moved. Only two South African embassies—both led by English-speaking liberals—formally acknowledged the assassination and the anger and grief caused by it. The Washington embassy flew the South African flag at half-mast while London held a prayer service for peace and to express their sympathy for Hani's family. No one from the government or National Party attended the funeral.

In the residential area immediately around the stadium, gangs of youth were attacking and burning houses. Police and ANC marshals tried to repel them, but they were outnumbered. Gunmen fired automatic weapons at police helicopters flying overhead. Smoke billowed into the sky from burning houses.

Archbishop Desmond Tutu was the preacher that day. He adopted Romans 8:31 as his lesson for the day: "If God be for us, who can be against us?" After greeting the mourners in five languages, he started his own call-and-response.

"Is there anyone here who doubts that Chris was a great son of the soil?"

"No!" the stadium roared back.

"I don't hear you?"

"No!" even louder, wilder.

The crowd went even wilder when he took a dig at those who were obsessed with the demonization of communism. "Those who oppressed us were not communists!" he said.

He said just as the resurrection followed the crucifixion, Hani's death could become a victory: "The death of Chris Hani gives the government and all the key players another chance. We want to make a demand today . . . we demand democracy and freedom. When?"

"Now!" the crowd roared back.

"They don't hear you in Pretoria. They don't hear you in Cape Town. We demand democracy and freedom. When?"

"Now!"

And finally, he made the key demand of the ANC and its allies: "We demand a date for the first democratic elections in this country. When?"

"Now!"

Tutu then told the crowd that South Africa was "the rainbow nation of God," a term he had coined and used several times before and which resonated with Mandela, who would popularize it in later years. "No one can stop us on our march to victory! No one, no guns, nothing! Nothing will stop us, for we are moving to freedom! God is on our side! . . . We are marching to freedom, all of us, Black and white," he said.

Joe Slovo gave one of the most moving tributes to Hani that day. He said those who sought killing as the only answer to the assassination could not step into Hani's shoes. "Chris was neither a hawk nor a dove," he said. "When the time came to fight, he fought like a tiger, and when a peaceful way became possible, he fought like a tiger to say so.

"The assassin and those behind him think they have killed a man and all he stood for. But they have mobilized the greatest army this country has ever seen. It is an army for democracy."

Finally, it was Mandela's turn to speak. His speech was long, the longest he had given that week, but it was expertly crafted for a moment of great doubt for him and the country.

Mandela's address started with the personal. He asked the stadium to stand for a moment of silence in tribute to Hani. Every bit of space in the stadium, its capacity 90,000, was taken up by a human body. Some estimates put the number of people inside the stadium at 120,000. There were tens of thousands more outside.

Then he spoke about Sabalele, the village he had flown to nine days before. "Chris Hani's passion for justice, for addressing the problems that plague the rural poor, were rooted in his childhood in Sabalele," he said. "His roots were so deep, so true, that he never lost them." It was, and is, a very familiar way of paying tribute in Black South Africa, saying that a person remained humble, a man or woman of the people, despite one's fortune or travels or education. Indeed, any sign that one has changed, assumed airs because of wealth or travel, is a sign of betrayal.

To this day, this ideal of Hani still grips South Africa. Whenever corruption scandals roil the country, the first question—and answer—is almost always: "Would Chris Hani have done this? No, Chris was a man of the people."

"Chris Hani touched the very heart of millions of us because he knew our pain, and eased it by giving us hope, giving us courage, giving us a way forward," Mandela continued. "Chris Hani loved life and lived it to the full. But he loved freedom more. Chris Hani loved our people, our organizations, our South African nation, and for that love he was brutally murdered."

Mandela then turned to culpability. Hani's murder, he said, was no aberration, but consistent with the patterns of scores of apartheid assassinations that remained "unsolved." He named a few: The revered trade union organizer and academic Rick Turner, shot dead at his home in Durban in 1978 in front of his then thirteen-year-old daughter, who was in the stadium that day. The Eastern Cape activists Matthew Goniwe and Sparrow Mkhonto, tortured and murdered in 1985. The popular academic David Webster, shot and killed in Johannesburg in 1989. The activist, academic, and writer Ruth First, Joe Slovo's wife, killed via parcel bomb in Mozambique in 1982. ANC official Dulcie September, killed in 1988 in a manner similar to the way Hani was murdered—five shots with a gun fitted with a silencer as she opened the door of the party's office in Paris.

"Their killers remain unnamed because the criminals investigate themselves," he said.

His anger was palpable as he turned his sights on the culpability of the government that De Klerk led. He called for Clive Derby-Lewis to be brought to court swiftly.

Part of the rupture between Mandela and De Klerk was that the state president had failed, in public and in private, to acknowledge that the government he led could be involved in dirty tricks. In 1992, five policemen had been convicted for carrying out the Trust Feed Massacre, in which eleven people, mainly women and two children, were sprayed with bullets and killed in a home in an area known as Trust Feed in KwaZulu-Natal. Initially, the 1988 massacre was portrayed as the work of "ANC terrorists," but two detectives from the area dug into and exposed it as a government security operation carried out by five policemen, including the local chief of police. Many other security police operations similar to Trust Feed had also been exposed, yet De Klerk still largely blamed the ANC for violence that, in fact, often emanated from elements in his security establishment.

Mandela made the point in his speech, saying: "In 1991, when we spoke of a Third Force being responsible for the violence, we were ridiculed and criticized by everyone. Now both South Africa and the world recognize not only the existence of that same Third Force, but also the extent of its activities. That is why De Klerk retired army and police generals with golden handshakes, but neither we nor the country know what activities they were dismissed for."

Mandela said Hani had warned that weapons stolen from the Pretoria Air Force Base in 1991 were to be used in covert operations and was ridiculed. "Guns from those same stolen weapons were used to kill him. This secret web of hit men and covert operations is funded by our taxes," he said.

It was a tough speech. Mandela turned next to the demonization of Hani. No effort had been spared to criminalize both MK and Chris Hani, he said.

"To criminalize is to outlaw, and the hunting down of an outlaw is regarded as legitimate. That is why, although millions of people have been outraged at the murder of Chris Hani, few were really surprised. Those who have deliberately created this climate that legitimates political assassinations are as much responsible for the death of Chris Hani as the man who pulled the trigger, and the conspiracy that plotted his murder. In this regard, the Minister of Law and Order and the Chief of the Army both have a great deal to answer for."

Mandela then turned on De Klerk, saying the president's first response after Hani's murder was to call a meeting of the State Security Council and to deploy 23,000 more troops. Mandela's anger showed. He had run out of patience.

"They say we cannot control our forces. We are not cattle to be controlled. And we say to De Klerk: it is your forces that lost control and, completely unprovoked, shot innocent marchers in Protea," he charged, referring to the Wednesday killing of four protesters and wounding of over a hundred people by unprovoked police in a suburb of Soweto.

Mandela then went on to speak in a manner that recalled the militant speeches of the night before by Gwala and Holomisa. He directly addressed his critics, those who wanted to create a false dichotomy between Mandela the freedom fighter and Mandela the negotiator. He was both, just like the ANC: "They talk of peace as if wanting peace is pacifism . . . We want peace, but we are not pacifists. We are all militants. We are all radicals. That is the very essence of the ANC, for it is a liberation movement fighting for freedom for all our people. It is our unceasing struggles— in the prisons, in mass campaigns, through the armed struggle that has brought the regime to the negotiating table. And those negotiations are themselves a site of struggle." Mandela had taken up Hani's language of being a militant for peace.

At the end of his oration, Mandela made an impassioned call for peace and restraint.

"Chris Hani has a very special place in our hearts. But each and every one of you is precious to us. You are our people, our pride and joy, our future. We love you all. And we want all of you to reach home safely. When we leave here, let us do so with the pride and dignity of our nation. Let us not be provoked . . . Let Chris Hani live on through all of us."

At the conclusion of the funeral program, Ramaphosa took the microphone and told the mourners that the Hani family had requested that everyone go home, as they wanted the ceremony at the cemetery to be private. But the announcement was too late. Hundreds of overloaded buses had already headed out.

This is where the agreement signed by Mbeki, Calitz, and Harris saved the day. In the South Africa before that day, the police would have been blocking the roads to the cemetery, trying to ensure that mourners did not go to a white area, and tear gas, water cannons, dogs, barbed wire, and even armored vehicles would have been used to try and control the crowds heading toward Elspark Cemetery. In that neighborhood, hundreds of white right-wingers, armed to the teeth, were waiting.

On the fifty-three kilometers from the stadium to the cemetery, most of the cars and buses broke every conceivable law possible. As the journalist Stengel described it: "People perched on top of buses, hanging out the windows—which had been punched out, sitting on top of each other inside. Many of those station wagons had sets of legs protruding from the rear." Ordinarily, the police would have tried to intervene. Because of the agreement, the police received strict instructions from Calitz to take a "low profile." This time, ANC marshals and peace monitors were in charge.

Along the highway, some militants tried to cause chaos, throwing rocks and all kinds of paraphernalia on the roadway. They wanted to trigger an accident, an event, that might set off some other chaos. The ANC marshals, in some instances helped by the police, cleared the obstacles.

As the buses entered Elspark the armed right-wingers stood behind their gates, watching. More than 20,000 people arrived at the cemetery for the burial ceremony. One of those people was Mondli Gungubele. At first, when he saw the right-wingers along the route to the cemetery, he was angry.

Idiots, he thought. Only later did he realize that, over and above the hatred, these people were afraid. It dawned on him then that Mandela was never weak during the entire negotiation process. His strength was that he appreciated the "authentic fears" of his opponents, that for many white South Africans to imagine the freedom of the people they had humiliated for centuries—and that such freedom would come without vengeance— was impossible.

Gungubele told me he felt profoundly sad for them.

"They didn't believe anything we were saying," he said.

"Hamba kahle, Mkhonto," the slow, moving, mournful dirge of every ANC funeral, rose. The right-wingers listening to it from the houses opposite the ceremony would have been chilled had they understood the Zulu lyrics: "We, the people of Spear of the Nation, have committed ourselves to kill these Boers."

Then an honor guard raised its guns, whereupon many in the crowd pulled pistols and machine guns from under their coats and fired their own salute into the air. The shooting ended only after Tokyo Sexwale, in a voice that boomed over the loudspeakers, demanded: "Cease your fire! The twenty-one-gun salute has ended."

Then it was over. The mourners returned to their buses and spread out across the country, heading home. Things were generally peaceful and orderly. But police fought small bands of looters near the stadium and cemetery. At least six deaths and a dozen injuries were reported, police said.

That night Gungubele sighed with relief. Harris, too, was reflective: the violence of that week was perhaps 5 percent of what could have happened, thanks to the calming words of Mandela and other leaders.

"Imagine if it was ninety percent," he told me. At least seventy people had died in violence directly linked to Hani's assassination.

For that Monday, though, Chris Hani had been buried with dignity. Tomorrow would be another day.

2 p.m.
Cape Town

Monday the nineteenth was supposed to be an ordinary working day in South Africa. And so, defying the ANC's call for a total stayaway, the country's still whites-only Parliament refused to cancel its sitting scheduled for that day, despite the fact that it would be totally eclipsed by the Hani funeral. De Klerk had a speech scheduled and he had flown from Pretoria to Cape Town for it.

The liberal opposition Democratic Party asked De Klerk to postpone that day's sitting in honor of Hani. He refused. It had then asked him to move the starting time by three hours to 5 p.m., after Hani's funeral had ended, to at least show respect. De Klerk had turned that request down as well. Instead, he proceeded with his speech at 2 p.m. as scheduled, while the nation watched Hani's funeral. It was the petty, nasty side of De Klerk on display, the one that many progressive South Africans were never to forget even when his positive role in the democratization process was to be recognized. His speech to Parliament made things even worse. Not caring that his decision to continue with his address right in the middle of Hani's live televised funeral was an insult to many, he said there was anger "among the leaders and supporters of the ANC" and those of Inkatha because there were "murders of members of the public, women and children, Black and white, murder of policemen and women." He failed to acknowledge that Hani had died at the hands of a white right-winger, someone radicalized by militant breakaways from his own party. Someone he, as a leader, had failed to control.

TUESDAY TO THURSDAY

April 20–22, 1993

There is a tide in the affairs of men.
Which, taken at the flood, leads on to fortune;
Omitted, all the voyage of their life
Is bound in shallows and in miseries.
On such a full sea are we now afloat,
And we must take the current when it serves,
Or lose our ventures.

Julius Caesar, Act 4, Scene 3

Dawn
April 20, 1993
South Africa

Immediately after Hani's assassination, Holomisa had thought that "there was no way that the talks in Kempton Park could go ahead."

But the events of the following week proved him wrong.

"Miraculously," he wrote in his autobiography, "Hani's death had the opposite effect . . . Hani's killing helped to push the process of democratization forward and faster. If those who plotted to kill Hani were praying for bloodshed, their prayers had failed dismally."

Even on the day of the funeral, a day full of anger, sadness, death, and general mayhem, the country did not descend into war. Even in Elspark, where the AWB was fearfully lying in wait for violence as 20,000 mourners arrived, the clash of white against Black did not happen.

Why? Largely because of the quiet, unheralded three-tier ring of marshals, peace monitors, and police negotiated by Thabo Mbeki, Koos Calitz, and Peter Harris three nights before. It worked largely because the kind of anger elicited by the police among communities and youth frustrated by the relentless political violence of previous years was removed from the front line; troubleshooting was done by ANC marshals and peacekeepers, who had legitimacy and authority among mourners; and police were not there to retaliate against every move they deemed a provocation. Crucially, the language of restraint, peace, and negotiation as the ultimate path to victory had never left the ANC leaders' lips that week. Even for some among those who spoke tough, such as Mokaba and Holomisa, the language tended toward temperance.

A year after Hani's assassination, Mandela told a gathering at the unveiling of the communist leader's tombstone: "At the time of Chris's death, prophets of doom predicted that our country would go up in flames. They said that the leadership of our people could not control 'young militants.' The political maturity of our nation has disproved them."

No other single event proved so conclusively that, whatever the trauma that was yet to come, South Africa's center would hold, wrote Patti Waldmeir, the *Financial Times* correspondent. "The crisis clarified, once and for all, the balance of power. Symbolically, De Klerk was all but unseated by it . . . De Klerk was still president; but Mandela was the nation's leader; he shouldered the task of racial reconciliation shirked by De Klerk."

In almost all Black South African cultures, a weeklong mourning period is observed by relatives before burial. The relatives, particularly immediate family, are confined to the home, receive visitors, and are comforted. In that period the bereaved are kept so busy telling, and retelling, the final days of the deceased that by the end of the period they are exhausted and feel the need to move on. It is very much like sitting shiva in the Jewish religion or Hidaad among Muslims.

In many ways, the decision by Mandela and his comrades to embark on the mass action of that week was to enact, at a national level, a period of mourning and expression of grief. It diverted the nation from destroying itself in an uncontrolled explosion of anger. Yet it would be naïve to think that this was the only reason why the ANC embarked on the commemorations and marches.

The actions were also about power. After three years of talks, the ANC desperately needed to conclude the "endless negotiations" and extract maximum concessions from the government. And so it had to show the extent of its support. It also had to be ruthless and, as Ramaphosa put it, go "for the jugular" following Hani's death. That is why it pressed for an election date and joint control of the state through a Transitional Executive Council. Once the National Party agreed to an election date, it could not turn back unless the right wing found some way to violently oust De Klerk. Once it had agreed to joint control of the state, white minority rule was at an end. Even in his grief for Hani, Mandela was enough of a strategist to see the opportunities ahead. The pressure assured a clear path to a new South Africa.

In many ways, Mandela knew that the violence that engulfed South Africa that week was a necessary price for what lay ahead. What he had to do was wrestle with the monster that was the people's anger, ensuring it would dissipate and pass. When I asked Holomisa why, ultimately, his anger at Hani's death did not turn to angry retaliation, he answered simply: "Mandela, the leader of Chris Hani, had called for calm . . ."

Mandela's triumph is that Holomisa and others listened to him. They listened to the man Hani would have listened to.

9 a.m.
April 20, 1993
Johannesburg and Cape Town

The day after the funeral, Meyer and Ramaphosa began meeting and setting down a grueling agenda for the talks. But De Klerk still wanted to get the last word. On the day after Hani's funeral he stood up in Parliament to criticize Mandela's speech at the funeral. It was only in his third speech to Parliament in three days, on April 21, eleven days after Hani's

assassination, that he seemed to get a hold of himself, to rise above parti-
san politics, and find a measure of statesmanship and even humanity.

"As we seek to rise above the human frailties that collectively and in-
variably tend to destroy cohesion and understanding among people, we
have to be motivated by the certain knowledge that we dare not fail. We
have recently experienced how one senseless deed has the potential to
undo, in a fleeting moment, that which was built up with much effort over
a long period of time," he said.

He outlined a road map to the establishment of a transitional executive committee, one which coincided with the ANC's demand that agreement on the TEC be signed by June 1. He held out an olive branch, saying:
"A wonderful future lies within our grasp. Let us grasp the opportunity of
the moment and move on together to the creation of a new and better
South Africa."

10 a.m.
April 20, 1993
Johannesburg

Muhammad Ali and Nelson Mandela finally had their meeting at Mandela's house in Johannesburg. Ali had attended Hani's funeral on Monday
and had been seated with the ANC leaders on the stage, but this was the
first time the two men got to talk. Mandela told journalists that Ali "was
not just my hero, but the hero of millions of young, Black South Africans
because he brought dignity to boxing." He said he particularly admired
Ali's stance against the Vietnam War and his refusal to enlist. He revealed
that when he met Ali for the first time on his tour of the US in 1990, he
was "extremely apprehensive."

"I wanted to say so many things to him. He was an inspiration to me,
even in prison, because I thought of his courage and his commitment to
his sport. I was overwhelmed by his gentleness and his expressive eyes.
He seemed to understand what I could not say and actually we conversed
very little."

In later years, Mandela made up for not being able to spend time with Ali that week. The two men were to meet again on numerous occasions, with Mandela going out of his way to meet the boxer. Ali was a hero in South Africa, his impact and influence more like that of a freedom fighter than a boxing champion. To this day, those who remember the week of Hani's murder remember that Ali had thrown in his lot with ordinary people, marching with them, visiting the Hani family and ANC leader Oliver Tambo, choosing the side of those who sought freedom. It is what Chris Hani would have done.

Morning
April 21, 1993
Jan Smuts Airport, Johannesburg

Mathews Phosa and deputy justice minister Sheila Camerer stood together at Jan Smuts Airport and welcomed the UK's Metropolitan Police fraud and antiterrorism branch head, Commander George Churchill-Coleman, to South Africa. Churchill-Coleman, later to be joined by the German judge and former prosecutor Dr. Ralf Kruger, was nominated by the British government to help with the Hani assassination. The two men's brief was to report their concerns to the attorney general directly. A month later Churchill-Coleman and Kruger declared that the police investigation into Hani's murder was professional and conducted with integrity. "Equal to the very best in the world," commented Churchill-Coleman on his departure from South Africa in May. In November 1993, when Waluś and Derby-Lewis were convicted, Phosa said the police had done a "phenomenal" job.

9 a.m.
April 22, 1993
Kempton Park

The Multi-Party Negotiating Forum, led by Ramaphosa and Meyer, re-started negotiations in Johannesburg. The previous week had taken a

heavy toll on the nation. An independent inquiry into informal repression by the South African Council of Churches said violence related to
the Hani assassination left at least eighty people dead in the economic hub
of the PWV region. In a particularly gruesome act, two men were burned
to death on the day of Chris Hani's funeral. They were trapped in their
houses near FNB Stadium when hundreds of youths who had come to
attend the funeral veered off into the nearby residential area and went on
a rampage. Statistics from the NGO the Human Rights Committee for
the period April 10 to April 19 indicated that more than 60 percent of
deaths and 80 percent of injuries were attributable to the security forces
and right-wing vigilantes.

As the negotiations restarted some political violence continued, but it
was not especially linked to the death of Chris Hani and no longer threatened the talks. That danger had passed.

THURSDAY, JUNE 3, 1993, AND TUESDAY, DECEMBER 7, 1993

And now what rests but that we spend the time
With stately triumphs, mirthful comic shows,
Such as befits the pleasure of the court?
Sound drums and trumpets! Farewell, sour annoy,
For here I hope begins our lasting joy.
      Henry VI, Act 5, Scene 7

The images that flowed out of South Africa on April 27, 1994, are heart-warming and iconic. A people who had struggled for centuries to remove the yoke of oppression from their backs were finally free. Lines of voters stretching kilometers, laughing, crying, smiling, were beamed across the globe. Everyone remembers the historic day when the first ever nonracial elections were held in South Africa. Few remember June 3, 1993.

That was the day the Multi-Party Negotiating Forum voted to set a date for the country's first national, nonracial, one-person-one-vote election.

It was not a special date; it had no significance. It was chosen because by then everyone was tired and a date had to be set. And so, fifty-four days after Hani's murder to try and scupper the arrival of a democratic South Africa, the election date was announced. Ramaphosa, reflecting back on Hani's murder, said this was the moment of victory for the ANC: "For me, the real victory in this negotiation process was not the signing of the interim constitution. It was setting the election date. I knew that if we didn't set that date, the whole process could have gone on forever. In our own constituency, the people felt that these negotiations had been going on for too long and, indeed, they had been going on for much too long."

Not everyone was pleased. "It's unattainable," said Walter Felgate, an Inkatha Freedom Party delegate at the talks. "At this point, I've got no confidence in that date."

Tokyo Sexwale told me that "Chris gave us that date."

After Hani's assassination, he said, the ANC made it clear that it was "now or never." "We said: 'You give us a date for elections on the death of Chris.' They realized that, look, it's all a mess. They must agree to an election date to appease the nation. So Chris gave us that date, which we wanted."

10 a.m.
December 7, 1993
Cape Town

Cyril Ramaphosa could not wipe the grin from his face. He was, to use his own words, "ecstatic."

He was standing inside the glass-roofed banquet hall of the former Good Hope Masonic Lodge. The chamber was previously used by the apartheid-era President's Council. Started as a think tank for P. W. Botha's reforms, the President's Council had for more than a decade used its veto power to block meaningful reforms, thus keeping grand apartheid alive. Now the room was about to start a new journey as the home of the Transitional Executive Council.

On every desk was a folder with a blood-red cover and a simple title in bold: "First Meeting of the Transitional Executive Council." Nestled inside were documents containing what seemed like boring rules and regulations of behavior, agendas, pieces of legislation written in turgid official parlance. Every member of the council, all thirty-two of them, was provided with the folder. The first item on the one-page agenda was "Prayer/Meditation."

"We are standing on the hill," Ramaphosa said. "And we can finally see the promised land of democracy."

After 341 years of colonialism and white minority rule, Black South Africans were about to share power with their former oppressors. Until that day, no Black people had made any decisions in the chamber except to clean and clear the desks. The Transitional Executive Council that Mandela had demanded in the wake of Hani's death was finally holding its first meeting.

Power was shifting. History was being made. Even the moment of meditation at the beginning of proceedings seemed like a revolutionary act. Where once only the Christian faith would have been acknowledged, on this day all faiths would be welcomed.

The ironies of the day piled upon each other. It was in this building, at the beginning of that year, that Clive Derby-Lewis had sat as a member of the President's Council. His wife, Gaye, was in the city with him, a hit list among the papers she was carrying around, fresh from having it handed to her by Arthur Kemp. It was while on this trip, the last he would make to the halls of Parliament and Cape Town, that Derby-Lewis had traveled to the nearby suburb of Tokai to have a silencer fitted onto the gun he would give to Janusz Waluś when he returned to Johannesburg. Now sitting in the well-padded seats where Derby-Lewis had sat in January, with murder in his heart, were members of the ANC, the SA Communist Party, the National Party, and others—thirty-two men and women clutching the red folder containing the documents of the first seating of the Transitional Executive Council.

President F. W. de Klerk would still be in office, but without the TEC he would not be able to make any major decisions.

Ramaphosa did not miss the significance and irony of the occasion. "Our entrance here means we have disinfected this chamber of the bad old odors," he said, his wide grin evident throughout the proceedings of the day. "This means the people have taken over what is theirs."

He was not alone in his enthusiasm. His opponent and partner in the negotiations, Roelf Meyer, said the historic session was "the final step in the process to bring about true democracy in South Africa."

But Mandela and De Klerk were not in the room. The two men were flying to Oslo, Norway, where they would jointly receive the Nobel Peace Prize. It was not a happy trip for either man.

A month before, when the announcement was made that they were jointly awarded the Nobel, there was friction between the two. When reporters asked what he thought De Klerk had done to deserve the prize, Mandela had snapped: "Just ask the Nobel Peace Prize Committee."

However, at the ceremony the two men were gracious with each other. In his Nobel Lecture, De Klerk said: "Five years ago, people would have seriously questioned the sanity of anyone who predicted that Mr. Mandela and I would be joint recipients of the 1993 Nobel Peace Prize. And yet both of us are here before you today.

"We are political opponents . . . It was not easy for the supporters of Mr. Mandela or mine to relinquish the ideals they had cherished for many decades. But we did it. And because we did it, there is hope."

Mandela paid tribute to De Klerk: "He had the courage to admit that a terrible wrong had been done to our country and people through the imposition of the system of apartheid. He had the foresight to understand and accept that all the people of South Africa must through negotiations and as equal participants in the process, together determine what they want to make of their future."

Mandela was, however, hurt that De Klerk had not acknowledged "the immorality of apartheid and the suffering it had caused the majority of South Africans in his acceptance speech." De Klerk had said that change in South Africa had come not from armed struggle or external pressure but from a "fundamental change of heart" and that this fundamental change had "occurred on both sides." For Mandela this was deplorable: Why would the ANC, which fought apartheid with everything it had for eighty-one years, be held up as just one side of a conflict that had changed its heart and mind?

In an off-the-cuff speech at a dinner attended by both men and hosted by the Norwegian prime minister the following evening, Mandela tore into De Klerk before some 150 guests. Mandela's friend George Bizos said it was "the one and only occasion that I would ever see Nelson lose control and allow his personal feelings to spill out in public."

Bizos said Mandela recounted an incident on Robben Island, when prison warders buried a man in the sand up to his neck and urinated on him. Mandela attacked De Klerk and the apartheid system for the oppression of Black people and for the murders committed by apartheid hit squads, asking why De Klerk had allegedly said "mistakes were made on both sides."

"What mistakes did we make when you were brutalizing us and locking us up and banning us and not allowing us to vote?" he asked.

After Mandela's dressing down, De Klerk vowed never to speak first again at any event where he appeared with Mandela. And yet the two men were to continue collaborating—and even forming a coalition government together—after this meeting. Frosty or not, they had come to share an obsession: to finish the job they had started and forge a democracy for South Africa, even if their conception of it was different.

Back in Cape Town, the thirty-two members of the TEC finally settled down. In just that first meeting, the men and women put an axe to apartheid with a ferocious swiftness. They adopted a resolution to establish the Independent Electoral Commission (IEC) and the Special Electoral Court that would run the elections on April 27, 1994. These bodies were headed up by respected, independent judges and community leaders. Harris, the young antiapartheid lawyer, went to work for the IEC, where the right wing tried to disrupt the elections by placing bombs in crowded areas such as taxi ranks, churches, and shopping malls.

With the launch of the TEC, the democratization process had reached the last mile. As it concluded its first meeting, the entire chamber ululated and danced. One of the delegates, Queen Vilankulu of the Intando Yesizwe Party, a minor party from the KwaNdebele homeland whose leader was keen to be part of the new democratic dispensation, summed it up: "With the end of this dark night, the weeping will end. Joy will come."

EPILOGUE

They didn't have to make me work on April 27, 1994. I had left the newsroom at 11 p.m. the night before and I was back at my desk by 5 a.m. The
Star published four print editions a day. I had filed a story the evening
before and was back to try and get out in the field and file something for
the 8 a.m. edition.

I was too late. The car pool was empty. All the company cars had already been taken by the senior reporters and the gung-ho photographers
who had driven out into the townships and suburbs around Johannesburg as early as 2 a.m., eager to get the first pictures and stories of the
historic day.

It was April 27, the day of South Africa's first nonracial national election after forty-six years of apartheid and more than three hundred years
of colonialism. The journalists who had rushed out ahead of me did not
need to go and look for stories. The stories were everywhere. The night
before, I had written about men and women in townships across the country queuing outside polling stations at dinnertime to ensure that they were
among the first to cast their votes. The chill of autumn was in the air, biting into the bones. Women nearing ninety or older were in the queues.
They did not care.

This was a historic moment and they wanted to be part of it.

At about 6 a.m. I went back downstairs. There were still no pool cars.
Sally Shorkend, a freelance photographer I had worked with covering
violence in the townships in the past year, was standing about, looking

as forlorn as I felt. Sally drove an old, battered VW Beetle at the time. We both looked at it. It was fine for driving around in the city, but would it make it to Soweto?

What the hell. We got into the Beetle and drove to Mofolo, a suburb of Soweto.

It was 6:40 a.m. when we got there. The line snaked around the school for more than a kilometer, and the people at the head of it were old enough to be my grandparents. Virtually every one of the first fifteen or so people in the queue was over seventy-five.

They had been there since the night before. We did a few interviews, and I wrote my story in my notebook on my lap in the passenger seat as Sally drove the Beetle back to the city. We filed our pictures and story by 8:30 a.m. for the edition of the paper that would hit the streets at 11 a.m.

Mandela had voted that morning, choosing to go to the violence-torn KwaZulu-Natal province where the Inkatha Freedom Party (IFP) was strongest. Right until just April 20—seven days before voting—the IFP had threatened to scupper the polls. Then it had agreed to participate after some late-night negotiating.

It had been an incredible year. Violence had spiked to such an extent that at times a new country did not seem achievable, as a free and fair election could just not be held in most affected areas. The right-wing extremists who supported Janusz Waluś continued to loom large. Just under two months after Hani's assassination, the AWB leader Eugène Terre'Blanche and a group of heavily armed supporters rammed an armored vehicle through the World Trade Centre in Kempton Park, Johannesburg, where negotiators were deliberating. In March 1994, I was on the scene when AWB members randomly attacked residents in Mafikeng, the capital of the Bophuthatswana homeland, killing forty-two people. An angry Bophuthatswana Defence Force soldier shot three AWB members in front of news cameras. The right-wingers fled, defeated.

The transition to democracy was blood-soaked: by the time Hani was murdered in April 1993, more than 11,000 people had died in political violence since Mandela had walked out of prison. In 1993 alone 3,794 people were killed in political violence—the highest in any year since 1985. Two days before the election a car bomb planted by right-wingers went off at Park Station, the main train and taxi terminus in downtown Johannesburg, killing nine people and leaving a waist-deep crater in the street.

Yet on that election day things went off peacefully. In the days and months afterward, political killings dropped off dramatically. Peace and freedom had finally come to South Africa.

"Never, never, and never again shall it be that this beautiful land will again experience the oppression of one by another and suffer the indignity of being the skunk of the world," Mandela said at his inauguration on May 10, 1994. He had won 62.6 percent of the vote while De Klerk's National Party came a distant second with 20.3 percent. Mangosuthu Buthelezi's Inkatha Freedom Party came third with 10 percent of the vote. Mandela invited De Klerk into his cabinet as one of his two deputy presidents, alongside Thabo Mbeki. He invited Buthelezi to join his cabinet as home affairs minister.

Chris Hani remains one of the most evocative figures in South African politics today. Every year memorial lectures are held and the constant refrain is where South Africa would be today had Hani not been assassinated. Often, these questions are accompanied by a quote attributed to him: "What I fear is that the liberators emerge as elitists who drive around in Mercedes-Benzes and use the resources of this country . . . to live in palaces and to gather riches."

Every president since Mandela stepped down in 1999 has been compared to Hani and been found wanting. It is an unfair comparison in many ways. Hani's contemporaries all used to hold the kind of views that he did. But as they ascended to the leadership of the country, they changed—or power changed them. Had he lived, Hani, too, might have changed. Or he might have surprised us all and, on assuming power, remained faithful to the plight of the poor.

This book is about leadership in a time of crisis. The great heroes of that week are ordinary South Africans, Black and white, young and old, who refused to be manipulated into war. The murder of Chris Hani was an attempt to set Black against white, to tip fury and fear into murder and mayhem. A country that had endured forty-five years of formalized racism and segregation was just the right tinder for Derby-Lewis and Waluś's racist fantasies.

That week, South Africans chose a different path: peace.

There is one more hero. I have written before of my admiration for George Orwell's slim anti-imperialist essay "Shooting an Elephant." In this story a young British policeman stationed in Burma walks toward an elephant that has just killed a villager. There are 2,000 Burmese following him. He is the only one with a gun. They expect, or want, him to kill the elephant. He knows that it would be wrong to do so because the elephant no longer poses a threat to anyone. But he is scared of looking like a fool—and being regarded as one—by the villagers. So he shoots the elephant.

When Mandela came out of prison there were millions of us behind him. We all urged him at the top of our voices to act radical and cause a conflagration. We did it most loudly in that week of Hani's assassination. Mandela chose an unpopular path—to tell his followers that he would not kill the elephant, would not pull the trigger, and that peace was better than war.

He is the greatest, most courageous and honest leader we ever had. He gave us the gift of a new future.

If only Chris Hani could have lived to see it too.

WHERE ARE THEY NOW?

Bantu Holomisa was appointed deputy minister of environment and tourism of South Africa by Nelson Mandela in 1994. In the same year he was elected to the National Executive Committee of the ANC. He was expelled two years later after he defied the party and testified about the corruption of one of his ANC comrades. He went on to cofound the United Democratic Movement with Roelf Meyer in 1997 and won a seat in Parliament in 1999, which he retains today. Despite Holomisa's expulsion from the ANC, his relationship with Mandela strengthened—he was the Mandela family's lead spokesman when Mandela died in 2013. He delivered the "vote of thanks" at the funeral. In Xhosa culture this "vote of thanks" is usually delivered by a senior family member. Mandela treated him like a son.

Mondli Gungubele has served in various public positions: as the mayor of Ekurhuleni, the eastern metropolitan area that includes Dawn Park; as a member of the national parliament; as a deputy minister of finance. He is currently minister in the Office of the President, overseeing five ministries, including state intelligence, under President Cyril Ramaphosa.

Peter Harris was seconded to head the Monitoring Directorate of South Africa's Independent Electoral Commission for the 1994 election. The directorate's role was to ensure a free and fair election. After 1994, he became an international consultant for the United Nations, advising on elections and conflict resolution programs in Mexico, Haiti, Sierra Leone, and other countries. He cofounded the Resolve Group Management

Consultancy, wrote three best-selling books, and still practices as a me-
diator and a lawyer, including representing the president of South Africa.

Niël Barnard became a director-general of the Western Cape province in 1994. He has written two books about his role in the transition to
democracy.

Kobie Coetsee was elected president of the National Council of
Provinces (the second house of South Africa's Parliament) in a gesture
of reconciliation by the ANC, which had a comfortable majority in the
chamber. He died in 2000. In 2020, it emerged that, on his retirement,
Coetsee had taken 13,000 pages of transcriptions of secret recordings
made of Mandela during his imprisonment in Victor Verster Prison.

In March 2022, an inquest into the 1982 death of antiapartheid activist Dr. Neil Aggett found that he had been tortured for sixty-two hours by
police, including Captain Nic Deetlefs, before he was killed. Judge Mot-
samai Makume said Deetlefs had admitted to torturing activist Barbara
Hogan and to helping cover up the murder of Aggett. At the time of writing, the National Prosecuting Authority said it was considering charges
against Deetlefs. He denies the charges.

F. W. de Klerk's tenure as the last apartheid president of South Africa
ended in April 1994. He served as one of President Nelson Mandela's two
deputies in the first nonracial and democratic government of South Africa
until 1996, when he withdrew his National Party from the government of
national unity. He died in November 2021. In a video released hours after
his death, he apologized for apartheid crimes committed against people
of color.

Clive Derby-Lewis and Janusz Waluś were sentenced to death for the
murder of Chris Hani. The two men's sentences were commuted to life
when Mandela, in one of the first acts of his administration, abolished the
death penalty. Given a chance to walk free if they disclosed everything
to the Truth and Reconciliation Commission in 1997, Derby-Lewis and
Waluś did not convince the body that they were telling the truth. As a
result, they were denied amnesty. Clive Derby-Lewis was granted medi-
cal parole due to his terminal lung cancer and was released from prison

in June 2015 after serving twenty-two years. He died in 2016. He never renounced his views. On November 21, 2022, South Africa's highest court ordered that Waluś be released. It said the justice minister's refusal to grant him parole was "irrational." He was released from prison on December 7, 2022, to begin serving two years of parole. Limpho Hani said the court's judgment was "diabolical" and a miscarriage of justice.

Gaye Derby-Lewis stood trial with her husband and Janus Waluś but was acquitted. She lives in South Africa.

Harry Gwala was elected to the position of chief whip of the ANC in the KwaZulu-Natal legislature after the 1994 elections. He died from a heart attack in June 1995.

Retha Harmse continues to be attacked online by the right wing in South Africa. After the Waluś trial she changed her surname. She moved to the UK for about ten years and then returned to South Africa.

Nelson Mandela became South Africa's first democratically elected president in 1994. He stepped down in 1999. He died on December 5, 2013, at the age of ninety-five. Ninety-one world leaders, including four US presidents, attended his memorial service in Johannesburg.

Gill Marcus became a member of Parliament in 1994, deputy minister of finance from 1996 to 1999, and deputy governor of the Reserve Bank until 2004. She left for academia and business. In 2009, she was appointed to the position of governor of the Reserve Bank, the ninth person and the first and only woman to hold the position.

Thabo Mbeki became deputy president of South Africa (with F. W. de Klerk) in 1994. He was president from 1999 to 2008.

Roelf Meyer helps governments and institutions across the globe manage transitions from autocracy to democracy.

Peter Mokaba became a member of Parliament in 1994 and served as the deputy minister of Environmental Affairs and Tourism in the Mandela administration. He died of an undisclosed illness in 2002 after denying the existence of HIV and describing antiretroviral medication for AIDS as "poison."

Carl Niehaus became South Africa's ambassador to the Netherlands during the Mandela administration. After several prominent positions he returned to the ANC as spokesperson but was forced to step down after being exposed for extensive borrowing of money from political contacts, including pretending his mother had died in order to get out of paying money owed to a landlord. In 2022, he was expelled from the ANC.

Cyril Ramaphosa headed up the body that wrote the final South African constitution, adopted in December 1996. In 1997, he went into private business and became one of South Africa's wealthiest entrepreneurs. He returned to politics in 2012 and became president of South Africa in 2018.

Tokyo Sexwale became premier of the Gauteng province in 1994. He left politics for business in the late 1990s and became a multimillionaire. He returned to politics in 2007 and twice ran for the position of ANC president but lost to Jacob Zuma.

Mathews Phosa became premier of the Mpumalanga province during the Mandela presidency. In 1999, he went into business, wrote a book of Afrikaans poetry, and was a key member of Mandela's program of reconciliation with the Afrikaans community.

Phumelele Civilian Hermans, Lungile Mazwi, and Mlulamisi Maxhayi were arrested and sentenced to twenty-five-year terms for the murders of the Weakley brothers and the attempted murder of Keith Rumble, Brett Rumble, and Thomas O'Keeffe. Fundisile Guleni was never prosecuted, while Zongezile Mxhize skipped bail. In 1998, Hermans, Mazwi, Maxhayi, and Guleni applied to the Truth and Reconciliation Commission for amnesty, which all four were granted the following year. In testimony before the TRC's amnesty committee, Guleni said that had he and his accomplices realized their targets were innocent holidaymakers, they would not have gone ahead with the attack. "We are so sorry for the families and would like to apologize to all those affected by our actions," he said. Guleni is a senior official in the Port St. Johns municipality. Hermans's whereabouts are unknown.

ACKNOWLEDGMENTS

A book like this is a bit like a child—it really does take a village to raise one. Many people brought this book to fruition and I would like to thank them all—many not named here—for their advice, generosity, enthusiasm, and patience.

This book started life with a few "what next" discussions with my sister Gloria. She has been a source of constant encouragement, advice, admonishment, and intelligence since our first chat on the subject in 2015. In 2018, with less than 5,000 words written, Isobel Dixon of Blake Friedmann in London introduced me to George Lucas at InkWell Management, and suddenly there was the possibility of a book. George was this book's first champion. He worked tirelessly, guiding the proposal and numerous drafts over the past few years. Writers say this a lot about their agents, but it is true: this book would not have happened without George's expertise, enthusiasm, patience, encouragement, and guidance.

No one writing about Nelson Mandela can do justice to the man and South Africa's transition to democracy without the hundreds of interviews and writings of Richard Stengel, John Carlin, and Padraig O'Malley. In the transition to democracy O'Malley interviewed hundreds of the key politicians in the country and collected thousands of materials, now housed at the Nelson Mandela Centre of Memory. It is a treasure trove for any historian, and I am grateful to have had the opportunity to be exposed to it and to have used it here. Carlin reported on South Africa's transition to democracy for the *Independent* in London. His journalism was illuminating, engaged, and an incredible record of how South Africa was changing.

I am grateful to Richard Stengel, who at the time of this story was working with Nelson Mandela on his monumental autobiography *Long Walk to Freedom*. Richard's book *Mandela's Way: Lessons on Life* inspired me to take just a slice of Mandela's life and try to reconstruct it. Sometimes, in journalism, you catch a break that changes everything on your project. My break came when Richard offered to show me his private diary from the day Hani was murdered to the day he was buried. Richard's observations and reflections helped make up the backbone of this book, and I am grateful to him for allowing me to use some of his private and public thoughts here.

Thousands of journalists covered the events of the week described here. Many investigative reporters tried to uncover the truth behind Hani's assassination. I am grateful to all of them for their "first draft of history." I am particularly grateful for Hanlie Retief's insightful profile of Retha Harmse, carried in the Afrikaans newspaper *Rapport*, and the many others written that week.

Few ANC leaders want to be interviewed about Chris Hani because of the conspiracy theories that have been peddled inside the party about his assassination. Of the hundreds that I approached, a few agreed to speak to me anonymously. Many on the side of the apartheid government also refused interviews, yet some agreed. I thank them.

I am particularly grateful to the following people who shared their recollections of that period: Gill Marcus, Joel Netshitenzhe, Niël Barnard, F. W. de Klerk, Tokyo Sexwale, Roelf Meyer, Barbara Masekela, Dave Steward, Pallo Jordan, Ronnie Kasrils, Bantu Holomisa, Carl Niehaus, Mac Maharaj, Peter Harris, Mondli Gungubele, Esther Waugh, Zirk Gouws, Victor Zazeraj, Mbhazima Shilowa, Valli Moosa, and Saki Macozoma. Writer, ANC leader, and philosopher Mandla Langa has been an inspiration for this book.

I would like to thank the many wonderful people working in libraries and archival institutions who contributed to this book. Debora Matthews of the South African History Archive, Verne Harris and Zanele Riba at the Nelson Mandela Foundation, Leonie Klootwyk at the Media24 library in Johannesburg, and Thabang Khanye at the University of the Free State were enthusiastic and extremely helpful. I am grateful to Hennie van Vuuren of the nonprofit organization Open Secrets, who pointed me to places where some apartheid documents that survived the mass shreddings of the 1990s might still be hidden. Thabisile Mbete and Mava Kuselo opened the Talk Radio 702 audio archives to me, while Phillip Kgaphola at Arena Holdings Library helped me with thousands of newspaper cuttings. Angie Hammond helped me understand the SABC's audiences now and in the 1990s.

Zamuxolo Nduna, Nadine Martin, Aba Mbengashe, and Fose Segodi helped me with research and weird things I could not do from the US, where a large part of this book was written, such as ascertaining that a building exists. Nozuko Vundla opened doors in SA that were firmly closed to me. My friend Donny Mothoa accompanied me everywhere, making me laugh, and think, and eat. I am extremely grateful for their help.

Robin Comley doggedly researched and found the photographs that make up an important part of this book. I am grateful to Chloe Thomas and Professor Steve Olivier for their permission to use their private pictures of Alastair "Ally" Weakley. I would like to acknowledge Paul Velasco for the generous use of his photos.

Kirsty Lang, Claudia Manning, and Caroline Southey read the rough first drafts of this book. I thank them for their suggestions, corrections, comments, and many helpful pieces of advice over the years. All errors are mine, all improvements are from their reading and their advice to "cut, cut, cut."

During the COVID-19 pandemic I gave up on this book. Kirsty Lang and Misha Glenny sat me down, gave me a talking to, and put me on Kirsty's "three-week writing program." I would not have restarted without their hospitality, friendship, and encouragement. The legendary Alice Mayhew acquired this book for Simon & Schuster in the US in 2019. After her passing Megan Hogan took over as editor. I could not have asked for a more assiduous, committed, patient, encouraging, and talented editor, and I would like to thank her for shepherding this book to print. I would like to thank Ian Marshall at Simon & Schuster in London for believing in the book. Jeremy Boraine of Jonathan Ball Publishers in South Africa has been a great friend and champion of my work for years, and I am grateful for his encouragement of this book. When Jeremy moved to London, Gill Moodie brought her expertise, insight, energy, and enthusiasm to bear on the final stages of the book.

My friend David Jammy and his colleagues at Done and Dusted gave me a space to read the voluminous TRC transcripts and reports in the peace and quiet of their offices during COVID-19 lockdown. Johnny Dorfmann gave me encouragement and an office when I needed to run one last mile. Nick Boraine, Louise Barnes, Nadine Zylstra, Jenny Lee, Stephen Lee, Kim Turner, and Akin Omotoso were always available for walks and lunches where I would bore them senseless about what I was working on.

This book is for my wife, Justine, and my daughters, Ayanda and Freya. They were patient, understanding, and encouraging while going through several life-changing transitions—including relocating across three continents! And they loved me, still.

NOTES

EASTER SATURDAY, APRIL 10, 1993
10 A.M.

7   Nelson Mandela walked: Richard Stengel, *Mandela's Way: Lessons on Life* (London: Virgin Books, 2010), 44. The material in this chapter is drawn largely from Stengel's book, Mandela's autobiography, and press reports.

7   "That was my first": Nelson Mandela, *Long Walk to Freedom* (London: Abacus, 1994), 16.

8   Mandela had been: Anthony Sampson, *Mandela: The Authorised Biography* (London: HarperPress, 1999), 3.

8   its genesis was an oddity for many: "For Burial, Mandela Will Return to His Beloved Boyhood Village," National Public Radio, December 13, 2013, accessed May 20, 2022.

9   After nine months of acrimony: "A fresh beginning for talks," *Star*, April 1, 1993.

9   The siege in Waco: *Beeld*, April 4, 1993; *Saturday Star*, April 10, 1993.

10 This is how everyone referred: Nelson Mandela Foundation, "Names," at https://www.nelsonmandela.org/content/page/names, accessed May 20, 2022.

10 The person on the line was: Richard Stengel, private diary, used with permission.

10 Masekela was street-smart: Barbara Masekela, *Poli Poli* (Johannesburg: Jonathan Ball Publishers, 2021), 112.

10 She was often so worried about Mandela: Author interview with Barbara Masekela, November 22, 2021.

11 Mandela loved Chris Hani: Janet Smith and Beauregard Tromp, *Chris Hani: A Life Too Short* (Johannesburg: Jonathan Ball Publishers, 2007), 249.

12   He put the phone down: Richard Stengel, private diary.

12   He was also deeply afraid: Nelson Mandela, *Long Walk to Freedom* (London: Abacus, 1994), 79.

10 A.M.

12   The stalking of Chris Hani had started: The stalking and murder of Chris Hani are detailed in police statements, court appearances, amnesty applications, and hearings at the Truth and Reconciliation Commission. To re-create the story of Janusz Waluś on the day he assassinated Chris Hani, I threaded many of these narratives together, often reconciling obvious lies and contradictions that have cropped up in the numerous testimonies. The transcripts at the TRC, which run to hundreds of thousands of words, can be accessed online at https://www.justice.gov.za/trc/amntrans/.

12   The athletic-looking killer with the blazing blue eyes and the blue shirt: Evelyn Groenink, *Incorruptible: The Story of the Murders of Dulcie September, Anton Lubowski and Chris Hani* (self-published, 2018).

12   "five minutes to midnight": See, for example, John D. Brewer, ed., *Can South Africa Survive? Five Minutes to Midnight* (London: Macmillan, 1989).

13   the two men had enjoyed breakfast: Testimony of the Derby-Lewises' domestic worker, Elizabeth Motswane, available at *State v. Waluś and Others* (70/93) [1993] ZAGPHC 1 (October 14, 1993), Supreme Court of South Africa (Witwatersrand Local Division). Available at http://www.saflii.org/cgi-bin/disp.pl?file=za/cases/ZAGPHC/1993/1 .html&query=Janusz%20Walus, accessed May 19, 2022.

13   liked to put on the quaint mannerisms: Among others, *Sunday Times*, November 6, 2016.

13   The list was fastidiously compiled by Gaye: Gaye provided the names and Arthur Kemp confessed to supplying the addresses and security details. In 2016, Gaye let slip to Hani's daughter Lindiwe that she did more work on the list than she initially let on, saying that she had found the Hanis' address herself: *News24*, March 19, 2017. Available at https://www.news24.com /News24/what-daddys-killers-said-20170318, accessed May 19, 2022; and see Arthur Kemp's role in his own words at https://omalley.nelson mandela.org/omalley/cis/omalley/OMalleyWeb/03lv02424/04lv03370 /05lv03422.htm.

13   Whether this was a hit list or not was to become a subject of contention: TRC Final Report (vol. 6, section 3, chap. 6, subsection 16, p. [original] 479, paragraphs 175–76) reads: "175. In determining whether the

applicants had made full disclosure, the Committee gave consideration to the purpose of the list of names. The applicants testified that Mrs. Derby-Lewis had prepared the list of names for innocuous reasons and that Derby-Lewis had decided to use it for a totally different purpose. The Committee found that the reason Mrs. Derby-Lewis gave for requiring the addresses of the persons on the list was unconvincing. Her explanation that she needed addresses in order to arrange interviews makes little sense in view of her concession that there was no likelihood of Mr. Hani giving her an interview in his home. 176. The Committee found that the names constituted a hit list compiled for the purpose of planning assassinations. The evidence of the applicants that the list was to assist them to communicate confidentially was wholly unconvincing and the Committee found their version to be untrue in this regard."

14 In 2000, the Cape High Court dismissed an application by Derby-Lewis and Waluś: "Hani Killers Lose Appeal," *News24*, August 13, 2001. Available at https://www.news24.com/news24/hani-killers-lose-appeal-20010813.

14 tried to go for the big prize, Mandela: SA Press Association, November 24, 1997. Available at https://www.justice.gov.za/trc/media/1997/9711/s971124k.htm, accessed May 19, 2022.

15 Waluś had left a wife and daughter: eNCA, Feature: "Searching for Janusz," January 30, 2015. Available at https://www.enca.com/south-africa/promo-searching-janusz, accessed May 20, 2022.

15 He followed his father and brother: For the history of the Polish community in South Africa, I relied partly on the academic work of Arkadiusz Żukowski, Institute of Philosophy and Social Sciences, Pedagogic University, Olsztyn, Poland. Available at https://journals.co.za/doi/pdf/10.10520/AJA10113053_105, accessed May 22, 2022.

17 "Keep Dawn Park White": "Affluent Blacks Start Shift to White Suburbs," *Star*, April 4, 1993; and Jon Qwelane, *Sunday Star*, April 18, 1993.

17 Chris Hani had woken up early: Janet Smith and Beauregard Tromp, *Hani: A Life Too Short* (Johannesburg: Jonathan Ball Publishers, 2007), 250.

18 But he needed Gungubele: Author interview (one of two) with Mondli Gungubele, Cape Town, March 3, 2022.

18 he read every available newspaper—across the language: Crain Soudien, ed., *Nelson Mandela: Comparative Perspectives of his Significance for Education* (Rotterdam: Sense Publishers, 2017), 52.

18 "Dawn Park: Where The Future Is": "For Many, the Past Improved the Future," *Daily Dispatch*, April 20, 1993.

19   He'd had a chance to study him a few days: Janet Smith and Beauregard
     Tromp, *Hani: A Life Too Short* (Johannesburg: Jonathan Ball Publishers),
     231.

19   "They will destroy this wonderful": Continued from the transcript at the
     TRC amnesty hearings. Available at https://omalley.nelsonmandela.org
     /omalley/index.php/site/q/03lv02167/04lv02264/05lv02267/06lv022
     68/07lv02272.htm, accessed May 22, 2022.

20   "He is greeting you," she said: "A Wave, Then Silent Killer Gunned Down
     Hani," *Sunday Star*, April 11, 1993.

20   aim for a large target: Waluś admitted to this under cross-examination by
     the Hani family lawyer, George Bizos, at the TRC. https://omalley.nelson
     mandela.org/omalley/index.php/site/q/03lv02167/04lv02264/05lv022
     67/06lv02268/07lv02272.htm, accessed May 22, 2022.

20   Chris Hani's lifeless body lay: "I Saw Him Killed," *Sunday Times*, April 11,
     1993.

21   he was a hero: Synopsis of *SA Dialogue*, March 1993 issue. Also "Hani Was
     Tipped As Next ANC President," *City Press*, April 18, 1993.

22   He dreamed of becoming: "My Life: Chris Hani's Short Autobiography
     in His Own Words." Available at https://ewn.co.za/2018/04/10/my-life
     -chris-hani-s-short-autobiography-in-his-own-words, accessed January 4,
     2021.

22   "became openly involved in the struggle": "Chris Hani," South African
     History Online. Available at https://www.sahistory.org.za/people/chris
     -hani, accessed May 21, 2022.

22   It was here that Hani's reputation as a heroic fighter was born: Janet Smith
     and Beauregard Tromp, *Hani: A Life Too Short* (Johannesburg: Jonathan
     Ball Publishers), 125.

22   half of the fifty ANC combatants: Hugh Macmillan, "After Wankie: The
     'Hani Memorandum' and Its Repercussions at Morogoro and on the ANC
     in Zambia, 1968–71," paper presented to the Workshop on Liberation
     Struggles in Southern Africa, University of Cape Town, 2008.

23   He was not at home: "Thembisile Chris Hani Timeline 1942–2003," South
     African History Online. Available at https://www.sahistory.org.za/article
     /thembisile-chris-hani-timeline-1942-2003, accessed January 5, 2021.

24   knew of the horrors in the camps: "Chris Hani: A Problem of History,"
     Paul Trewhela, Politicsweb, October 23, 2009. Available at https://www
     .politicsweb.co.za/news-and-analysis/chris-hani-a-problem-of-history, ac-
     cessed January 4, 2021.

24 MK cadres detonated a car bomb: List of MK Operations, ANC 2nd Submission to TRC—Appendix Four. Available at https://omalley.nelson mandela.org/omalley/index.php/site/q/03lv02424/04lv02730/05lv029 18/06lv02949.htm, accessed January 4, 2021.

24 "we are still around": Unattributed interview with Chris Hani (1988), quoted in Janet Smith and Beauregard Tromp, *Hani: A Life Too Short* (Johannesburg: Jonathan Ball Publishers, 2007), 157.

24 By the late 1980s, the apartheid state was under siege: "From the Archive: Sanctions Agreed Against Apartheid-Era South Africa," *The Commonwealth.* Available at https://thecommonwealth.org/news/archive -sanctions-agreed-against-apartheid-era-south-africa, accessed January 4, 2021. Also "How Margaret Thatcher Helped End Apartheid—Despite Herself," *Guardian*, April 10, 2013. Available at https://www .theguardian.com/world/2013/apr/10/margaret-thatcher-apartheid -mandela, accessed May 20, 2022.

25 Hani received the highest number: Report of the Independent Electoral Commission, July 6, 1991. Available at https://new.anc1912 .org.za/48th-national-conference-report-of-the-independent/, accessed May 7, 2022.

25 But F. W. de Klerk's eyes lit up: Author interview with F. W. de Klerk, Plattekloof, South Africa, September 7, 2018.

26 Hani made a beeline for Viljoen: Grant Parker, "Mixed Capital: Classicism in Unexpected Places" (Princeton/Stanford Working Papers in Classics, February 2–4, 2012).

26 floored him at their first meeting in 1990: John Allen, *Rabble-Rouser for Peace: The Authorised Biography of Desmond Tutu* (London: Random House, 2006), 333.

26 He also recognized that a Hani who was not fully on board with the negotiations: "Key ANC Negotiator Assassinated in S. Africa: Violence: Chris Hani's Murder Threatens to Undermine Constitutional Talks and Raises Fears of a Bloody Township Uprising," Scott Kraft, *Los Angeles Times*, April, 11, 1993. Available at https://www.latimes.com/archives/la-xpm -1993-04-11-mn-21786-story.html.

27 Hani was fully committed to peace negotiations: "Demons of Their Own Making Bedevil the Peace," John Kane-Berman, *Business Day*, April 23, 1993.

28 Its best-known slogan was: "SAHRC Takes PAC to Court for Using 'One Settler, One Bullet' Phrase During March," South African Human Rights Commission, November 25, 2020. Available at https://www

.sahrc.org.za/index.php/sahrc-media/news/item/2527-sahrc-takes
-pac-to-court-for-using-one-settler-one-bullet-phrase-during-march,
accessed May 22, 2022.

28   "the bullet cannot be abandoned": Niël Barnard, with Tobie Wiese, *Peaceful Revolution: Inside the War Room at the Negotiations* (Cape Town: Tafelberg Publishers, 2017), loc. 2669 (Kindle edition).

28   Five days before Hani's assassination: TRC Final Report, vol. 2, chap. 7,
subsection 36, p. 685. Available at https://sabctrc.saha.org.za/reports
/volume2/chapter7/subsection36.htm, accessed May 22, 2022.

28   He spoke of transforming ANC self-defense units: "A Belief He Was
Prepared to Die For," *Star*, April 13, 1993. Also *New Nation*, April 8, 1993.

28   Six days before his murder: "No Truth in Breakaway Army, says Hani," *Star*,
April 5, 1993.

28   UK prime minister Margaret Thatcher: "Margaret Thatcher Branded
ANC 'Terrorist' While Urging Nelson Mandela's Release," *Independent*,
December 9, 2013. Available at https://www.independent.co.uk/news/uk
/politics/margaret-thatcher-branded-anc-terrorist-while-urging-nelson
-mandela-s-release-8994191.html, accessed May 22, 2022.

10:10 A.M.

29   Nothing about Retha Harmse: This section draws largely and gratefully
from reporting by South African and international press, particularly the
South African *Sunday Times*, *Rapport's* profile columnist Hanlie Retief
(whose profile of Harmse appeared on April 18), John Carlin of the UK's
the *Independent*, and others. I have used pictures of Harmse from the *Sunday Times* and *Rapport* for descriptive purposes: "I saw him killed, says
Hani witness," *Sunday Times*, April 11, 1993.

29   When the Hani family moved into the neighborhood: "The Woman Who
Saw Everything," *Rapport*, April 18, 1993.

29   The local council had voted to retain apartheid: "Amid the Darkness," Jon
Qwelane, *Sunday Star*, April 18, 1993.

30   they found places such as Boksburg Lake: " 'Whites Only' Signs Reappear-
ing in South Africa," *Washington Post*, November 10, 1988.

30   the place was awash with posters: "Amid the Darkness," Jon Qwelane, *Sunday Star*, April 18, 1993.

30   She was set on going to Shoe City: "Point Blank Shots Fired at Lifeless
Body," *Sunday Times*, April 11, 1993.

30   he wanted to be fit: "A Belief He Was Prepared to Die For," *Star*, April 13, 1993. Also *New Nation*, April 8, 1993.

31   It was a common misconception: Testimony by Gaye Derby-Lewis at the TRC amnesty hearing of Clive Derby-Lewis, Day 4, December 1, 1997. Available at https://omalley.nelsonmandela.org/omalley/index.php/site /q/03lv02167/04lv02264/05lv02267/06lv02268/07lv02273.htm, accessed May 21, 2022.

31   She needed to collect milk bottles: "Point Blank Shots Fired at Lifeless Body," *Sunday Times*, April 11, 1993.

32   She put her foot on the brakes: Ibid.

32   "Somebody has just been shot": Police transcript, conversation between Sergeant Dearham and Mrs Harmse, SA Police Service, April 10, 1993, South African History Archive, Call Number B1.5.5.1.

34   "If it was Chris Hani that was shot": "The Woman Who Saw Everything," *Rapport*, April 18, 1993.

10:45 A.M.

34   Waluś's assassination of Hani was swift and professional: The sections on Waluś's actions and thoughts are culled from various sources as indicated above, but primarily his amnesty hearing testimony and cross-examination by various counsel, particularly George Bizos on behalf of the Hani family. TRC amnesty hearings, available at https://omalley.nelsonmandela.org /omalley/index.php/site/q/03lv02167/04lv02264/05lv02267/06lv022 68/07lv02272.htm, accessed May 22, 2022.

10:30 A.M.

36   It was just before 11 a.m. and David O'Sullivan had his feet: "The Day Chris Hani Was Assassinated," David O'Sullivan, Kaya959.co.za. Available at https://www.kaya959.co.za/the-day-chris-hani-was-assassinated/, accessed May 22, 2022.

36   Marcus had left South Africa as a twenty-year-old university student: Milton Shain and Miriam Pimstone and JWA staff, "Gill Marcus," in Shalvi/ Hyman Encyclopedia of Jewish Women, December 31, 1999, Jewish Women's Archive. Available at https://jwa.org/encyclopedia/article /marcus-gill, accessed June 23, 2021.

37   Then she ran outside and saw Nomakhwezi: "A Wave, Then Silent Killer Gunned Down Hani," *Sunday Star*, April 11, 1993.

37   his face clouds over: Author interview with Mondli Gungubele, Cape Town, March 3 and March 7, 2022.

39   Hani's murder has become a "where were you when...": "Where Were You When Chris Hani Was Killed?" *Sunday Independent*, April 9, 2017.

39   "It was like the sky": Email interview with author, December 18, 2020, and "Hani's Light Still Burns Brightly," *News24*, April 10, 2003.

39   Sitting in his apartment in Hillbrow: Email interview with author, January 14, 2021.

39   In Bisho, in September 1992, twenty-eight ANC supporters were killed: Report of the Truth and Reconciliation Commission, vol. 3, chap. 6, para. 547.

40   The name referred to an incident when, in 1838: "Origins of the Battle of Blood River 1838," South African History Online, available at https://www.sahistory.org.za/article/origins-battle-blood-river-1838, accessed May 21, 2022.

41   At the meeting, Mbeki informed the government delegation: Niël Barnard, with Tobie Wiese, *Peaceful Revolution: Inside the War Room at the Negotiations* (Cape Town: Tafelberg Publishers, 2017), loc. 197 (Kindle edition).

41   Ronnie Kasrils also had his suspicions: Author interview with Ronnie Kasrils, February 2, 2021. Also "Where Were You When Chris Hani Was Killed?" *Sunday Independent*, April 9, 2017.

11:15 A.M.

41   Clive Derby-Lewis and his wife, Gaye: This and the following sections on the Derby-Lewises are drawn from testimony at the TRC amnesty application of Clive Derby-Lewis and Janusz Waluś. The Truth and Reconciliation Commission of South Africa final report is available at https://www.justice.gov.za/trc/report/finalreport/Volume%201.pdf, accessed May 19, 2022.

41   A third-generation white South African: "Clive Derby-Lewis: Murderer Who Provided Gun Used to Kill Hani in Bid to Spark Bloodbath," *Sunday Times*, November 6, 2016.

42   hard-line adherents of apartheid split off from the National Party: "Afrikaner Founds Right-Wing Party," *New York Times*, March 21, 1982.

42   Even by the standards of the Conservative Party: "Obituary: Clive Derby-Lewis," *News24*, November 3, 2016. Available at https://www.news24.com/news24/obituaries/obituary-clive-derby-lewis-20161103, accessed May 22, 2022.

43   He befriended David Irving, the Holocaust denier: "Obituary: Clive

Derby-Lewis—South African Politician Sentenced to Death for the Murder of Chris Hani," *The Times*, November 05, 2016. Available at https://www.thetimes.co.uk/article/clive-derby-lewis-dfblppnt8, accessed November 18, 2022.

43 Irving visited South Africa, sponsored by the Stallard Foundation: "Holocaust Denier Jailed," Ian Traynor, *Guardian Weekly*. Available at https://www.theguardian.com/guardianweekly/story/0,,1715580,00.html, accessed January 12, 2021.

44 Born in Australia into a devoutly Roman: "Apartheid's Fanatic in a Polka-Dot Frock: John Carlin Investigates What Lies Behind the English-Style Respectability Exuded by Some of South Africa's Far-Right," *Independent*, May 2, 1993. Available at https://www.independent.co.uk/news/world/apartheid-s-fanatic-polka-dot-frock-john-carlin-investigates-what-lies-behind-english-style-respectability-exuded-some-south-africa-s-far-right-2320389.html, accessed January 12, 2021.

44 Using secret Swiss bank accounts: Mervyn Rees and Chris Day, *Muldergate: The Story of the Info Scandal* (Johannesburg: Macmillan South Africa, 1980). Also "The Info Scandal," South African History Online. Available at https://www.sahistory.org.za/article/information-scandal, accessed May 19, 2022.

45 The Waluśes were doing well: Janet Smith and Beauregard Tromp, *Hani: A Life Too Short* (Johannesburg: Jonathan Ball Publishers), 239.

45 He listened to the fiery rhetoric: "Big Read: The Cruelty, Violence, Absurdity and Hope of 1986," *Business Day*, May 4, 2021. Available at https://www.businesslive.co.za/bd/life/2021-05-04-big-read-the-cruelty-violence-absurdity-and-hope-of-1986/, accessed May 22, 2022.

11:15 A.M.

46 The people sipping tea at the Venters' house: This section threads together testimony in the trial of Waluś and the Derby-Lewises in 1993, their appeal in 1994, and testimonies by all the players and their associates at the Truth and Reconciliation Commission amnesty hearings beginning in 1997.

47 "Don't worry, it's not that weapon": TRC amnesty hearings, available at https://www.justice.gov.za/trc/amntrans/bok/bok2_3hani1.htm, accessed May 22, 2022.

12 P.M.

47 Among those who descended: Peter Harris, *Birth: The Conspiracy to Stop the '94 Elections* (Cape Town: Penguin Random House South Africa, 2011), 22.

47   the regional structure of the National Peace Accord: Phiroshaw Camay and Anne J. Gordon, "The National Peace Accord and Its Structures," South Africa Civil Society and Governance Case Study No. 1, Co-operative for Research and Education (CORE), Johannesburg, South Africa. Available at https://omalley.nelsonmandela.org/omalley/index.php/site/q/03lv0 2424/04lv03275/05lv03294/06lv03321.htm, accessed January 21, 2021.

48   They had no guns, little equipment: Author interview with Peter Harris, Zoom, March 16, 2022.

48   For both men, the murder of Hani: Author interviews with Harris, March 16, 2022; and Gungubele, March 3, 2022.

50   "I don't know what we are going to tell these youth now": "Key ANC Negotiator Assassinated in S. Africa: Violence: Chris Hani's Murder Threatens to Undermine Constitutional Talks and Raises Fears of a Bloody Township Uprising," *Los Angeles Times*, April 11, 1993.

12 P.M.

51   Prime Minister Hendrik Frensch Verwoerd was dead: F. W. de Klerk, *The Last Trek—A New Beginning: The Autobiography* (London: Macmillan, 1998), 41.

51   Not that there wasn't white supremacy: "The History of Separate Development in South Africa," South African History Online. Available at https://www.sahistory.org.za/article/history-separate-development-south-africa, accessed May 20, 2022.

51   The legacy of that dispossession: "The Land Audit Report," Department of Rural Development and Land Reform, Government of South Africa, November 2017. Available at https://www.gov.za/sites/default/files/gcis-document/201802/landauditreport13feb2018.pdf, accessed May 20, 2022.

52   They are buried, silent and bitter: F. W. de Klerk, *The Last Trek—A New Beginning: The Autobiography* (London: Macmillan, 1998), 4.

53   He was considered a traitor: "'Uncontrollable' Hani had to be killed—Derby-Lewis in last interview," *News24*, November 15, 2016. Available at https://www.news24.com/News24/uncontrollable-hani-had-to-be-killed-derby-lewis-in-last-interview-20161115, accessed May 20, 2022.

53   white South Africans' "most hated adversary": Willem de Klerk, *FW de Klerk: The Man in His Time* (Johannesburg: Jonathan Ball Publishers, 1991), 18.

53   Yet De Klerk had not come from the *verligte*: Ibid., 19.

53   De Klerk had learned at his mother's knee: F. W. de Klerk, *The Last Trek—A New Beginning: The Autobiography* (London, Macmillan, 1998), 4.

54   He sought the day when: "Interview: FW de Klerk," *Focus4*, Third Quarter 1996, Helen Suzman Foundation. Available at https://hsf.org.za/publica tions/focus/issue-4-third-quarter-1996/interview-fw-de-klerk, accessed May 20, 2022.

54   one of their three children, Willem: "How South Africa's Former First Lady Met a Violent, Lonely and Bitter End," *Guardian*, December 5, 2001. Available at https://www.theguardian.com/world/2001/dec/06 /chrismcgreal, accessed May 20, 2022.

54   Ironically, it had been none other than De Klerk who in 1985: "The Romance that Rocked South Africa," David B. Ottaway, *Washington Post*, February 14, 1991. Available at https://www.washingtonpost.com/archive /lifestyle/1991/02/14/the-romance-that-rocked-south-africa/6d361e2a -b31c-4178-8b72-2ac78e253d53/?noredirect=on&utm_term=.7d3bdb 0046dc, accessed May 20, 2022.

54   Marike would press Willem to end the engagement: "Nicole's Life of Drama," *News24*, April 17, 2003. Available at https://www.news24.com /Entertainment/CelebNews/Nicoles-life-of-drama-20030416, accessed May 20, 2022.

55   South Africa had become the first country ever: F. W. de Klerk, *The Last Trek—A New Beginning: The Autobiography* (London: Macmillan, 1998), 273.

55   The ANC was skeptical of De Klerk's assertions: Anthony Sampson, *Mandela: The Authorised Biography* (London: HarperPress, 1999), 468.

55   De Klerk, needing an experienced communicator: World Summit of Nobel Laureates website. Available at http://www.nobelpeacesummit.com/mr -david-steward/, accessed May 20, 2022.

56   Steward was on a rare Easter break: Author interview with Dave Steward, Cape Town, July 27, 2018.

56   De Klerk said he knew that: Author interview with F. W. de Klerk, Cape Town, September 7, 2018. Recollection also in *The Last Trek—A New Beginning*, 275.

12 P.M.

56   Back at the Hani home, ANC leaders: Author interview with Gill Marcus, virtual, February 19, 2021. Visuals of the press briefing available on

YouTube at https://www.youtube.com/watch?v=mcOjx4SFYLI, last accessed May 20, 2022.

57   This time, however, Sexwale called for calm: Author interview with Tokyo Sexwale, Johannesburg, October 9, 2019. Remarks also in "How Chris Hani Died," *Sunday Times*, April 11, 1993.

57   Adelaide reached over: "A Wave, Then Silent Killer Gunned Down Hani," *Sunday Star*, April 11, 1993.

12 P.M.

58   That is former world boxing heavyweight champion Muhammad: "The Greatest: Heavyweight Fighter, Man of Intelligence and Depth," Gavin Evans, *Mail & Guardian*, December 23, 1999. Available at https://mg.co.za/article/1999-12-23-the-greatest-heavyweight-fighter-man-of/, accessed May 20, 2022.

58   He was notorious back then: Joe Matthews recounts being put through a rigorous exercise routine by Mandela in an interview on PBS. Joe Matthews interviewed by John Carlin, PBS. Available at https://www.pbs.org/wgbh/pages/frontline/shows/mandela/interviews/matthews.html, accessed May 20, 2022.

58   Mandela had met Ali: "Nelson Mandela's 1990 and 1993 Visits to L.A. Recalled," *Los Angeles Daily News*, December 5, 2013.

59   A wildly popular young Soweto boxer: "The Greatest: Heavyweight Fighter, Man of Intelligence and Depth," Gavin Evans, *Mail & Guardian*, December 23, 1999. Available at https://mg.co.za/article/1999-12-23-the-greatest-heavyweight-fighter-man-of/, accessed May 20, 2022.

59   In October 1979, at the height of apartheid: This surreal boxing match is recounted in "A Hollow Sporting Footnote in Apartheid-Era South Africa," by Trevor Sacks in the *New York Times*, October 20, 2012.

1 P.M.

60   General Bantu Holomisa was being feted: Author interview with Bantu Holomisa, December 7, 2020.

61   When the Transkei was established, the homeland: Eric Naki, *Bantu Holomisa: The Game Changer* (Johannesburg: Picador Africa, 2017), 36. The sections on Holomisa are mainly drawn from this biography, which he fully collaborated with, and the author interview of December 7, 2020. Extensive research has been published about the "homeland" system. For a quick and accurate guide, the O'Malley Archives at the Nelson

Mandela Foundation, which I have used extensively, is useful and can be accessed at https://omalley.nelsonmandela.org/omalley/index.php/site /q/03lv02424/04lv03370/05lv03413.htm.

63 Stengel recalled that Holomisa: Richard Stengel, *Mandela's Way* (New York: Crown Archetype, 2010), 154.

63 De Klerk had long seen in Holomisa: F. W. de Klerk, *The Last Trek—A New Beginning: The Autobiography* (London: Macmillan, 1998), 271.

1 P.M.

64 It was generally accepted that De Klerk's: Overwhelming evidence and argument of the disinformation campaign against Hani are carried in the *African Communist: Journal of the SA Communist Party*, no. 132 (First Quarter 1993), which can be accessed at https://omalley.nelsonmandela.org /omalley/index.php/site/q/03lv02424/04lv02730/05lv03005/06lv030 06/07lv03051/08lv03053.htm. The genesis of the government deception around the Black People's Army disinformation campaign was carried in "Army of the Night: Dreamed Up?," *Weekly Mail*, March 26, 1993.

65 he arranged for a statement: "A Black Leader in South Africa is Slain and a White is Arrested," Bill Keller, *New York Times*, April 11, 1993. Available at https://www.nytimes.com/1993/04/11/world/a-black-leader -in-south-africa-is-slain-and-a-white-is-arrested.html, accessed May 20, 2022.

66 He did not want the newly revived: Padraig O'Malley, "Ramaphosa and Meyer in Belfast—The South African Experience: How the New South Africa was Negotiated" (1996), John M. McCormack Graduate School of Policy and Global Studies Publications, 28, https://scholarworks.umb .edu/mccormack_pubs/28, accessed January 7, 2021.

66 At that time De Klerk had tried to show: "De Klerk's Visit to Massacre Site Brings New Eruption of Violence," Bill Keller, *New York Times*, June 21, 1993. Available at https://www.nytimes.com/1992/06/21/world/de -klerk-s-visit-to-massacre-site-brings-new-eruption-of-violence.html, accessed January 7, 2021.

66 "I am convinced we are no longer dealing with human beings": *City Press*, June 21, 1992, 1, and "Boipatong Massacre—17 June 1992," South African History Online. Available at https://www.sahistory.org.za/article/boipa tong-massacre-17-june-1992, accessed January 7, 2021.

66 "The continuing direct and indirect involvement": Memorandum from Nelson Mandela to F. W. de Klerk, June 26, 1992. Available at https://www

.theguardian.com/guardianweekly/story/0,,1715580,00.html, accessed December 21, 2022.

2 P.M.

67   Countries such as the newly minted Russia: "Yeltsin Exchanges Salutes with Soul Mate De Klerk," *Los Angeles Times,* June 2, 1992. UN Security Council Resolution 772, adopted on August 17, 1992, decided to deploy observers to South Africa.

67   Victor Zazeraj, director of the foreign affairs ministry: Victor Zazeraj, email correspondence with author, January 5, 2021. Also see Theresa Papenfus, *Pik Botha and His Times* (Pretoria: Litera Publications, 2010), 4.

68   In most of the international statements of grief: "EC Renews Call for Peace, Settlement," *The 11 Citizen,* April 13, 1993.

68   Nobel laureate Archbishop Desmond Tutu would call: "ANC Calls for Calm," *Sunday Times,* April 11, 1993. Further Tutu remarks in "Key ANC Negotiator Killed in S. Africa," *Los Angeles Times,* April 11, 1993, available at https://www.latimes.com/archives/la-xpm-1993-04-11-mn-21786-story .html, accessed December 21, 2022.

69   Mandela knew that Sexwale and other militant ANC leaders: Author interview with Tokyo Sexwale, Johannesburg, October 9, 2019.

69   On the streets, the violence that: "Black Anger at Assassination," *Sowetan,* April 13, 1993.

2 P.M.

70   "From the first I noticed that De Klerk listened": Nelson Mandela, *Long Walk to Freedom* (London: Abacus, 1994), 663.

70   His friend Archbishop Desmond Tutu also praised De Klerk: The Tutu remarks from "Dismantling Apartheid" by Subry Govender, June 18, 2015. Available at https://www.dw.com/en/how-south-africa-dismantled -apartheid/a-18524662, accessed May 20, 2022.

70   "Even the head of an illegitimate": Assessment by Tom Cohen in "Nelson Mandela: Man of Many Handshakes," CNN, December 5, 2013. Available at http://edition.cnn.com/2013/12/05/world/africa/nelson-mandela -handshakes, accessed December 21, 2022.

71   After excoriating De Klerk following: Shaun Johnson, "From the Archive: An Interview with Nelson Mandela on Bisho, De Klerk and the New South Africa," *New Statesman,* July 4, 2013. Available at https://www.newstates

man.com/world/2013/07/archive-interview-nelson-mandela-bisho-de
-klerk-and-new-south-africa, accessed on July 17, 2017.

72 Asked what his view of De Klerk was as the negotiations continued: Princeton N. Lyman, "Mandela and De Klerk: Essential Partners," blog post, *The Great Debate*, December 9, 2013. Available at www.blogs.reuters .com/great-debate, accessed July 17, 2017.

72 Despite their ability to transcend their differences: Mandela interview with Richard Stengel, Nelson Mandela Centre of Memory, April 29, 1993.

2 P.M.

73 Just south of the Midlands is another: *Explore Wild Coast*, Eastern Cape Parks and Recreation Agency. Available at https://visiteasterncape.co.za /regions/wild-coast/, accessed November 17, 2022.

74 It was a place that forty-four-year-old Alastair Weakley loved: The sections on Alastair and Glen Weakley are mainly culled from testimony at the amnesty hearings and other sources. Particularly moving is the testimony of their sister, Roslyn Stratford, found in the second part of this transcript: https://www.justice.gov.za/trc/hrvtrans/hrvpe1/day3.htm.

74 Weakley loved this land: Grant Fowlds and Graham Spence, *Saving the Last Rhinos: The Life of a Frontline Conservationist* (New York: Pegasus Books, 2019), chap. 3.

2 P.M.

75 "He was so sad": John Carlin, *Playing the Enemy: Nelson Mandela and the Game That Made a Nation.* (New York: Grove Atlantic, 2008), 117.

75 "I loved you like the true son you were": Address by ANC president Nelson R. Mandela at the funeral of Martin Chris Hani, FNB Stadium, Soweto, April 19, 1993. The funeral and speech can be viewed in full at https://reuters.screenocean.com/record/895586.

76 "In the days after the assassination": Richard Stengel, *Mandela's Way* (New York: Crown Archetype, 2010), 48.

76 In Sexwale's view, Mandela found himself: Author interview with Tokyo Sexwale, Johannesburg, October 9, 2019.

76 He described the state of the country as "fragile": Nelson Mandela, *Long Walk to Freedom* (London: Abacus, 1994), 729.

77 Cofimvaba was a harsh place: Address by ANC president Nelson R.

Mandela at the funeral of Martin Chris Hani, FNB Stadium, Soweto, April 19, 1993.

77   with Gilbert contorted by grief: Janet Smith and Beauregard Tromp, *Hani: A Life Too Short*, (Johannesburg: Jonathan Ball Publishers, 2007), 250.

3 P.M.

78   Only hours after the assassination: "Blacks Taunted in Streets," *Sunday Times*, April 11, 1993.

78   In Khayelitsha township just outside: "Barricades Burn in Khayelitsha," *Cape Times*, April 12, 1993.

5–6 P.M.

79   It was evening when Holomisa's plane: Author interview with Bantu Holomisa, Pretoria, December 7, 2020.

80   With nightfall looming, what would happen?: Author interview with Saki Macozoma, January 27, 2021.

5 P.M.

80   When Janusz Waluś had left at 7 a.m.: This section relies on Maria Ras's testimony at the trial of Janusz Waluś, Clive Derby-Lewis, and Gaye Derby-Lewis. The case is *State v. Waluś and Others* (70/93) [1993] ZAGPHC 1 (October 14, 1993), Supreme Court of South Africa (Witwatersrand Local Division). Available at http://www.saflii.org/cgi-bin/disp.pl?file=za/cases/ZAGPHC/1993/1.html&query=Janusz%20Walus, accessed May 19, 2022.

80   The two had been together for ten years: "Lawyer Admits Suspect's Guilt," Associated Press, October 13, 1993.

81   He told her not to worry: "Toe val Derby-Lewis flou," *Vrye Weekblad*, October 28, 1993. Available at https://www.vryeweekblad.com/nuus-en-politiek/2021-08-10-toe-val-derby-lewis-flou/, accessed May 19, 2020.

6 P.M.

81   police sergeant Mike Holmes had arrived: Waluś testimony at Truth and Reconciliation Commission amnesty hearing, November 24, 1997). Available at https://omalley.nelsonmandela.org/index.php/site/q/03lv02167/04lv02264/05lv02267/06lv02268/07lv02272.htm, accessed November 17, 2022.

83   "Mike, I think something made you happy": *State v. Waluś and Another* (585/93,586/93) [1994] ZASCA 189 (November 30, 1994), South Africa Supreme Court of Appeal. Available at http://www.saflii.org/cgi-bin

/disp.pl?file=za/cases/ZASCA/1994/189.html&query=janusz%20
walus, accessed May 19, 2022.

7 P.M.

83   ANC Youth League member Phumelele Civilian Hermans: Transcripts of
     Hermans and his comrades' testimonies can be accessed through the TRC
     archives at https://www.justice.gov.za/trc/amntrans/am1998.htm. These
     sections thread together their various testimonies.

84   Despite its beauty: South African unemployment trends collated under
     "South Africa Unemployment Rate 1991–2022" by Macrotrends. Avail-
     able at https://www.macrotrends.net/countries/ZAF/south-africa/un
     employment-rate.

84   Port St. Johns was a study in racial segregation: "My Hometown: Port
     St Johns, Eastern Cape," eNCA, July 28, 2016. Available at https://www
     .enca.com/south-africa/my-hometown-port-st-johns-eastern-cape. A use-
     ful pictorial map of Port St. Johns and Mthumbane can be found here:
     https://www.google.com/maps/d/viewer?mid=1aGRhZpf7Waz3UcF9Ss
     4z9L_Lho4&hl=en&near&mrt=yp&fb=1&ie=UTF8&t=h&msa=0&ll=-
     31.645612860525894%2C29.53287079598682&spn=0.140454%2C0.21
     9727&z=16&iwloc=0004a468764b1910b1c10&source=embed.

7 P.M.

86   When the Boipatong Massacre: Author interview with F. W. de Klerk,
     Plattekloof, South Africa, September 7, 2018.

87   It had taken nine months of secret talks: Catherine Barnes and Eldred
     De Klerk, "South Africa's Multi-Party Constitutional Negotiation Pro-
     cess," *Accord*, no.13, December 2002, 26. Available at https://www.c-r.org
     /accord/public-participation/south-africas-multi-party-constitutional
     -negotiation-process, accessed November 17, 2022.

87   Harris said he was petrified: Peter Harris, *Birth: The Conspiracy to Stop
     the '94 Elections* (Cape Town: Penguin Random House South Africa,
     2011), 23.

87   "closest to a race war of Black against white": Richard Stengel, *Mandela's
     Way* (New York: Crown Archetype, 2010), 50.

8 P.M.

88   In his memoir De Klerk: F. W. de Klerk, *The Last Trek—A New Beginning:
     The Autobiography* (London: Macmillan, 1998), 276.

88   "asked to speak on the SABC that night to address the nation": Nelson Mandela, *Long Walk to Freedom* (London: Abacus, 1994), 729.

88   even Hani's biographers: In Smith and Tromp, *Hani: A Life Too Short*, 249. Stengel in *Mandela's Way*, 48. O'Sullivan in his reflection piece on the KayaFM site. Available at https://www.kaya959.co.za/the-day-chris-hani-was-assassinated/, accessed December 21, 2022.

9 P.M.

88   Arrangements had already been made: "Mandela Speaks to the Nation," *Sunday Star*, April 11, 1993.

89   it was already past the main "Black" news bulletin at 7 p.m.: All Media and Products Survey (AMPS) Meter: Weekly Report, April 5, 1993, to April 11, 1993, published by South African Advertising Research Foundation.

89   television would come to South Africa "over his dead body": "The First Ever TV Broadcast in SA," SABC website, available at http://web.sabc .co.za/sabc/home/tvob/events/details?id=c01a1640-7f2b-4270-82c3 -caea284ad8ad&title=The%20First%20Ever%20SABC%20TV%20 Broadcast%20in%20SA, accessed May 22, 2022.

89   The killing of Chris Hani, it turns out, attracted a bigger television audience: AMPS Meter weekly report. Audience figures interpreted by senior SABC analyst (name withheld).

90   He had cataracts in his left eye: "Prison Work Hurt Mandela's Tear Glands," Reuters, July 13, 1994. Available at https://www.deseret .com/1994/7/13/19119585/prison-work-hurt-mandela-s-tear-glands, accessed May 20, 2022.

90   Mandela had to wear "his glasses": Email correspondence with Pallo Jordan, December 18, 2020.

90   "took clothes—and their power—seriously": "How Nelson Mandela's Example Offers Style Lessons for a New Year," Vanessa Friedman, *Financial Times*, December 27, 2013. Available at https://www.ft.com/content /d3f7320c-6669-11e3-aa10-00144feabdc0, accessed December 21, 2022.

90   As a young lawyer in the 1950s, he had worn the finest suits: This story is recounted by Richard Stengel in a PBS *Frontline* series of interviews conducted by John Carlin. It is available at https://www.pbs.org/wgbh /pages/frontline/shows/mandela/boy/stengel.html. A slightly different version is recounted by Bizos in his book *65 Years of Friendship* (p. 46), where he says when he saw Mandela, the tailor Alfred Kahn was on his

knees in front of Mandela, fitting him for a suit, much to the bemusement of the white clientele.

91   a suit that looked slightly too big for him: The suit can be viewed during Mandela's address at https://www.youtube.com/watch?v=_1uG2ND wzZU, accessed on May 20, 2022.

91   There were no greetings: The full Mandela speech can be accessed on the Mandela Foundation website at https://omalley.nelsonmandela .org/omalley/index.php/site/q/03lv02039/04lv02133/05lv02149/0 6lv02150.htm, accessed May 19, 2022.

93   "It was fine": "Mandela Speaks to the Nation," *Sunday Star*, April 11, 1993.

93   In 1992, Mandela took a small plane: This anecdote was recounted by Richard Stengel at a meeting of the International Peace Institute held at the Trygve Lie Center for Peace, Security & International Peace in New York City on July 26, 2010. The transcript can be accessed at https:// www.ipinst.org/wp-content/uploads/2010/07/pdfs_transcript_stengel _july26.pdf, accessed May 22, 2022.

94   Mandela knew what it was like to lose a son: Nelson Mandela, *Long Walk to Freedom* (London: Abacus, 1994), 531.

EASTER SUNDAY, APRIL 11, 1993
5:30 A.M.

97   Back in his prison cell, Waluś: This section draws from testimony by Waluś and others from the amnesty hearings in 1997–1999, as indicated above. I have also used the South African History Archive's De Wet Potgieter Collection, which includes the SA Police investigation diary kept throughout the week of April 11. It can be viewed at SAHA, which has now been moved to the Department of Historical Papers, University of the Witwatersrand. The call number is B1.5.5.2.2.

97   But under the Internal Security Act, he could be held for up to twelve months: Lawrence Baxter, "Section 29 of the Internal Security Act and the Rule of Law," *Reality* 17, no. 6 (1985): 4–6. Available at https://disa.ukzn .ac.za/sites/default/files/pdf_files/renov85.4.pdf.

97   According to the Human Rights Committee: Max Coleman, ed., *A Crime Against Humanity—Analysing the Repression of the Apartheid State* (Johannesburg: Human Rights Commitee of South Africa, 1998).

98   Holmes had ordered a Sergeant J. Slingerland: *State v. Waluś and Another* (585/93,586/93) [1994] ZASCA 189 (November 30, 1994). South Africa Supreme Court of Appeal. Available at http://www.saflii.org/cgi-bin

/disp.pl?file=za/cases/ZASCA/1994/189.html&query=janusz%20 walus, accessed May 19, 2022.

98   It was one of a large arsenal stolen: "Gun that Killed South African Linked to Theft by Right-Winger," Paul Taylor, *Washington Post*, April 14, 1993. Available at https://www.washingtonpost.com/archive/politics /1993/04/14/gun-that-killed-s-african-linked-to-theft-by-right-wing ers/73b4b8f3-56ee-4f76-a94f-a6f03f5f6695/, accessed May 20, 2022.

99   "I remember him saying that those weapons": Ibid.

99   For Holmes, it meant he had to get something: "Police 'Cannot Get Hani Murder Suspect to Talk,'" *Business Day*, April 14, 1993.

MIDDAY

99   If Mandela's historic televised speech: "Storm Warnings in South Africa: 'Big War' Feared After Killing of ANC Activist," John Carlin, *Independent* (London), April 11, 1993. Available at https://www.independent.co.uk /news/storm-warnings-in-south-africa-big-war-feared-after-killing-of -anc-activist-police-guard-was-refused-two-whites-burnt-to-death-in -township-1454762.html, accessed May 24, 2022.

100 That morning the SA Communist Party chairman, Joe Slovo, had stopped a radio interviewer: "A Martyr for the Young Lions," Scott Macleod, *Time*, April 19, 1993. Available at http://content.time.com/time/subscriber/ar ticle/0,33009,978235,00.html, accessed May 24, 2022.

100 Shilowa, at the time an avowed communist who only wore red socks: Author interview with Mbhazima Shilowa, July 14, 2021.

100 At the Dutch Reformed Church, just ten minutes' drive from Hani's home: "Tragedy Hangs Over Church Service," *Star*, April 12, 1993.

101 was a somber affair: Author interview with Joel Netshitenzhe, April 14, 2021.

101 Others were not as delicate: "Harry Gwala, Man of Steel," *African Communist*, no. 142 (Third Quarter 1995). Available at https://omalley.nelson mandela.org/omalley/index.php/site/q/03lv02424/04lv02730/05lv030 05/06lv03006/07lv03105/08lv03115.htm, accessed December 21, 2022.

102 He told a mass rally: Niël Barnard, with Tobie Wiese, *Peaceful Revolution: Inside the War Room at the Negotiations* (Cape Town: Tafelberg Publishers, 2017).

102 "The NP elite is getting into bed": Winnie Madikizela-Mandela's opinion piece was published in both the *Sunday Times* and *Sunday Star* on January 24, 1993.

102 shared similar traits: Alexander Johnston, "The ANC Populists," *Indicator SA* 12, no. 2 (Autumn 1995).

103 As the NEC members filed into their conference room: "ANC Rejects Call to Walk Out of Talks," *Los Angeles Times*, April 12, 1993. Available at https://www.latimes.com/archives/la-xpm-1993-04-12-mn-22043-story .html, accessed December 21, 2022.

103 As the meeting deliberated, the ANC Western Cape leader, Tony Yengeni: "High Tension as Thousands March on Police Station," *The Argus*, April 13, 1993.

103 In this meeting, too, there was despair, confusion, anger—and venting: Author interview with Ronnie Kasrils, February 2, 2021.

104 "like lambs to the slaughter": Nelson Mandela and Mandla Langa, *Dare Not Linger: The Presidential Years* (London: Macmillan, 2017), 21.

104 Julius Nyerere, the president of Tanzania: Ibid., 22.

104 "This is their purpose": "ANC Rejects Call to Walk Out of Talks," *Los Angeles Times*, April 12, 1993. Available at https://www.latimes.com/archives /la-xpm-1993-04-12-mn-22043-story.html.

104 Mandela said the ANC "had to do something to channel away": Nelson Mandela interview with Richard Stengel, Johannesburg, April 23, 1993, Nelson Mandela Centre of Memory, Nelson Mandela Foundation.

105 the ANC decided to stage marches, memorial services, rallies, and other gatherings: Ibid.

105 And Hani was merely the latest in a long line: "Political Assassinations 1974 to 1994," South African History Online. Available at https://www .sahistory.org.za/article/political-assassinations-1974-1994. Also, "Focus on Security," *Sowetan*, April 13, 1993.

105 ANC leaders were still investigating the murder: "The Erasure of Dulcie September," Africa Is a Country, August 20, 2019. Available at https:// africasacountry.com/2019/08/the-erasure-of-dulcie-september.

105 The lawyer Griffiths Mxenge was killed: "South Africa Appoints Judicial Inquiry in Death of Black Close to Mandelas," John F. Burns, *New York Times*, February 1, 1990. Available at https://www.nytimes.com/1990/02/01 /world/south-africa-appoints-judicial-inquiry-in-death-of-black-close-to -mandelas.html, accessed December 21, 2022.

105 The men and women in the room knew one thing, though: Niël Barnard, with Tobie Wiese, *Peaceful Revolution: Inside the War Room at the Negotiations* (Cape Town: Tafelberg Publishers, 2017), loc. 346 (Kindle edition).

106   In 1989, for example, Ramaphosa and other leaders: Anthony Butler, *Cyril Ramaphosa* (Johannesburg: Jacana Media, 2007), 239.

106   The leaders held her indirectly responsible for the beating: "Black Groups Ostracize Mrs. Mandela," William Claiborne, *Washington Post*, February 17, 1989. Available at https://www.washingtonpost.com/archive/politics/1989/02/17/black-groups-ostracize-mrs-mandela/fb59e4a7-e978-4c0d-8013-ef586cd596c4/, accessed December 21, 2022.

107   It was in this Sunday morning meeting that the skeleton of Mandela's plan: Author interview with Joel Netshitenzhe, April 14, 2021.

107   Mandela was always eager: "As the Going Gets Tougher, So Does Mandela," Christopher S. Wren, *New York Times*, May 5, 1991. Available at https://www.nytimes.com/1991/05/05/weekinreview/the-world-as-the-going-gets-tougher-so-does-mandela.html, accessed December 21, 2022.

108   The negotiations process had become bogged down: "The Story of Chris Hani's Assassination and its Aftermath," Constitution Hill. Archive material available at https://ourconstitution.constitutionhill.org.za/the-assassination-of-chris-hani/, accessed December 21, 2022.

108   If an election date was not set in the next round of negotiations: "Many ready to take up arms," *Weekly Mail*, April 16, 1993.

108   go "for the kill": Since July 1991, when he became the ANC's chief negotiator, Ramaphosa's view was that the government had to be pushed to "the precipice." "We pushed it to the precipice, to the point where everything could break down. Government could not risk the breakdown of negotiations. We knew by force of argument and what was at stake that we would come out victorious." The assassination of Chris Hani boosted the cause. "The objective had been there but it tended to be a bit fuzzy at times. After Chris Hani died we went for the kill." The original source of this quote is the *Observer* newspaper, April 24, 1994, headlined "Hooked on Peace By Heir Apparent" (22).

109   An agitated Mandela detailed how Walter Sisulu: "ANC Blames Police for Not Protecting Hani," the *Citizen*, April 12, 1993.

110   Ramaphosa reserved his greatest anger for: "South African Communist Leader Assassinated, Suspect Arrested," United Press International, April 10, 1993. Available at https://www.upi.com/Archives/1993/04/10/South-African-Communist-leader-assassinated-suspect-arrested/5833734414400/, accessed December 21, 2022.

110   was a friend of Gaye Derby-Lewis: "Apartheid's Fanatic in a Polka-Dot Frock," John Carlin, *Independent*, May 2, 1993. Available at https://www

.independent.co.uk/news/world/apartheid-s-fanatic-polka-dot-frock-john -carlin-investigates-what-lies-behind-english-style-respectability-exuded -some-south-africa-s-far-right-2320389.html, accessed January 12, 2021.

110   Of course, that assumed the police weren't behind the plot: Elinor Sisulu, *Walter and Albertina Sisulu: In Our Lifetime* (Cape Town: David Philip, 2002), 619.

111   In townships in the East Rand, groups of activists gathered: Author interview (one of two) with Mondli Gungubele, Cape Town, March 3, 2022.

111   Mandela was alive to his friend Desmond Tutu's warning: "ANC Rejects Call to Walk Out of Talks," *Los Angeles Times*, April 12, 1993. Available at https://www.latimes.com/archives/la-xpm-1993-04-12-mn-22043-story .html.

MIDDAY

112   Chris Hani's office was spartan: "A Note on Desk Pad Said 'Peace Corp,'" *The Argus*, April 13, 1993.

112   Guleni had received basic training: "Further submissions and responses by the African National Congress to questions raised by the Commission for Truth and Reconciliation—May 12, 1997." Available at https://www .justice.gov.za/trc/hrvtrans/submit/anc2.htm#Appendix%207, accessed December 21, 2022.

112   in the next twelve months Guleni: "TRC Told SDUs Killed Four Apla Members," SA Press Association, November 3, 1999. Available at https:// www.justice.gov.za/trc/media/1999/9911/p991103b.htm, accessed December 21, 2022.

114   In one famous incident in 1990: "Mandela Finds His Mission Impeded," David B. Ottaway, *Washington Post*, April 7, 1990. Available at https:// www.washingtonpost.com/archive/politics/1990/04/07/mandela -finds-his-mission-impeded/b7fcecdc-de35-44fe-a364-e7725e260ce0/, accessed December 21, 2022.

114   So, in its fax statement to the branches: This statement was faxed from the SACP's Eastern Cape regional office and is in tone far more militant than the national statement. It calls for all international sporting links to be reviewed, all government buildings "to be occupied," and for the deputy minister of law and order to be fired immediately. It declares a Black weekend—no shopping between April 16 and 19. SACP Eastern Cape statement, April 11, 1993. Collection 228, Liberation Movements Archives, University of Fort Hare.

MIDDAY

116　On the evening of Sunday, June 22, 1992: "This Won't Be the First Time Cyril Ramaphosa Keeps His Friends Close, and His Enemies Closer," Bruce Whitfield, *Business Insider*, February 27, 2018. Available at https://www.businessinsider.co.za/whitfield-on-the-reshuffle-2018-2, accessed December 21, 2022.

116　He said the massacre had turned the clock back three decades: "Mandela Halts All Talks with White Leadership," *Los Angeles Times*, June 22, 1992. Available at https://www.latimes.com/archives/la-xpm-1992-06-22-mn-657-story.html, accessed December 21, 2022.

117　Ramaphosa, raised in the hard-knuckle township of Soweto: "How Cyril Lands the Big Fish," *Mail & Guardian*, May 26, 1995. Available at https://mg.co.za/article/1995-05-26-how-cyril-lands-the-big-fish/, accessed January 8, 2021.

117　Meyer, on the other hand, had never fished: Tom Lodge, "Thabo Mbeki and Cyril Ramaphosa: Crown Princes to Nelson Mandela's Throne," *World Policy Journal* 10, no. 3 (Fall 1993): 65–71.

117　When the heated emotions: Padraig O'Malley, *Shades of Difference: Mac Maharaj and the Struggle for South Africa* (New York: Viking, 2007), 392.

AFTERNOON

118　started to "eat me inside like a worm": Eric Naki, *Bantu Holomisa: The Game Changer* (Johannesburg: Picador Africa, 2017), 177.

119　The assassination of Hani was part of the alleged operation: TRC Final Report, vol. 6, sec. 3, chap. 1, p. 243. Available at https://sabctrc.saha.org.za/reports/volume6/section3/chapter1/subsection26.htm?t=%2BOperation+%2BKatzen&tab=report, accessed December 21, 2022.

9 P.M.

120　the threatening calls had started: The Harmse sections draw on reporting by Hanlie Retief in "The Woman Who Saw Everything," *Rapport*, April 18, 1993; in "I Saw Him Killed," *Sunday Times*, April 11, 1993; Harmse's court testimony in October 1993; and other reporting such as the Associated Press's "Woman Who Helped Catch Hani Suspect Now under Fire," April 15, 1993.

AFTERNOON

121　Steward had arranged for him to give a television interview: "Politicians' Security Beefed Up," *Star*, April 12, 1993.

122   De Klerk knew that there was danger ahead: Niël Barnard, with Tobie
       Wiese, *Peaceful Revolution: Inside the War Room at the Negotiations* (Cape
       Town: Tafelberg Publishers, 2017), loc. 2348 (Kindle edition).

EASTER MONDAY, APRIL 12, 1993
LUNCHTIME

127   Instead, that afternoon Clive retired: Janet Smith and Beauregard Tromp,
       Hani: A Life Too Short (Johannesburg: Jonathan Ball Publishers, 2007),
       257.

127   The leader of the AWB, Eugène Terre'Blanche: " 'An Atrocious Deed,'
       Says Terre'Blanche," *Citizen*, April 12, 1993. Also, "Terre'Blanche: Loved
       or Hated," *News24*, June 4, 2010. Available at https://www.news24.com
       /news24/terreblanche-loved-or-hated-20100406, accessed December 21,
       2022.

DAYTIME

128   It was becoming clear that Hani had been marked: *Daily Dispatch*, April 13,
       1993, and "Hani Talks About His Death," *Weekly Mail*, April 16, 1993.

129   The five-page note repeated Holomisa's suspicion of state involvement:
       "Holomisa Links Death to Govt's E Cape Plan," *Citizen*, April 12, 1993.

129   he decided to respond with a terse statement: *Daily Dispatch*, April 13,
       1993.

DAYTIME

129   He repeated the messages from Mandela's press conference on Sunday:
       "Violence Flares in Townships," *Star*, April 13, 1993.

129   Sometimes, however, words went awry: Author interview with Mondli
       Gungubele, Cape Town, March 3, 2022.

130   It is a chant that continues today: " 'Kill the Boer' Case a Veiled Attempt
       at Halting Pursuit of Economic Emancipation—Malema," *News24*, Febru-
       ary 16, 2022. Available at https://www.news24.com/news24/southafrica
       /news/afriforums-kill-the-boer-case-a-veiled-attempt-at-halting-pursuit
       -of-economic-emancipation-malema-20220216, accessed December 21,
       2022.

131   Mokaba, having lost sight of his own transport: "ANC Leaders Struggle to
       Avert War," John Carlin, *Independent*, April 13, 1993. Available at https://
       www.independent.co.uk/news/anc-leaders-struggle-to-avert-war-john
       -carlin-joins-black-south-africans-marching-to-their-murdered-hero-s

-home-yes-we-are-an-angry-people-but-we-will-act-with-calm-there-will
-be-no-racial-war-1455026.html, accessed December 21, 2022.

131   Gungubele was doing the same, marching with the crowds: "20,000 march
on Dawn Park," *Star*, April 13, 1993.

DAYTIME

132   They needed something to calm their nerves: "The Woman Who Saw
Everything," *Rapport*, April 18, 1993.

4:40 P.M.

132   plumes of smoke covered a police helicopter: "Black Anger at Assassination," *Sowetan*, April 13, 1993.

133   Many spoke of disillusionment with the government : "Leaders at Militant
Rallies Call for Peace, Discipline," *Star*, April 13, 1993.

133   Houses of Blacks linked to the government: "Mass Protests to Mark Hani
Assassination," *Business Day*, April 13, 1993.

133   "It is the masses who should call the shots": "Yengeni Lashes Leaders," *The
Argus*, April 13, 1993.

134   If there was Black anger, there was also white hate: "Sympathy for the
Devil," *Weekly Mail*, April 16, 1993.

135   However, that evening he used the communication channel: Author interview with Roelf Meyer, October 7, 2019.

135   His mind was made up that this second address: Author interview with
Gill Marcus, February 19, 2021.

TUESDAY, APRIL 13, 1993
5 A.M.

137   Nelson Mandela, usually up at 4 a.m.: Richard Stengel, private diary entry,
April 13, 1993.

137   after his separation from Winnie: Anthony Sampson, *Mandela: The Authorised Biography* (London: HarperPress, 1999), 453.

138   For example, in June 1990, Hani's contingent of bodyguards: Janet Smith
and Beauregard Tromp, *Hani: A Life Too Short* (Johannesburg: Jonathan
Ball Publishers, 2007), 207.

138   The Swedish government had announced that its long-standing funding of
the ANC: "ANC May Lose Its Yearly Grant," *Sowetan*, April 13, 1993.

139   Marcus was negotiating a spot on the news: "SABC Unbowed Over
Speech," *Business Day*, April 15, 1993.

8 A.M.

139 They expected protests outside court: "Violence Flares on Reef and E Cape," *Star,* April 14, 1993.

140 Waluś appeared before a magistrate promptly at 8 a.m: "Drama by hof toe Waluś verskyn" (Drama in court as Waluś appears), *Beeld,* April 14, 1993.

140 Two members of the Afrikaner Weerstandsbeweging: "Mandela Warns of Looming Disaster," John Carlin, *Independent,* April 14, 1993. Available at https://www.independent.co.uk/news/world/mandela-warns-looming -disaster-man-accused-killing-chris-hani-appears-court-amid-fears-he -was-part-right-wing-plot-1455136.html. Also in *Star,* April 14, 1993, accessed December 21, 2022.

141 In 1990, Terre'Blanche had visited Law and Order minister: Christopher S. Wren "Rumblings on the Right," *New York Times Magazine,* July 10, 1990. Available at https://www.nytimes.com/1990/10/07/mag azine/rumblings-on-the-right.html, accessed December 21, 2022.

142 But Sexwale and Niehaus could see that the crowd: Author interview with Carl Niehaus, Johannesburg, December 4, 2020.

143 Sexwale was angered and pained at the assassination: Author interview with Tokyo Sexwale, Johannesburg, October 9, 2019.

10 A.M.

144 groups of angry youth attacked police stations: Reports from *Beeld, The Argus, Cape Times, Star, Daily Dispatch, EP Herald* on April 14, 1993.

9 A.M.

144 meeting with the two men overseeing the Hani investigation: "23000 van-dag ontplooi" (23,000 deployed today), *Beeld,* April 14, 1993.

145 He once complained to an interviewer: Don Foster, Paul Haupt, and Marésa de Beer, *The Theatre of Violence: Narratives of Protagonists in the South African Conflict* (Cape Town: HSRC Press, 2005), 117.

145 There had been 222 separate "unrest-related": "23000 vandag ontplooi" (23,000 deployed today), *Beeld,* April 14, 1993.

145 They wanted to clamp down hard: See *Beeld* ("23000 vandag ontplooi") and SA Press Association, "Clash Leaves Peace Process Tottering," *EP Herald,* April 16, 1993.

MIDMORNING

146 ANC leaders in Cape Town announced that Ali would attend commemorations: "High Tension as Thousands March on Police Station," *The Argus*, April 13, 1993.

146 Ali wrote to Mandela: The letter can be viewed via the *Irish Mirror* here: https://www.irishmirror.ie/news/world-news/amazing-letter-muhammad-ali-nelson-9425156, accessed December 21, 2022.

2 P.M.

146 The ANC had very little investigative capacity: Author interview with ANC NEC member Mathews Phosa, March 11, 2021.

147 He had to rely on the SA Police investigators: "For Mandela, a Perilous Road Ahead," *New York Times*, April 16, 1993.

147 "It's because your police have been chasing me so hard": Herman Giliomee, *The Last Afrikaner Leaders: A Supreme Test of Power* (Cape Town: Tafelberg, 2012), 323.

147 An ANC intelligence operative, a burly former rugby player: "Nog nege op moordlys" (Another nine on murder list), *Beeld*, April 12, 1993. The ANC agent Ronnie Watson is also quoted extensively by Evelyn Groenink in *Incorruptible: The Story of the Murders of Dulcie September, Anton Lubowski and Chris Hani* (self-published, 2018).

5 P.M.

149 The 4x4 double cab pickup truck made its way up the hill: Section drawn from TRC testimonies of actors.

149 The legend of Ally Weakley stretched from: "Go well my teacher," BBC .co.uk, October 31, 1998. Available at http://news.bbc.co.uk/2/hi/programmes/from_our_own_correspondent/205063.stm, accessed December 21, 2022.

150 Grant Fowlds, another of Weakley's pupils: Grant Fowlds and Graham Spence, *Saving the Last Rhinos: The Life of a Frontline Conservationist* (New York: Pegasus Books, 2019), loc. 251 (Kindle edition).

5 P.M.

151 Early on Tuesday, April 13, 1993, Mlulamisi Maxhayi: Section drawn from TRC testimonies of actors.

EVENING

155 Now, just three days later, he had reached a turning point: F. W. de Klerk, *The Last Trek—A New Beginning: The Autobiography* (London: Macmillan, 1998), 276.

155 In 1990, Craig Kotze, a crime reporter: "Craig Kotze: Police Commissioner George Fivaz's spokesman," *Mail & Guardian*, August 2, 1996. Available at https://mg.co.za/article/1996-08-02-craig-kotze-police-commissioner-george-fivazs/, accessed December 21, 2022.

155 This was a body whose participants were *hardegat*: Patti Waldmeir, *Anatomy of a Miracle* (London: Viking, 1997), 188.

6 P.M.

157 He scribbled them down himself at the top of the draft: Author interview with Carl Niehaus; remarks also asserted in this article at https://uncensoredopinion.co.za/night-nelson-mandela-became-de-facto-president-south-africa/, accessed December 21, 2022.

158 Arriving in 1994 to train SABC: "The Way We Were: The Unknown SABC Story," September 16, 2014. Available at http://www.thejournalist.org.za/the-craft/way/, accessed December 21, 2022.

159 Pretorius had described his job succinctly: Robert B. Horowitz, *Communication and Democratic Reform in South Africa* (Cambridge University Press, 2001), 72.

7:02 P.M.

161 For many, the address was a game changer: Anthony Sampson, *Mandela: The Authorised Biography* (London: HarperPress, 199), 469.

161 Archbishop Desmond Tutu said he believed: Tutu said this as part of the PBS series on him. Available at https://www.pbs.org/wgbh/pages/frontline/shows/mandela/interviews/tutu.html, accessed December 21, 2022.

161 As speeches go, Mandela's that night was a remarkably short one: Televised address to the nation by ANC president Nelson Rolihlahla Mandela, on the assassination of Chris Hani, April 13, 1993. Available at http://db.nelsonmandela.org/speeches/pub_view.asp?pg=item&ItemID=NMS135&txtstr=Chris%20Hani, accessed December 21, 2022.

162 In a widely circulated academic paper: Kenneth S. Zagacki, "Rhetoric, Dialogue, and Performance in Nelson Mandela's 'Televised Address on the Assassination of Chris Hani,'" *Rhetoric and Public Affairs* 6, no. 4 (Winter 2003): 709–35.

162   Gungubele had, since the age of sixteen: Interview with author.

164   "If we had not done so the right wing and these sinister elements": Transcript of Mandela interview with Richard Stengel, Nelson Mandela Foundation, April 23, 1994.

8:15 P.M.

166   Carl Niehaus was in tears: Author interview with Niehaus.

167   He was not to know until the next day: "SABC Unbowed Over Speech," *Business Day*, April 15, 1993.

WEDNESDAY, APRIL 14, 1993
9 A.M.

169   Retha Harmse did not go to work on Wednesday morning: "Woman Who Helped Catch Hani Suspect Now Under Fire," Associated Press, April 15, 1993. Available at https://apnews.com/article/81da3789f34cb3f4cc4d23 3f57753ba3, accessed December 21, 2022. Also, *Rapport* profile by Hanlie Retief.

9 A.M.

170   Across the country, those who wanted to commemorate: These sections are pulled together from multiple news sources and interviews as per the text.

170   The people inside were singing and lustily partaking: " 'Een verskriklikke stofwolk' voordat trein van spoor spring," ('Terrible dust cloud' before train derails), *Beeld*, April 15, 1993.

9 A.M.

171   As the movement to churches, stadiums, and other: "Treurnicht Goes For Tests After Heart Attack," *Beeld*, April 14, 1993.

171   Treurnicht was a giant: "Obituaries: Andries Treurnicht, 72, Leader of Hard-Line Pro-Apartheid party," Bruce Lambert, *New York Times*, April 23, 1993. Available at https://www.nytimes.com/1993/04/23/obituaries /andries-p-treurnicht-72-leader-of-hard-line-pro-apartheid-party.html, accessed December 21, 2022.

171   Three months after Mandela's release: "60,000 Afrikaners Protest De Klerk's Dialogue with the ANC," David B. Ottaway, *Washington Post*, May 27, 1990. Available at https://www.washingtonpost.com/archive /politics/1990/05/27/6000-afrikaners-protest-de-klerks-dialogue-with

-anc/90315eba-95bb-475d-bc06-a3c54fb304fd/, accessed December 21, 2022.

172   His nickname was "Dr. No": Patrick Laurence, "Dr. No Baits De Klerk," *Financial Review*, March 13, 1992. Available at https://www.afr.com/poli tics/dr-no-baits-de-klerk-19920313-k4u5a, accessed December 21, 2022.

173   the Mandela who was being vilified onstage was speaking twelve kilometers away: "Pro-Apartheid Rally Denounces De Klerk," *Greensboro News & Record*, May 27, 1990. Available at https://greensboro.com/pro-apartheid-rally-de nounces-de-klerk/article_07a4cead-3590-5ca3-b0e4-405226309af9.html, accessed December 21, 2022.

173   Back among the right-wingers, Derby-Lewis: Clive Derby-Lewis statement on Afrikaner Volksparty website. Available at http://www.afrikanervolk sparty.org/index.php/media/160-artikels/4907-clive-derby-lewis-parole -refusal-prejudice.html, accessed December 21, 2022.

10 A.M.

174   The day started off peacefully enough in Cape Town: "Hani Chaos— Demos Blamed, "*Saturday Star*, July 10, 1993.

174   "It has no beginning and no end, this crowd": "An Anger That Couldn't Be Controlled," *Weekly Mail*, April 16, 1993.

174   Tutu's famous church was overwhelmed: "South Africa Riots Lead to 7 Deaths; Tensions Run High," *New York Times*, April 15, 1993.

175   In all these skirmishes, ANC marshals tried to stop looters: "Youth Turn to Looting as Hani March Ends in Chaos," *Business Day*, April 15, 1993.

175   ANC National Executive Committee member Trevor Manuel tried, but he was punched: "S. Africa Protest of Hani Slaying Turns Violent," *Los Angeles Times*, April 15, 1993.

11 A.M.

175   The previous day Mandela had been chided: Stengel, private diary.

175   By the time his motorcade arrived at Soweto's: "War and Peace," *Sowetan*, April 15, 1993.

177   "I understand your anger": "Mandela's Plea to Youths," *Sowetan*, April 15, 1993.

2 P.M.

177   Tokyo Sexwale was at Jabulani alongside Carl Niehaus: Interview with Carl Niehaus. The narrative that follows is culled from press reports quoted

above and published at the time, the admirable press releases and other work of the ANC in Soweto and in the Joburg suburb of Yeoville in the 1990s to seek justice for the victims, and the Congress of SA Trade Unions' attempts to remember and honor Sam Tambani.

177   An ANC local leader and trade unionist, Sam Tambani: Statement by COSATU, ANC-SACP PWV regions, and National Union of Mineworkers (April 22, 1993); corroborated in the documentary *People Under Fire: A Shooting in Soweto*, directed by Mandla Smit. Also see "S. Africa Protest of Hani Slaying Turns Violent," *Los Angeles Times*, April 15, 1993, and Patti Waldmeir, *Anatomy of a Miracle* (London: Viking, 1997), 224.

2 P.M.

179   Ali's bus had returned from Mitchells Plain early: "Ali Visits Hani Widow," *Sunday Times*, April 18, 1993.

2 P.M.

181   Tensions were high by the time the crowd: "Police Deployed at Transkei Resorts," *Daily Dispatch*, April 16, 1993.

181   The man did not appear: "Angry Mob Turns on Reporters at Embassy," *Daily Dispatch*, April 16, 1993.

182   personnel at the embassy were escorted home and the government released a statement saying spouses and children: "Nog Transkeise polisiemanne by vakansieoorde ontplooi" (More Transkei police deployed at holiday resorts), *Beeld*, April 16, 1993.

2 P.M.

182   Nelson Mandela was hungry: Richard Stengel, private diary.

2 P.M.

184   Peter Mokaba was back trying to talk down not just his angry supporters but provocative white extremists: "Hani's Death Widens Gulf," *Saturday Star*, April 17, 1993.

2 P.M.

185   Janusz Waluś had refused to cooperate with the police for three days: "Police Cannot Get Hani Murder Suspect to Talk," *Business Day*, April 14, 1993. Also interviews with Sexwale and Phosa.

185   The SA Police weren't in the habit of handling suspects gently: See

exhibition of "Detention without trial in John Vorster Square" at https://artsandculture.google.com/story/8AXhQ-3oNAMA8A?hl=en, accessed December 21, 2022.

185   renowned pathologist Dr. Jonathan Gluckman released: "Pathologist Who Alleged Police Murders Gets Death Threats," United Press International, July 27, 1992. Available at https://www.upi.com/Archives/1992/07/27/Pathologist-who-alleged-police-murders-gets-death-threats/9974712209600/, accessed December 21, 2022.

185   So he called a man he could trust: "Ex-Cop Says He Had No Choice But to Conceal Bopape's Death," SA Press Association, June 2, 1998. Available at https://www.justice.gov.za/trc/media/1998/9806/s980602b.htm, accessed December 21, 2022.

186   Deetlefs was a particularly nasty piece of work: "We Covered Up Assault, Torture of Detainees - Deetlefs," SA Broadcasting Corporation News, February 18, 2020. Available at https://www.sabcnews.com/sabcnews/we-covered-up-assault-torture-of-prisoners-deetlefs/, accessed November 17, 2022.

186   Deetlefs was known to begin his torture session by saying: "Ebrahim Ismail Ebrahim: A Gentle Revolutionary," Ahmed Kathrada Foundation. Available at https://www.sahistory.org.za/sites/default/files/archive-files/ebrahim_ismail_ebrahim_book_pdf.pdf, accessed December 21, 2022.

186   One of Deetlefs's most notorious cases was: "Neil Aggett Inquest: Nicholas Deetlefs to Face Prosecution," *Star*, February 21, 2020. Available at https://www.iol.co.za/news/politics/neil-aggett-inquest-nicholas-deetlefs-to-face-prosecution-43119441, accessed December 21, 2022.

2 P.M.

187   There were seven cabinet ministers in the room: Minutes of the State Security Council, April 14, 1993. Provided to author by anonymous source. All documents and audio related to this book will be donated by the author to the Nelson Mandela Centre of Memory and Dialogue, 107 Central Street, Houghton Estate, Johannesburg, 2001, South Africa.

187   Launched in 1972 to "advise the government": Context and quotes drawn from Kenneth Grundy, *The Militarisation of South African Society* (Oxford University Press, 1986). Conclusions are author's.

188   "shorten the list of politically sensitive individuals": "Apartheid-Era Murder of Sleeping Teenagers Returns to Haunt De Klerk," *Guardian*, August 5, 2007. Available at https://www.theguardian.com/world/2007/aug/06/southafrica.topstories3, accessed December 21, 2022.

188   De Klerk had dismantled the "state security management system": "South Africa to Overhaul Security Net," William Claiborne, *Washington Post*, November 29, 1989. Available at https://www.washingtonpost.com /archive/politics/1989/11/29/south-africa-to-overhaul-security-net/06 da88a7-a57c-43b4-b505-3f5a54aada34/, accessed December 21, 2022.

188   There was Adriaan Vlok—the only man in the room: Minutes of ANC Extended National Executive Committee Meeting, May 17, 1991. Available at https://omalley.nelsonmandela.org/omalley/cis/omalley/OMal leyWeb/03lv03445/04lv04015/05lv04051/06lv04064/07lv04066.htm, accessed December 21, 2022.

189   Vlok was, ironically, later to be the only member of apartheid's leaders to approach: Eve Fairbanks, "'I Have Sinned Against the Lord and Against You! Will You Forgive Me?'" *New Republic*, June 19, 2014. Available at https://newrepublic.com/article/118135/adriaan-vlok-ex-apartheid -leader-washes-feet-and-seeks-redemption, accessed December 21, 2022.

189   The hard-smoking, hard-drinking Kriel: "Obituary: Hernus Kriel, Nat police minister," Chris Barron, *Sunday Times*, July 12, 2015. Available at https://www.timeslive.co.za/sunday-times/opinion-and-analysis/2015 -07-12-obituary-hernus-kriel-hardline-nat-police-minister/, accessed December 21, 2022.

190   "Kobie" Coetsee, the former prisons minister: Nelson Mandela, *Long Walk to Freedom* (London: Abacus, 1994), 624.

190   Danie Schutte, the minister of home affairs: "Four White Men and Truth," *Mail & Guardian*, May 19, 1995. Available at https://mg.co.za /article/1995-05-19-four-white-men-and-truth/, accessed December 21, 2022.

191   APLA commander Sabelo Phama had reportedly been spotted: "APLA Chief Bolts Home After TV Talk," *Sunday Times*, April 11, 1993.

191   De Klerk ordered that the South African army be positioned at the border with the Transkei: SSC Minutes, April 14, 1993.

192   Delport, said future marches would have to adhere to strict legal requirements: "Urgent New Moves in Government Drive for Peace," *Daily Dispatch*, April 16, 1993.

193   At least forty tons of apartheid government files are estimated to have been destroyed by the National Intelligence Service: "Apartheid's History in Shreds," *Mail & Guardian*, October 23, 1998. Available at https://mg.co .za/article/1998-10-23-apartheids-history-in-shreds/, accessed December 21, 2022.

194   The meeting's other big decision was to mandate Roelf Meyer: This detail is not in the minutes but is revealed by De Klerk in *The Last Trek*, where he says this was the government's "carrot" to the ANC (p. 276).

194   The ANC had demanded such a council for years: "Presidency Proposal Rejected by Mandela," David B. Ottaway, *Washington Post*, April 26, 1992. Available at https://www.washingtonpost.com/archive/politics /1992/04/26/presidency-proposal-rejected-by-mandela/6ad6f38d -0700-479a-94e9-aded945586f6/, accessed December 21, 2022.

195   "the first grip on state power for the extra-parliamentary liberation movements": "Transitional Executive Council" by Padraig O'Malley at https:// omalley.nelsonmandela.org/omalley/index.php/site/q/03lv02424 /04lv02730/05lv03162.htm, accessed December 21, 2022.

8 P.M.

196   De Klerk was seething: F. W. de Klerk, *The Last Trek—A New Beginning: The Autobiography* (London: Macmillan, 1998), 276.

9 P.M.

197   Between 90 and 100 percent of employees: "Wegbly aksie 'een van die grootstes nog'" (Stayaway "one of the biggest yet"), *Beeld*, April 15, 1993.

198   Yet the toll was high: "South African Violence Leaves at Least 8 Dead," *Washington Post*, April 15, 1993.

MIDNIGHT

199   A return to talks was inevitable, he said: Mark Gevisser, *Thabo Mbeki: The Dream Deferred* (Johannesburg: Jonathan Ball Publishers, 2007), 610.

199   "The idea of negotiations as the only option": Willie Esterhuyse, *Endgame: Secret Talks and the End of Apartheid* (Cape Town: Tafelberg, 2012), 147.

199   "The apartheid regime could not defeat us": "Why Did it Take a Prisoner to Bring Down Apartheid?," Anita Powell, VOA News, April 24, 2014. Available at https://www.voanews.com/a/years-on-why-did-it-take-a-prisoner -to-bring-down-apartheid/1899993.html, accessed December 21, 2022.

THURSDAY, APRIL 15, 1993
8 A.M.

201   Deetlefs and his sidekick, Warrant Officer Andre Beetge, were friendly: TRC Amnesty Hearing: Janusz Waluś, November 24, 1997, Pretoria. The

transcripts have no page numbers but discussion can be found at page 12 of 158 in the document pasted into MS Word. Available online at https:// www.justice.gov.za/trc/amntrans/pta/2derby1.htm, accessed December 21, 2022.

204   "typical South American junta": "A New Colonialism is Being Fostered: Interview with Tienie Groenewald," *Executive Intelligence Review*, July 16, 1993.

204   The apartheid security network was full of stories about the use of chemical weapons: "Plague War: What Happened in South Africa?," PBS, *Frontline*. Available at https://www.pbs.org/wgbh/pages/frontline/shows/plague /sa/. To read about sodium thiopental, visit the BBC's write-up here: "Can a Drug Make You Tell the Truth?," BBC, October 3, 2013, at https://www .bbc.com/news/magazine-24371140, accessed December 21, 2022.

8 A.M.

206   Members of the AWB that Waluś belonged to had fired guns: *Covert Action Magazine*, summer 1993. Available at https://covertactionmagazine.com /wp-content/uploads/2020/01/CAQ45-1993-2.pdf), accessed December 21, 2022.

206   "Our post box is overfilling": "Assassination in South Africa Galvanizes Right-Wing Whites," Scott Kraft, *Los Angeles Times*, April 17, 1993. Available at https://www.latimes.com/archives/la-xpm-1993-04-17-mn-240 12-story.html, accessed December 21, 2022.

206   Sam Shilowa believes that the danger of the moment: Author interview with Mbhazima Shilowa, July 14, 2021.

9 A.M.

207   The meeting, described as "steamy": "Door Opens for Militants to Take Leadership in Mass Mobilisation," *Southscan*, April 20, 1990.

9 A.M.

208   Roelf Meyer and Cyril Ramaphosa met that morning: "Clash leaves peace process tottering," *EP Herald*, April 16, 1993.

209   "in the end it is not in the interests of the democratic forces in this country for De Klerk to lose power": Author interview with Mbhazima Shilowa, July 14, 2021.

9 P.M.

209 "These are the reflexes of a P. W. Botha": ANC–SA Communist Party–Congress of SA Trade Unions Alliance press statement, April 16, 1993.

210 Ramaphosa, drawing on the tactics he had learned: Interviewee preferred to not name Ramaphosa. This sentiment accords with the view Ramaphosa expressed in "Hooked on Peace by Heir Apparent," *Observer*, April 24, 1994, 22.

210 "We pushed it to the precipice": Ibid.

211 "We are radicals. We are a radical organization": "ANC verhard sy houding oor massa-aksie" (ANC adopts tougher stance on mass action), *Beeld*, April 17, 1993.

211 "If the government issued regulations meant to prevent the alliance's supporters": Ibid.

FRIDAY, APRIL 16, 1993
AFTERNOON

214 Mandela was the ANC's most effective fundraiser: "Mandela Tour Receipts Have Yet to Leave the US," Lynne Duke, *Washington Post*, December 9, 1990. Available at https://www.washingtonpost.com/archive/politics/1990/12/09/mandela-tour-receipts-have-yet-to-leave-us/fcca2cf6-9eb5-4a85-b020-326fe45bbeed/, accessed December 21, 2022.

215 He didn't like it: According to Raymond Suttner (email correspondence).

215 The country was shutting down: "Rand Show to Close Early for Hani's Funeral," *Business Day*, April 16, 1993.

215 Violence linked to, or sparked by, anger at Hani's murder: "More Killings Countrywide Lift Toll to 28," *Star*, April 16, 1993.

215 The funeral would be a big affair: "Hani Burial Live on TV," and "Special Trains Laid On," *Saturday Star*, April 17, 1993.

216 The hawkish law and order minister, Hernus Kriel, was back: "ANC radikale wil situasie om Hani uitbuit" (ANC radicals want to exploit Hani situation), *Beeld*, April 19, 1993.

11 P.M.

217 The delegates and leaders of the Wits-Vaal Regional Peace Secretariat had worked through the night: Author interview with Peter Harris, Zoom, March 16, 2022.

218 That handshake nearly didn't happen: Email interview with Zirk Gouws.

218   the police would step back and would "under-police" the events of the next
        few days: "Joburg Steeled for Mass March," *Saturday Star*, April 17, 1993.

SATURDAY, APRIL 17, 1993
11 A.M.

221   Muhammad Ali was back in Johannesburg: "Ali Parade Postponed," *Satur-
        day Star*, April 17, 1993.

221   Ali had a message of peace: "Ali Visits Hani Widow," *Sunday Times*, April 18,
        1993.

2 P.M.

222   The militant talk began to ratchet up again: "Winnie verklaar nou oorlog
        teen Nelson" (Winnie declares war against Nelson), *Rapport*, April 18, 1993,
        and "Winnie Tells Youth to Take Over," *Sunday Times*, April 18, 1993.

222   Kriel accused the ANC of making "political propaganda" out of Hani's
        death: "ANC radikale wil situasie om Hani uitbuit" (ANC radicals want to
        exploit Hani situation), *Beeld*, April 19, 1993.

6 P.M.

222   They came for Clive Derby-Lewis as the sun was setting: "Toe val Derby-
        Lewis flou" (Derby-Lewis then faints), *Vrye Weekblad*, October 28, 1993.

224   treated badly by the police: Testimony at the TRC, which unraveled under
        questioning by the Hani family lawyer, George Bizos.

224   "I want to send out a message": *State v. Waluś and Another* (585/93,586/93)
        [1994] ZASCA 189 (November 30, 1994), South Africa Supreme Court of
        Appeal. Available at http://www.saflii.org/cgi-bin/disp.pl?file=za/cases
        /ZASCA/1994/189.html&query=janusz%20walus, accessed May 19, 2022.

226   Kemp . . . was reportedly a former member of the SA Police and the Secu-
        rity Branch: "Hani Conspirator Was Intelligence Man," *Mail & Guardian*,
        February 14, 1994. Available at https://mg.co.za/article/1997-02-14-hani
        -conspirator-was-intelligence-man/, accessed December 21, 2022.

226   SAA flight 232 took off from Johannesburg: Janet Smith and Beauregard
        Tromp, *Hani: A Life Too Short* (Johannesburg: Jonathan Ball Publishers,
        2007), 255. This link was first uncovered by the *Mail & Guardian*'s Ste-
        faans Brümmer in 1997 after Kemp went around to UK newspapers hawk-
        ing the story of his participation in the Hani affair. The full write-up is in
        "Hani's Flight of 'Coincidence,'" *Mail & Guardian*, February 21, 1997.

226   Then, later, she admitted she lied at the trial: Gaye admitted to lying in her

testimony at the TRC amnesty hearings of her husband and Waluś, where she said: "I prevaricated on that matter." Transcript of Truth and Reconciliation Commission Amnesty hearing, December 1, 1997. Available at https:// omalley.nelsonmandela.org/omalley/index.php/site/q/03lv02167/04lv0 2264/05lv02267/06lv02268/07lv02273.htm, accessed July 19, 2022.

229   One of Gaye's best friends was Craig Kotze: "Apartheid's Fanatic in a Polka-Dot Frock: John Carlin Investigates What Lies Behind the English-Style Respectability Exuded by Some of South Africa's Far-Right," *Independent*, May 2, 1993. Available at https://www.independent.co.uk/news /world/apartheid-s-fanatic-polka-dot-frock-john-carlin-investigates-what -lies-behind-english-style-respectability-exuded-some-south-africa-s-far -right-2320389.html, accessed January 12, 2021.

229   The big mystery of the case is that the arrest of Derby-Lewis: Evelyn Groenink, *Incorruptible: The Story of the Murders of Dulcie September, Anton Lubowski and Chris Hani* (self-published, 2018), 289–90.

230   Tellingly, in 2016, Gaye boasted to Hani's daughter Lindiwe: "What Daddy's Killers Said," *News24*, March 18, 2017. Available at https://www .news24.com/News24/what-daddys-killers-said-20170318, accessed December 21, 2022.

231   "a waste of time and people's taxes": "Talking to Chris," *Sunday Times*, April 22, 1993.

231   "In that court we have the killers, not the plotters": "ANC Will Not Close its Files on Assassinations," *Business Day*, June 25, 1993.

231   In 2001, Steve Tshwete, the safety and security minister: "ANC Veterans Accused of Plot to Harm Mbeki," Chris McGreal, *Guardian*, April 25, 2001. Available at https://www.theguardian.com/world/2001/apr/26/chrismc greal, accessed December 21, 2022.

233   "You can choose to believe Hani's murder was just the work of a lone Polish immigrant": "Chris Hani's Assassination Had Wider Contexts and Consequences," Jeremy Cronin, *Politicsweb*, April 15, 2019. Available at https:// www.politicsweb.co.za/opinion/chris-hanis-assassination-had-wider -context-and-co, accessed December 21, 2022.

SUNDAY, APRIL 18, 1993
1–8 P.M.

235   The public broadcaster had undertaken to air most of it live: "ANC Signs March Pact," *The Argus*, April 17, 1993.

235   it was "unbearable": "Moving, in More Ways Than One," *Star*, April 20, 1993.

236 While MK combatants standing at attention nearby cried: "A Daughter Mourns," *The Argus*, April 19, 1993.

236 The stadium was festooned with the red flags of the Congress of SA Trade Unions: "Tears for Chris," *Sowetan*, April 19, 1993.

236 Mandela's cavalcade entered the stadium at 6:15 p.m.: "Thousands Gather to Mourn Hani," *Business Day*, April 19, 1993.

6 P.M.

237 "If we are all dead by the end of today there will be only 100 blacks left": The gathering of armed vigilantes in Elspark and elsewhere in the country was covered in numerous publications. Some of these quotes were collated from the *Sunday Times* ("People Brace Themselves for Burial Crowds," April 18, 1993), *Daily Dispatch* ("For Many, the Past Improved on the Future," April 20, 1993), *Star*, and many other local and international publications.

237 "Most people here are peace-loving people": "80,000 Mourners, 21-Gun Salute Bid Farewell to Apartheid Foe," *Los Angeles Times*, April 20, 1993. Available at https://www.latimes.com/archives/la-xpm-1993-04-20-mn -25048-story.html, accessed November 17, 2022.

9 P.M.

238 Outside the stadium, death was still stalking: Truth Commission Final Report, vol. 3, chap. 6. Available at https://sabctrc.saha.org.za/reports /volume3/chapter6/subsection88.htm, accessed December 21, 2022.

11 P.M.

239 By midnight the stadium was shaking: "Moving, In More Ways Than One," *Star*, April 20, 1993.

239 "I feel that it will take a miracle to survive this crisis": Peter Harris, *Birth: The Conspiracy to Stop the '94 Elections* (Cape Town: Penguin Random House South Africa, 2011), 23.

MIDNIGHT

240 The firebrand Gwala stood up to speak: The Gwala and Holomisa speeches were carried by one newspaper, the *Citizen*, April 19, 1993, which ran a long SA Press Association report, and the quotes are corroborated in Richard Stengel's private diary. Other, slight coverage in the *Star*: "Mandela Greeted with Stomping Cheers," April 20, 1993; "An Army for Democracy," April 20, 1993.

MONDAY, APRIL 19, 1993
9 A.M.

243 the funeral matched the previous Wednesday for the biggest work stayaway: "Business Counts Cost of Protest," SA Press Association, April 20, 1993.

244 Archbishop Desmond Tutu was the preacher that day: John Allen, *Rabble-Rouser for Peace: The Authorised Biography of Desmond Tutu* (New York and London: Random House, 2006), 334.

245 Joe Slovo gave one of the most moving tributes: "An Army For Democracy," *Star*, April 20, 1993.

245 Mandela's address started with the personal: Address by ANC President Nelson R. Mandela at the funeral of Martin Chris Hani, FNB Stadium, Soweto, April 19, 1993. The funeral and speech can be viewed in full at https://reuters.screenocean.com/record/895586, accessed December 21, 2022.

245 To this day, this ideal of Hani still grips South Africa: "Chris Hani Would Not Be Proud of South Africa Today," *Star*, April 11, 2021. Available at https://www.iol.co.za/news/opinion/chris-hani-would-not-be-proud-of -sa-today-83568455-e582-46f7-ba09-9cb4c73e9380, accessed December 21, 2022.

248 This is where the agreement signed by Mbeki, Calitz, and Harris: "Monitors Keep Violence in Check," *Business Day*, April 20, 1993.

249 Then an honor guard raised its guns: "Assassinated Black Militant, a Communist, is Buried Next to White Neighborhood," Scott Kraft, *Los Angeles Times*, April 20, 1993. Available at https://www.latimes.com/archives/la -xpm-1993-04-20-mn-25048-story.html, accessed December 21, 2022.

TUESDAY TO THURSDAY, APRIL 20–22, 1993
DAWN, APRIL 20, 1993

254 "At the time of Chris's death, prophets of doom predicted": Mandela speech, April 14, 1994, Chris Hani tombstone unveiling.

254 No other single event proved so conclusively: Patti Waldmeir, *Anatomy of a Miracle* (London: Viking, 1997), 224.

9 A.M., APRIL 20, 1993

256 "As we seek to rise above the human frailties": F. W. de Klerk speech to Parliament, April 20, 1993.

10 A.M.

256   "I wanted to say so many things to him": Howard L. Bingham, *Muhammad Ali: A Thirty-Year Journey* (New York: Simon & Schuster, 1993).

MORNING, APRIL 21, 1993

257   "Equal to the very best in the world": "Chris Hani: The State's Case," *Sunday Star*, June 20, 1993.

257   had done a "phenomenal" job: "Two Convicted in South African Assassination," Paul Taylor, *Washington Post*, October 15, 1993. Available at https://www.washingtonpost.com/archive/politics/1993/10/15/2-convicted-in-s-african-assassination/5bda7248-f2a8-4587-b76f-9dac68e61c9e/, accessed December 21, 2022.

9 A.M.

257   The previous week had taken a heavy toll on the nation: Alliance press statement, April 20, 1993. Available at http://www.historicalpapers.wits.ac.za/inventories/inv_pdfo/AG2543/AG2543-2-2-34-01-jpeg.pdf, accessed December 21, 2022.

THURSDAY, JUNE 3, 1993, AND TUESDAY, DECEMBER 7, 1993

259   "For me, the real victory": "The Story of Chris Hani's Assassination and Its Aftermath," Constitution Hill. Archive material available at https://ourconstitution.constitutionhill.org.za/the-assassination-of-chris-hani/, accessed December 21, 2022.

10 A.M., DECEMBER 7, 1993

260   He was, to use his own words, "ecstatic": "Multi-Racial Council Begins South Africa Oversight Role," Bob Drogin, *Los Angeles Times*, December 8, 1993. Available at https://www.latimes.com/archives/la-xpm-1993-12-08-mn-65100-story.html, accessed December 21, 2022.

263   "the one and only occasion that I would ever see Nelson lose control": George Bizos, *65 Years of Friendship* (Johannesburg: Umuzi, 2017), 214.

SELECT BIBLIOGRAPHY

LEGAL PROCEEDINGS

State v. Waluś and Others (70/93) [1993] ZAGPHC 1 (October 14, 1993), the Supreme Court of South Africa (Witwatersrand Local Division). Available at http://www.saflii.org/cgi-bin/disp.pl?file=za/cases/ZAGPHC /1993/1.html&query=Janusz%20Walus, accessed May 19, 2022.

State v. Waluś and Another (585/93,586/93) [1994] ZASCA 189 (November 30, 1994), South Africa Supreme Court of Appeal. Available at http://www.saflii.org/cgi-bin/disp.pl?file=za/cases/ZASCA/1994/189 .html&query=janusz%20walus, accessed May 19, 2022.

Truth and Reconciliation Commission of South Africa Report, Cape Town, the Commission. Available at https://www.justice.gov.za/trc/re port, accessed May 19, 2022.

TRC 1998 AMNESTY HEARING TRANSCRIPTS

A huge amount of the thoughts, emotions, and intentions of the protagonists in this book are drawn from their testimony at the TRC. The transcripts, which run to hundreds of thousands of words, can be accessed online at https://www.justice.gov.za/trc/amntrans/am1998.htm. The testimonies of the Clive Derby-Lewis circle and those of the Phumelele Hermans circle can be accessed using this site. Among the key transcripts are Clive Derby-Lewis's amnesty hearing (accessed May 19, 2022). An alternative to the TRC site is the Nelson Mandela Foundation's O'Malley archives, which carry numerous resources and transcripts from the TRC, such as the testimony of Janusz Waluś. Available at https://omalley.nelson mandela.org/omalley/index.php/site/q/03lv02167/04lv02264/05lv022 67/06lv02268/07lv02272.htm.

Allen, John. *Rabble-Rouser for Peace: The Authorised Biography of Desmond Tutu.* New York and London: Random House, 2006.

Andrews, Penelope, and Stephen Ellmann, eds. *The Post-Apartheid Constitutions: Perspectives on South Africa's Basic Law.* Johannesburg: Wits University Press, 2001.

Barnard, Niël, with Tobie Wiese. *Peaceful Revolution: Inside the War Room at the Negotiations.* Cape Town: Tafelberg Publishers, 2017.

———. *Secret Revolution: Memoirs of a Spy Boss.* Cape Town: Tafelberg, 2015.

Bizos, George. *65 Years of Friendship.* Johannesburg: Umuzi, 2017.

Butler, Anthony. *Cyril Ramaphosa.* Johannesburg: Jacana Media, 2007.

Carlin, John. *Playing the Enemy: Nelson Mandela and the Game That Made a Nation.* London: Atlantic, 2008.

De Klerk, F. W. *The Last Trek—A New Beginning: The Autobiography.* London: Macmillan, 1998.

Esterhuyse, Willie. *Endgame: Secret Talks and the End of Apartheid.* Cape Town: Tafelberg, 2012.

Fowlds, Grant, and Graham Spence. *Saving the Last Rhinos: The Life of a Frontline Conservationist.* New York: Pegasus Books, 2019.

Gevisser, Mark. *Thabo Mbeki: The Dream Deferred.* Johannesburg: Jonathan Ball Publishers, 2007.

Groenink, Evelyn. *Incorruptible: The Story of the Murders of Dulcie September, Anton Lubowski and Chris Hani.* Self-published, 2018.

Gumede, William Mervin. *Thabo Mbeki and the Battle for the Soul of the ANC.* Cape Town: Struik Publishers, 2005.

Harris, Peter. *Birth: The Conspiracy to Stop the '94 Elections.* Johannesburg: Penguin Random House South Africa, 2011.

Harrison, David. *The White Tribe of Africa: South Africa in Perspective.* Los Angeles: University of California Press, 1981.

Hartley, Ray. *Ramaphosa: The Man Who Would Be King.* Johannesburg: Jonathan Ball Publishers, 2017.

Johnson, Shaun. *Strange Days Indeed: South Africa from Insurrection to Post-Election.* London: Transworld Publishers, 1993.

Macmillan, Hugh. "After Wankie: The 'Hani Memorandum' and Its Repercussions at Morogoro and on the ANC in Zambia, 1968–71," paper presented to the Workshop on Liberation Struggles in Southern Africa, University of Cape Town, 2008.

———. *Chris Hani.* Johannesburg: Jacana Media, 2014.

Mali, Themba. *Chris Hani: The Sun That Set Before Dawn*. Johannesburg: SACHED Trust, 1993.

Mandela, Nelson. *Conversations with Myself*. London: Macmillan, 2010.

———. *Long Walk to Freedom*. London: Little, Brown, 1994.

Mandela, Nelson, and Mandla Langa. *Dare Not Linger: The Presidential Years*. London: Macmillan, 2017.

Meredith, Martin. *Mandela: A Biography*. London: Public Affairs, 1997.

Naki, Eric. *Bantu Holomisa: The Game Changer*. Johannesburg: Picador Africa, 2017.

Niehaus, Carl. *Fighting for Hope*. Cape Town: Human & Rousseau, 1993.

Nqakula, Charles. *The People's War: Reflections of an ANC Cadre*. Johannesburg: Mutloatse Arts Heritage Trust, 2017.

O'Malley, Padraig. *Shades of Difference: Mac Maharaj and the Struggle for South Africa*. London: Viking, 2007.

Papenfus, Theresa. *Pik Botha and His Times*. Pretoria: Litera Publications, 2010.

Sampson, Anthony. *Mandela: The Authorised Biography*. London: HarperPress, 1999.

Sisulu, Elinor. *Walter and Albertina Sisulu: In Our Lifetime*. Cape Town: David Philip, 2002.

Smith, Janet, and Beauregard Tromp. *Hani: A Life Too Short*. Johannesburg: Jonathan Ball Publishers, 2007.

Stengel, Richard. *Mandela's Way: Lessons on Life*. London: Virgin Books, 2010.

———. Unpublished Private Diary, April 9, 1993, to April 19, 1993.

Waldmeir, Patti. *Anatomy of a Miracle*. London: Viking, 1997.

Van Wyk, Barry. "The Balance of Power and the Transition to Democracy in South Africa." Department of Historical and Heritage Studies, University of Pretoria, 2005.

Zagacki, Kenneth S. "Rhetoric, Dialogue, and Performance in Nelson Mandela's 'Televised Address on the Assassination of Chris Hani.'" *Rhetoric and Public Affairs* 6, no. 4 (Winter 2003): 709–735.

PHOTO CREDITS

INDEX

Adams, Erica, 54
African National Congress (ANC), xiii
　actions organized by, 107–8, 117, 133–34, 140,
　　145, 154–55
　and Boipatong Massacre, xv, 39, 66–67, 86–87,
　　147
　in Cape Town, 144, 146, 174–75, 179, 180, 250
　Kobie Coetsee and, 270
　day of mourning announced by, 169
　F. W. de Klerk and, 55, 70, 122, 155, 164, 189,
　　192, 196, 213, 246
　and Easter church services, 100
　as exile organization, 69, 104
　at FNB Stadium, 236, 239–41, 244, 246, 249
　fundraising by, 214
　Fundisile Guleni and, 84
　Mondli Gungubele and, 38, 111, 129
　Harry Gwala and, 101, 102, 129–30, 271
　Chris Hani and, 2, 17, 18, 21–28, 30, 31, 39, 57,
　　69, 78, 112, 131
　Peter Harris and, 50
　Phumele Civilian Hermans and, 114–15
　Bantu Holomisa and, 61–63, 79, 80, 118, 128,
　　190–91, 269
　and IFP, 40, 93, 112
　Hernus Kriel and, 189, 190, 216, 218, 219, 222
　as legitimate political party, 139, 225
　Mac Maharaj and, 82
　Winnie Mandela and, 137–38
　and Mandela's address to the nation, 156–60
　Gill Marcus and, 36, 156
　Barbara Masekela and, 10
　mass support for, 106
　Thabo Mbeki and, 199, 217
　Peter Mokaba and, 102, 130–31, 222
　Carl Niehaus and, 76, 166–67, 177, 271–72
　Julius Nyerere and, 104
　and Operation Katzen, 119
　and PAC, 27–28
　Mathews Phosa and, 193, 200, 203

pro-apartheid extremists and, 141, 145, 172,
　173, 185–86, 204, 205, 230, 261
　Cyril Ramaphosa and, 87, 115, 198, 208–11,
　　236, 259
　and SACP, 114, 172, 218, 232–33
　and Security Branch, 202–3
　security measures of, 138, 153
　and Dulcie September murder, 105, 232, 246
　Tokyo Sexwale and, 38–39, 57, 134, 143, 185,
　　260, 272
　Sam Shilowa and, 207
　Walter Sisulu and, 11, 57, 109, 110
　Sam Tabani and, 177–78
　Oliver Tambo and, 11, 221–22, 257
　in Transkei, 181–82
　unbanning of, 3, 4, 25, 53, 83, 86
　and Waluś trial, 140–42
　Tony Yengeni and, 103
　Jacob Zuma and, 231
　see also ANC Youth League; MK (Umkhonto
　　we Sizwe, Spear of the Nation); National
　　Executive Committee (NEC)
Afrikaanse Protestantse Kerk, 43
Afrikaner Resistance Movement, see Afrikaner
　Weerstandsbeweging
Afrikaner Volksfront (AVF), 122
Afrikaner Weerstandsbeweging (AWB, Afrikaner
　Resistance Movement), xiii, 45, 63, 78, 80,
　113, 114, 122, 125–29, 140–42, 184, 206,
　237–38, 253, 266
Agenda (television program), 121
Aggett, Neil, 186–87, 270
Alexandra township, 10
Ali, Muhammad, xi, 58–60, 146, 179–80, 221–22,
　256–57
Amnesty Committee (TRC), 225
Amnesty International, 24
ANC Youth League, 83, 103, 179, 184–85,
　222
Anglo-Boer War, 25

Angola, 23, 24, 164–65, 190, 203
anthrax, 205
antiapartheid movement, 3–5, 12–15, 21, 22, 24–25, 42, 49–50, 60, 69, 84, 86, 102, 104–6, 165, 179, 206, 231–32, 237, 263
apartheid system, 3–5, 9, 12–15, 26, 29, 44, 51, 53, 55–56, 60–63, 104, 134, 145, 173, 188–90, 193, 225, 262–63
Apex, 98
APLA, see Azanian People's Liberation Army
Appeal Court of South Africa, 224
Asvat, Abu Baker, 106
Auckland Park, 90
Audience Ratings (ARs), 89
AVF, see Afrikaner Volksfront
AWB, see Afrikaner Weerstandsbeweging
Ayob, Ismail, 137
Azanian People's Liberation Army (APLA), xiv, 28, 63, 64, 112, 119, 191
Azanian People's Organisation, 87, 191

Baker, Herbert, 188
Barnard, Ferdi, 232
Barnard, Niël, 40–41, 65, 105–6, 190, 193, 270
Basotho people, 61
Bedfordview, 42
Beeld (newspaper), 126, 127, 171
Beetge, Andre, 201, 202, 217
Being Chris Hani's Daughter (Lindiwe Hani), 230–31
Benoni, 38
Benoni Police Station, 82, 83, 97–99, 125–26, 140, 185–87, 201–5, 216–17, 223
Beyers, Andries, 42
Bisho Massacre, 39, 55, 71
Bizos, George, 90–91, 227, 262–63
"Black channel," 89
Blades, Jack, 180
Boesak, Allan, 175
Boipatong Massacre, xv, 39–40, 55, 66–67, 71, 86–87, 104, 116, 117, 147, 199
Boksburg, 13, 20, 29–30, 32–36, 38, 81–82, 125, 134, 169–70, 184, 191–92, 206–7, 221–22, 237–38
    see also Dawn Park
Boksburg Civic Centre, 184
Boksburg Lake, 30
Boksburg Magistrate Court, 139–43, 140, 160, 177
Boksburg Police Station, 81
Booi, Mkhululi, 181–82
Booyse, Wim J., 206
Bophuthatswana Defence Force, 266
Bophuthatswana homeland, 61, 62, 191, 266
Boraine, Alex, 225

Botha, P. W. (prime minister), x, 25, 42, 53, 119, 159, 187–88, 190, 197, 203, 209, 260
Botha, Pik (minister of foreign affairs), 68, 82, 189–90
Botswana, 22
Brackenfell, 171
Branch Davidians, 9
British Commonwealth, 68
Brits, Dorne, 184
Brynard, Karin, 82
Buchenwald concentration camp, 80
Burgersdorp, 52
Business Day, 25, 157
Buthelezi, Mangosuthu, 47, 114, 267

Calitz, Koos, 217–18, 248, 254
Camerer, Sheila, 257
Canadian Broadcasting Corporation, 158
Cape High Court, 14
Cape Peninsula, 215
Cape Town, 5, 13, 17, 21, 22, 37, 41, 58, 67–70, 77, 78, 99, 103, 113, 133, 144, 146, 160, 161, 170–75, 179–80, 198, 207, 210, 223, 226–27, 250–51
Carlin, John, 76, 131
Carlton Hotel (Johannesburg), 182–83
CCV-TV, 78, 89
Chikane, Frank, 189
Chile, 68
cholera, 205
Christian Brothers College, 41
Cieniuch, Stanisław, 68
Ciskei homeland, xv, 39, 61, 119
Citizen, the, 44, 127–28, 226, 228, 230
Clarke, Edwin, 127, 226, 228
CODESA, see Convention for a Democratic South Africa
Coetsee, "Kobie," 190, 192, 232–33, 270
Coetzee, Dirk, 105
Coetzee, Gerrie, 59–60
Cofimvaba, 21, 75, 77
"colored" South Africans, 42, 52, 54, 89, 134, 179
Congress of South African Trade Unions (COSATU), xiii, 109, 207, 210, 211, 218, 236
Conservative Party (CP), xiii, xvi, 12, 17, 42–45, 53, 65, 70–71, 80, 87, 171, 173, 226, 230
Convention for a Democratic South Africa (CODESA), xiii, xv, 86
COSATU, see Congress of South African Trade Unions
CP, see Conservative Party
Cradock, 146
Craven, Danie, 150–51

Credo van 'n Afrikaner (Treurnicht), 172
Cronin, Jeremy, 232–33
Crossroads, 78
Cry, the Beloved Country (Paton), 73

Daily Dispatch, 119
D'Aubuisson, Roberto, 43
Davis, Gaye, 174
Dawn Park (Boksburg, Johannesburg), 2, 12–34, 37–41, 47–51, 56–58, 77, 80, 83, 85, 98, 100, 110, 120–21, 125, 131, 143, 184–85, 221, 269
Dearham, Sergeant, 32–34
Deetlefs, Nicolaas "Nic," x, 186–87, 201–5, 216–17, 229, 270
de Klerk, Barend, 52
de Klerk, Frederik Willem "F. W.," x
 and ANC "radicals," 211
 and apartheid system, 54
 Black anger toward, 206–7
 and Boipatong Massacre, 86–87
 and P. W. Botha, 24–25
 and Pik Botha, 189–90
 defeat of, at polls, 267, 270
 as deputy president, 271
 election of, 43
 family background, 51–54
 and Chris Hani, 25–26, 60, 65–66
 and Hani murder investigation, 144–45, 185
 and Bantu Holomisa, 62–64, 120, 128–29, 190–91
 and Hernus Kriel, 109, 189
 liberation organizations unbanned by, xv
 and Nelson Mandela, 65, 67, 70–73, 88, 115–16, 121–23, 193, 196, 197, 208, 209, 213, 246, 247, 262–63, 270
 and Winnie Mandela, 102
 and Mandela's address to the nation, 161
 and National Peace Accord, 47
 and negotiations process, 52–53, 62
 and news of Chris Hani's death, 55–56
 as Nobel laureate, 262
 and nuclear weapons, 55
 and Operation Katzen, 119
 and peace-making process, 3, 12, 199
 and peace-talks referendum, 30, 86, 143, 206
 and Johan Pretorius, 160
 and pro-apartheid extremists, 5, 140–41, 206
 reform process started by, 108
 residences of, 78
 rise to presidency, 25–26
 as role model, 6
 and Dulcie September murder, 105
 speech of, contemporaneous with Hani's funeral, 250, 255–56

 and State Security Council, 187–88, 192, 195, 196
 as target of pro-apartheid forces, 64, 176
 and Transitional Executive Council, 194–95, 261
 and Umkhonto we Sizwe, 103
 and unrest following Hani's murder, 154–55, 164, 167, 191–93, 215, 216, 218
 "unseating" of, by Mandela, 254
 and Adriaan Vlok, 189
de Klerk, Johannes Cornelis, 52
de Klerk, Marike, 51, 54
de Klerk, Willem, 54
Delport, Tertius, 190, 192
Democratic Party (South Africa), 43, 151
Department of Information (South African government), 44
Department of Information and Publicity (ANC), 36, 39
Department of Prisons, 141
Derby-Lewis, Clive, x, 12–14, 42–47, 53, 81, 125–27, 132, 171–73, 205, 222–31, 233–34, 237, 246, 257, 261, 268, 270–71
Derby-Lewis, Gabriella Maverna "Gaye," x, 13, 41, 44–47, 81, 110, 126, 127, 173–74, 223–31, 233, 261, 271
de Waal, J. H., 229
Dingane, King, 40
"Dingane Scenario," 40
Dishy, Les, 221
Dobsonville, 99
Drakensberg Mountains, 117
Duarte, Jessie, 75
du Plessis, Barend, 53
du Plessis, Tim, 82
du Preez, Max, 141
du Randt, Lionel, 46, 227–28
Durban, 58, 74, 79, 113, 114, 146, 179, 180, 246
Dutch Reformed Church, 43, 52, 100, 172
Du Toit, Constable, 35

Eastern Cape, 21, 48, 51–56, 77, 79, 84, 85, 114, 119, 144, 145, 147, 150, 180–81, 198, 246
 see also Port St. Johns; Qunu; Sabalele; Umtata
East Rand region and townships, 38, 48, 49, 111, 133, 162, 219
Ekurhuleni, 269
Elangeni Hotel, 146
Elliot (Khowa), 79
Eloff, Fritz, 224–25
El Salvador, 43
Elspark, 237, 253
Elspark Cemetery, 248–49
Esterhuyse, Willie, 199
European Community, 68

Federal Bureau of Investigation (FBI), 9
Felgate, Walter, 260
Financial Times, 90, 254
Finley, Ken, 238
First, Ruth, 14, 246
Flagstaff, 113–15, 152
FNB Stadium (Soweto), 215, 235–37, 239–41,
    243–50, 258
Fourie, Johan, 228–29
Fowlds, Grant, 150, 151
Frankel, Sidney, 116–17
Free State Homelands, 15

Galanakis, George, 181–82
Gallup International, 108
Gauteng province, 272
Gazankulu homeland, 61
Geldenhuys, Jannie, 119
Gere, Richard, 134
Gluckman, Jonathan, 185
Goldstone, Richard, 82
Goldstone Commission, 147
Goniwe, Matthew, 188, 246
Gouws, Zirk, 218, 219
Grahamstown, 75
Graser, Anton, 44, 45, 229
Grimbeek, Anton, 83
Groenewald, Jan, 229
Groenewald, Tienie, 122, 203–5, 229
Groenink, Evelyn, 148, 229, 230, 232
Grootboom, Noxolo, 37
Group Areas Act, 179
Guardian, 228
Guleni, Fundisile, 84, 85, 112–15, 151–54, 272
Gumede, Archie, 114
Gungubele, Mondli, ix, 18, 37–39, 47–50, 76, 85,
    87, 111, 129–32, 162, 216, 219, 249, 250,
    269
Gungubele, Rebecca "Queendy," 38, 49
Gwala, Harry, ix, 101–2, 129–30, 157, 236, 237,
    240, 247, 271

Haiti, 269
Hani, Chris, 2–3
    and ANC, 17, 18, 21–28, 31, 39, 57, 69, 78,
        112, 131, 138
    childhood and early career, 21–24
    and F. W. de Klerk, 25–26, 65
    demonization of, in Afrikaans press, 28–29
    disinformation campaign against, 64–65, 204
    as evocative figure in South African politics,
        267
    funeral of, 214–19, 235–41, 243–50, 256
    and Mondli Gungubele, 37–39, 48
    and Daan Harmse, 30–31

    as "hawk," 103, 107
    and Bantu Holomisa, 62, 63
    and Internal Security Act, 97
    and Nelson Mandela, 2–3, 11–12, 25–27, 38,
        109–10
    move to Dawn Park neighborhood, 29–30
    as peace advocate, 2–3, 27, 29
    premonitions of his own death, 128
    previous threats to life of, 109–10
    and Tokyo Sexwale, 143
    and Oliver Tambo, 57
    and Desmond Tutu, 26
    see also Hani assassination
Hani, Gilbert, 21, 22, 77, 78, 139, 157, 236
Hani, Limpho, 17, 31, 231, 236
Hani, Lindiwe, 17, 230–31, 233, 236
Hani, Martin Thembisile "Chris" (brother of
    Chris Hani), 14
Hani, Neo, 17, 18, 38, 236
Hani, Nomakhwezi, 17, 18, 20, 37, 39, 236
Hani, Nomayise Mary, 21, 77, 236
Hani, Victor, 77
Hani assassination, xvi, 2, 12–21
    Muhammad Ali and, 146, 179, 221–22, 257
    ANC and, 101, 105, 118–19, 133–34, 138, 195,
        206–8
    anticipated reaction to, 3
    AWB's response to, 127–28, 206
    Pik Botha's reaction to, 68
    convictions of Waluś and Derby-Lewis for,
        224, 270
    Day of Mourning following, 169, 171
    Nicolaas Deetlefs's response to, 202–3
    De Klerk government's response to, 64–65,
        148, 190–91, 196–97, 213, 222, 243,
        250–51
    F. W. de Klerk's fear of unrest following, 72, 73,
        255–56
    F. W. de Klerk's reaction to news of, 56
    Derby-Lewises and, 46–47, 126–27, 223, 224
    evidence incriminating Janusz Waluś in, 98
    goals of killers in, 85, 268
    Mondli Gungubele's response to, 37–38, 162
    Retha Harmse as witness to, 30–34
    Peter Harris's reaction to news of, 47, 48,
        50–51, 87
    Bantu Holomisa's response to, 118–20, 129,
        253, 255
    ignoring of, by white churches, 100
    Ronnie Kasrils's response to, 41, 208
    Mac Maharaj on, vii
    Mandela on De Klerk's response to, 209
    Mandela receiving news of, 11–12
    Mandela's address on two-year anniversary
        of, 254

Mandela's address to the nation following, 156–60, 163–66
Mandela's fear of unrest following, 76
Mandela's funeral oration following, 245–48
Mandela's public statement following, 92–93
Mandela's reaction to, 75–76, 94
Mandela's suspicions about, 162
Mandela's visit to the Hani homestead following, 77–78, 139, 157
media coverage of, 59, 81, 88–90, 100
Roelf Meyer's reaction to news of, 118
MK and, 151
Peter Mokaba's response to, 130–31, 184
national elections following, 259–60
official government announcement following, 148
police investigation into, 104, 110, 144–45, 169, 173–74, 176, 203, 217, 223, 257
Cyril Ramaphosa response to, 104, 210, 255
reactions to, 5
restarting of peace talks following, 3, 198, 253, 260
Tokyo Sexwale's response to, 57, 142, 143
Sam Shilowa's response to, 206–7
suspicions of conspiracy in, 129, 225–34
Desmond Tutu's response to, 68–69, 174, 244
unrest following, 99, 129, 133, 144, 154–55, 164, 167, 176–77, 182–84, 191–93, 198, 209, 211, 215, 216, 218, 222, 238–39, 254–55, 258
Janusz Waluś's flight and capture following, 34–36
Ally Weakley and, 74–75
white public's reaction to, 133–34
witnesses to, 30–34, 36–37
see also Waluś, Janusz
"Hani Memorandum," 23
Harmse, Daan, 30–32, 34, 120, 132, 170
Harmse, Retha, xi, 29–34, 120, 121, 162, 169, 271
Harris, Peter, xi, 47–51, 87, 130, 150, 184, 216–18, 248, 250, 254, 263, 269–70
Hartzenberg, Ferdi, 173–74, 226, 230
Heine, Edmund, 237–38
Henning, Eugene, 178
Hermans, Phumele Civilian, xi, 83–85, 112–15, 151–52, 272
Hertzog, Albert, 89
Hillbrow (Soweto neighborhood), 5, 39, 229
Hitler, Adolf, 43
HIV/AIDS, 42
Holmes, Mike, x, 81–83, 97–99, 125, 186, 202–5, 223, 224, 229–30
Holomisa, Bantu, ix, 60–64, 75, 78–80, 88–89, 94, 107, 118–20, 128–29, 138, 144, 145, 167,

180, 181, 190–91, 236, 240, 247, 253–55, 269
homeland system, 60–61, 77
homosexuality, 44
Houghton (Johannesburg suburb), 14, 137–39
Human, Ivor, 223, 229
Human Rights Committee, 97, 258

IEC, see Independent Electoral Commission
IFP, see Inkatha Freedom Party
Independent (newspaper), 131, 140
Independent Electoral Commission (IEC), 263, 269
Indian South Africans, 27, 42, 52, 89, 270
Inkatha Freedom Party (IFP), xiii, xv, 27, 38, 40, 47, 49, 93, 101, 108, 112, 114, 147, 250–51, 260, 266, 267
Intando Yesizwe Party, 263
Internal Security Act, 27, 97, 139
Internal Stability Unit, 132
Irving, David, 43, 45

Jabulani Amphitheatre (Soweto), 175–77, 197, 215–16
Jackson, Peter, 16, 229
Jan Smuts Airport, 58–60, 89, 138
Jim Crow laws, 3
Johannesburg, 3–5, 17, 36–37, 39, 45, 48, 58–61, 67–69, 76–80, 87–95, 99–111, 113, 132–35, 138–39, 143, 144, 146–49, 156–67, 175–77, 180, 182–84, 186, 187, 191–92, 197–200, 207–11, 214–19, 221–34, 236, 238–39, 246, 255–57, 265–67, 271
see also Boksburg; Dawn Park; FNB Stadium
Johannesburg Stock Exchange, 117
Jordan, Pallo, 39, 76, 88, 90, 139, 215

Kagiso Mall, 132
Karoo, 52, 56
Kasrils, Ronnie, 41, 103, 208
Katlehong township, 38, 129–32, 184
Kemp, Arthur, 126–27, 132, 226, 228, 230, 231, 261
Kempton Park, 119, 253, 257–58, 266
Khayelitsha township, 78, 215
Khowa (Elliot), 79
Kimberley, 41
King, Martin Luther, Jr., 163, 175
King David (film), 134
Knight, Tim, 158, 159
Knysna, 56
Koresh, David, 9
Kotze, Craig, x, 110, 148, 155, 186, 229
Kraai, Dudu, 148–49, 230

Kriel, Hernus, x, 64, 109, 144–45, 155, 189, 190,
    195, 216, 218–19, 222
Kruger, Ralf, 257
Krugersdorp, 41–47, 126–28, 132, 222, 226
KwaNdebele homeland, 61, 263
KwaZakhele, 144
KwaZulu-Natal, 61, 73, 93, 101, 102, 114, 157,
    215, 236, 240, 246, 266, 271

Langa Township, 22
Lebowa homeland, 61
Lesotho, 17, 23
Liebenberg, Andreas "Kat," 119, 190
Loftus Versfeld rugby stadium, 60
London, U.K., 43, 54, 188, 243, 273
Long Walk to Freedom (Mandela), 5, 88
Lourens, Johanna "Jansie," 186, 203, 205
Louw, Mike, 200
Louw, Raymond, 161
Lubowski, Anton, 232
Lusaka, Zambia, 138
Lwandle, 133
Lyman, Princeton, 72

Macozoma, Saki, 39, 80, 90, 93
Mafikeng, 266
Magoda, Alina Mapelo, 239
Maharaj, Mac, vii, 82, 109, 139, 214–15
Majola, 152
Makwetu, Clarence, 176
Malherbe, Frans, 36
Malindi, Gcina, 227
Mamelodi township, 133
Mandela, Nelson, ix
    addresses to the nation, 88–93, 99, 111,
        133–35, 139, 156–57, 159–67, 197–98, 218
    and Muhammad Ali, 58, 146, 256–57
    birth and childhood, 7–8
    and Boipatong Massacre, 66–67, 104
    book plans of, 5
    and Mangosuthu Buthelezi, 114
    clan name of, 38
    death of, 269
    and F. W. de Klerk, 65, 67, 70–73, 88, 115–16,
        121–23, 193, 196, 197, 208, 209, 213, 246,
        247, 262–63, 270
    English name of, 8
    FNB stadium speech of, 244–48, 255
    as fundraiser, 214
    and funeral of Chris Hani, 214–16, 236,
        244–48, 255
    and Chris Hani, 2–3, 11–12, 25–27, 38, 75–80,
        92–93
    as hero, 6
    and Bantu Holomisa, 60–63, 79–80, 138
    and homeland system, 61
    imprisonment of, 8–9, 57, 65, 69, 107, 109,
        143, 270
    international support for, 187
    and Mac Maharaj, 139, 214–15
    on making peace, vii
    and Winnie Mandela, 137–38
    and Roelf Meyer, 269
    and militant wing of ANC, 107
    and Peter Mokaba, 185
    as nation's leader, 254
    and negotiations with apartheid government,
        9, 30, 40, 70–73, 86, 103–4, 106, 108, 190,
        195
    and news of Chris Hani's death, 10–12, 75–78
    newspaper reading habits, 18
    and Carl Niehaus, 142, 143
    as Nobel laureate, 262
    press coverage of, 28, 102
    pro-apartheid movement's targeting of, 12, 14,
        28, 64, 82–83, 105, 171
    public vs. private persona of, 93–95, 158, 214
    and Cyril Ramaphosa, 101, 103
    release of, from prison, xv, 4, 25, 39, 53, 98–99,
        112, 171–72, 268
    Rivonia Trial speech of, 49–50
    and Tokyo Sexwale, 69, 143
    and Walter Sisulu, 109–10
    as South African president, 267, 271–72
    at Soweto rally, 175–77, 182–83
    and Transitional Executive Council, 261
    and transition to democracy, 266–67
    on Andries Treurnicht, 173
    and unrest following Hani's murder, 176–77,
        182–84, 198, 209, 215, 216, 222, 254–55
    vision of, 184
    and Adriaan Vlok, 188
    and Tony Yengeni, 133
    see also African National Congress (ANC)
Mandela, Thembi, 94
Mandela, Winnie, 10, 28, 64, 76, 100, 102, 106–7,
    130, 137, 222, 237, 240
Mandela, Zenani, 61
Mandela's Way (Stengel), 7
Mangope, Lucas, 191
Manuel, Trevor, 175
Marcus, Gill, ix, 36, 39, 56, 76, 78, 88–90, 93, 100,
    135, 139, 156, 271
Marker, Jamsheed, 68
Markinor Research Group, 108
Masekela, Barbara, 10–11, 27, 63, 71, 139, 175,
    198, 214
Masekela, Hugh, 10, 11
Maseko, Edward, 239
Maseru, Lesotho, 23

M*A*S*H, 89
Matanzima family, 77
Mauritius, 18
Maxhayi, Mlulamisi, 115, 151–54, 272
Maxwell, Keith, 228
Mayibuye, 39
Mazwi, Lungile, 115, 151, 272
Mbabane, 79
Mbeki, Thabo, 41, 57, 109, 184, 199, 211, 216–19, 231, 248, 254, 267, 271
Mdingane, Miss (teacher), 8
Mexico, 269
Meyer, Roelf, x, 65, 73, 87, 88, 116–18, 135, 160, 190, 193, 194, 198, 208–9, 255, 257, 261, 269, 271
Mhlahlo, Thobile, 133
Miriam (housekeeper), 10
Mitchells Plain, 179
MK (Umkhonto we Sizwe, Spear of the Nation), xiii, 23, 24, 41, 57, 103, 109, 112, 128, 151, 153, 179, 195, 235–37, 247
Mkhonto, Sparrow, 246
Mofolo, 266
Mokaba, Peter, ix, 102, 103, 108–9, 130–31, 184–85, 222, 240, 254, 271
Molobi, Saul, 5
Morogoro Conference, 23
Moshodi, Maria, 239
Moshodi, Paul, 239
Mozambique, 14, 203, 246
Mpande, 84, 152
MPLA (Movimento Popular de Libertação de Angola, Popular Movement for the Liberation of Angola), 24
MPNF (Multi-Party Negotiating Forum), xiii, xvi, 87, 257, 259
Mswati III, King, 61
Mthumbane township, 84
Mulder, Connie, 44
Multi-Party Negotiating Forum (MPNF), xiii, xvi, 87, 257, 259
Multi-Party Negotiating Process, 257–58
Mvezo (village), 8
Mxenge, Griffiths, 105
Mxenge, Victoria, 105
Mxhize, Zongezile, 152
Myburgh, Gert, x, 110, 144, 145, 148, 178, 190–92, 271
Mzilikazi, King, 40

Naidoo, Jay, 134, 199–200, 207
Namibia, 165
Natal, 38
National Action, 190
National Council of Provinces, 270

National Executive Committee (NEC), 10, 23, 25, 28, 39, 57, 101, 103, 107, 147, 175, 192, 209, 210, 214, 269
National Intelligence Service (NIS), 40–41, 128, 187, 193, 200, 233
National Party (NP), xiv, 24–26, 42, 43, 51, 53, 54, 58, 68, 85–87, 102, 107–8, 116, 117, 172, 176, 177, 187, 194, 195, 209, 210, 215–16, 243, 267, 270
National Peace Accord (NPA), xv, 47, 48, 130, 198
National Peace Committee, 192
National Union of Mineworkers, 210
NEC, *see* National Executive Committee
Netherlands, 271
Netshitenzhe, Joel, 39–41, 101, 107
New Nation (newspaper), 232
Newsweek, 29
New York Times, 65, 73, 141
Ngoepe, Bernard, 225
Niehaus, Carl, ix, 39, 76, 141–44, 157–60, 166–67, 177, 178, 186, 203–5, 217, 271–72
NIS, *see* National Intelligence Service
Njikelana, Paul, 99–100
North Carolina State University, 162
Northern Ndebele people, 61
NP, *see* National Party
NPA, *see* National Peace Accord
nuclear weapons, 55
Nyalukana, Viyani, 115, 151–54, 255, 261
Nyerere, Julius, 104

OK Bazaars (department store), 174
O'Keeffe, Chloë, 74
O'Keeffe, Thomas, 74, 149, 272
Olivier, Constable, 35
O'Malley, Padraig, 195
Operation Katzen, 119
Oppenheimer, Harry, 90
Organisation of African Unity, 68
Orsmond, Johan, 100
Orsmond, Reginald, 236
Orwell, George, 268
O'Sullivan, David, 36–37, 57, 88
Owen, Ken, 82, 161

PAC, *see* Pan Africanist Congress of Azania
Pakistan, 68
Pan Africanist Congress of Azania (PAC), xiv, 27–28, 131, 176, 191
Paris, France, 105, 188, 232, 246
Parker, Aida, 230
Paton, Alan, 73
Patriot, 45
Pedi people, 61
Phama, Sabelo, 28, 191

Philoctetes (Sophocles), 26
Phola Park, 99
Phosa, Mathews, 147–49, 193, 200, 203, 231, 257, 272
Poland, 68, 80, 202, 271
Polish United Workers' Party, 80
Pollsmoor Prison, 8
Port Elizabeth, 79, 133, 144, 146, 150–51, 180
Port St. Johns, 73–75, 83–85, 112–15, 149–54, 272
President's Council, 43, 260
Pretoria, 2, 14–16, 24, 35, 39, 45, 55, 60, 78, 80–83, 98–99, 115–19, 121–23, 125, 133, 141, 144–46, 148, 154–56, 172, 187–201, 206, 213, 217, 222, 224, 229, 232, 233, 243, 244, 247, 250
Pretoria Air Force Base, 247
Pretoria Maximum Prison, 243
Pretoria Prison, 217
Pretoria University, 26
Pretoria-Witwatersrand-Vereeniging (PWV), 30, 39, 134, 140, 150, 217, 243, 258
Pretorius, Johan, 139, 159–60, 166, 167
Pretorius, Paul, 49
Progressive Federal Party, 42
Progressive Party, 151
Protea, 247
Protea Police Station, 177, 182
PWV, *see* Pretoria-Witwatersrand-Vereeniging

Qunu, 7–12, 70–73, 79, 91, 94, 137
QwaQwa homeland, 15, 45, 61, 204, 229

Radio 702 (Johannesburg), 36, 57, 134
Raditapole, Tefo, 147–48
Radom, Poland, 15
Ramaphosa, Cyril, ix, 49, 87–89, 101, 103, 104, 106, 108, 110, 115–18, 135, 139, 198, 207–11, 231, 236, 248, 255, 257–61, 269, 272
Rand Stadium, 18
Rapport, 28, 170
Ras, Maria, 15, 80
Reagan, Ronald, 24
Reformed Church, 52
Reserve Bank, 271
Resolve Group Management Consultancy, 269–70
Retief, Hanlie, 31
Retief, Piet, 40
Rhodesia, 22
    see also Zimbabwe
Rivonia Trial (1964), 10, 49–50
Robben Island prison, 8, 39, 57, 82, 90, 94, 101, 139, 143, 214, 263

Robinson, Brian, 237
Roman Catholic Church, 43
Romera, Óscar, 43
Rosettenville, 18
Rotunda, 226
Rudolph, Piet "Skiet," 99, 233
rugby, 150–51
Rumble, Brett, 149
Rumble, Keith, 74, 149
Russia, 67, 68
Rutgers University, 10

SAAF, *see* South African Air Force
Sabalele, 21, 75–78, 94, 245
SABC, *see* South African Broadcasting Corporation
SACP, *see* South African Communist Party
SADF, *see* South African Defence Force
SAIMR, *see* South African Institute for Maritime Research
St. Andrew's College, 150
Sampson, Anthony, 161
Sandton, 98
Sanford and Son, 89
SAPA, *see* South African Press Association
SAPP, *see* South African People's Party
Savimbi, Jonas, 24
Schaeffer and Schaeffer (law firm), 22
Schutte, Danie, 190
Schwarz, Harry, 42, 216
SDUs, *see* self-defense units
Sebokeng Massacre, 9
Sebokeng township, 238–39
Security Branch, 138, 145, 185–86, 202, 226, 229
Seipei, Stompie, 106
self-defense units (SDUs), 83–84, 112, 115
September, Dulcie, 105, 232, 246
Serache, Nat, 181
Sexwale, Judy, 143
Sexwale, Tokyo, ix, 30, 38–39, 57, 69, 76–77, 80, 99, 100, 134, 141–44, 156, 177, 185, 231, 249, 260, 272
Shangaan people, 61
Shilowa, Mbhazima Sam, 100, 165, 206–8
Shoe City, 30
"Shooting an Elephant" (Orwell), 268
Shorkend, Sally, 265–66
Sierra Leone, 269
Sisulu, Walter, 11, 25, 57, 94, 109–11, 138, 207
Slingerland, J., 98
Slovo, Joe, 14, 25, 82, 83, 88, 100, 104, 105, 107, 175, 245, 246
Smal, Constable, 32–33
Smit, Basie, 147

Smuts, Jan, 51, 58
sodium thiopental, 205
Soga, Tiyo, 26
Sophocles, 26
South African Air Force (SAAF), 24, 98–99, 233, 247
South African Broadcasting Corporation (SABC), 85, 88–90, 93, 103, 111, 135, 139, 156–60, 166, 178, 206, 215
South African Citizen Force, 41–42
South African Communication Service, 55
South African Communist Party (SACP), xiv, 2, 3, 14, 17, 25, 41, 53, 78, 79, 92, 100, 109, 113, 114, 133, 172, 207, 208, 218, 232–33, 236, 261
South African Council of Churches, 258
South African Defence Force (SADF), xiv, 42, 119, 191, 219
South African Indian Congress, 27
South African Institute for Maritime Research (SAIMR), 228, 229
South African People's Party (SAPP), 64
South African Police, 40, 110, 147, 185, 226
South African Press Association (SAPA), 183
Soviet Union, 2, 22, 57
Soweto, 4, 58, 59, 99–100, 106, 109–10, 117, 131, 137, 175–79, 182, 197, 235, 247, 266
Soweto Massacre (1976), 4, 116, 172
Spear of the Nation, see MK
Special Branch (National Intelligence Service), 128
Special Electoral Court, 263
Spioenkop (farm), 52
Spruitview township, 18
SSC, see State Security Council
Stallard Foundation, 43, 45, 81, 125–26
Stan Schmidt School of Karate, 15, 16
Star, the (newspaper), 1–2, 4, 110, 155, 265
Starling, Daniel, 32
State of Emergency, 109
State Security Council (SSC), xiv, 119, 155, 187–89, 191–92, 194–96, 199, 208, 209, 213
Stengel, Richard, xi, 5, 7, 9, 10, 27, 63, 75–76, 88, 91, 93–94, 137, 138, 182–83, 214, 248–49
Steward, Dave, 55–56, 65, 73, 120, 121, 193
Steynsburg, 52, 64–67, 70–73, 87
Strauss, Brigadier, 177
Strijdom, J. G., 51
Strydom, Barend, 141
Sunday Star (newspaper), 1–2, 76, 93, 102
Sunday Times (Johannesburg), 43–44, 82, 99–100, 102, 128, 161, 170
Sunday Times (London), 65
Suppression of Communism Act, 22

Supreme Court (Witwatersrand Local Division), 224
Supreme Court of Appeal (Bloemfontein), 14
Sussex University, 109
Suttner, Raymond, 215
Suzman, Helen, 72
Swart, Pieter, 171
Swaziland, 60–64, 79
Sweden, 138–39

Tambani, Sam, 177–78
Tambo, Adelaide, 57
Tambo, Oliver, 11–12, 57, 138, 221–22, 257
Tanzania, 22, 23, 104
Tate, "Big" John, 59–60
TEC, see Transitional Executive Council
television, 89
    see also South African Broadcasting Corporation (SABC)
Terre'Blanche, Eugène, 45, 78, 127–29, 140, 141, 206, 266
Thatcher, Margaret, 24, 28
Third Force, 246–47
Thobela, Dingaan "Rose of Soweto," 59
Thokoza Township, 38
toyi-toyi, 143, 170, 181, 236
Transitional Executive Council (TEC), xiv, 194–95, 210, 213, 255, 256, 260–61, 263
Transkei, 10, 61–64, 76–80, 86–87, 118–20, 128, 138, 145, 167, 180–82, 190–91, 198, 208
Transkei Defence Force, 152, 236
Transvaal, 44
TRC, see Truth and Reconciliation Commission
Treurnicht, Andries, 17, 171–73
Truckers (gay bar), 44, 229
Trust Feed Massacre, 246
Truth and Reconciliation Commission (TRC), xiv, 5–6, 13–14, 193, 223–27, 230, 233, 239, 270, 272
Tshwete, Steve, 231
Tsonga people, 61
Tswana people, 61, 191
Turner, Rick, 105, 246
Tutu, Desmond, xi, 26, 68–70, 111, 133, 161, 174, 198, 225, 244
TV1, 78, 89, 121, 134

UDF, see United Democratic Front
Uitenhage, 146
Ukraine, 57
Umkhonto we Sizwe, see MK
Umtata, 61, 79, 80–81, 86–87, 90, 94, 118–20, 128–29, 180–82, 208

Umtata Airport, 78, 79, 119
Umzimvubu River, 84
Union Buildings, 144–46, 187–95
Unita, 24
United Democratic Front (UDF), xiv, 106
United Nations, 55, 60, 67, 68, 104, 269
United Party, 51
United States, 3, 6, 24, 72
University of Cape Town, 172
University of Fort Hare, 22
University of Port Elizabeth, 150
University of the Free State, 15
University of the Witwatersrand, 105
UN Security Council, 68

Vanderbijlpark, 40, 216
van der Merwe, Constable, 32
van der Merwe, Du Toit, 51
van der Merwe, Johan, x, 145–46, 149, 185–86,
    208, 218
van Gass, Chris, 1–2
van Niekerk, Adriaan, 185–87
van Rensburg, Horace, 181
van Rooy, J. C., 52
van Rooy family farm, 51–56
Venda homeland, 61
Venda people, 61
Venter, Faan, 41, 46, 227, 228
Venter, Maureen, 41, 46, 47
Vermeulen, Koos, 206, 233
Verwoerd, Hendrik Frensch, 51, 52
Victor Verster Prison, xv, 9
Vietnam War, 59, 256
Vilankulu, Queen, 263
Viljoen, Gerrit, 26
Villa-Vicencio, Charles, 193
Visser, Johannes, 226
Vlakplaas, 232
Vlok, Adriaan, x, 141, 188–90, 191
Volksunie, xvi, 87
Voortrekker Monument (Pretoria), 172
Vorster, John, 44
Vorster, Sergeant, 125
Vosloorus township, 38, 49, 184
Vrye Weekblad, 141

WAB, see World Apartheid Movement
Waco, Texas, siege, 9
Waldmeir, Patti, 178–79, 254
Wałęsa, Lech, 68
Waluś, Ewa, 15

Waluś, Janusz, x, 12–17, 19–20, 29, 34–36, 45–47,
    63, 64, 69, 80–83, 85, 97–99, 105, 120,
    125–27, 138–40, 147, 148, 157, 160–63,
    169, 171–73, 175, 177, 184–87, 201–6,
    216–17, 223–34, 237, 238, 257, 261, 266,
    268, 270–71
Waluś, Tadeusz, 15
Waluś, Wanda, 15
Waluś, Witold, 15–17, 126, 229
Wankie Campaign, 22
Washington Star, 44
Waterkloof, 45
Watson, Ronnie, 147
Weakley, Alastair, xi, 74–75, 149–51, 167, 272
Weakley, Debbie, 149
Weakley, Glen, xi, 74, 149, 272
Weakley, Trevor, 149
Webster, David, 105, 232, 246
Weekly Mail, 59, 174
Wellington, 170
Wende, Hamilton, 150, 151
Western Cape, 102, 144, 175, 270
Western Goals Institute, 43
Wild Coast, 73–74, 85
Wits-Vaal Regional Peace Secretariat, 47, 50–51,
    216, 217, 222
Witwatersrand, 39, 224
Wit Wolve (White Wolves), 27, 141
World Apartheid Movement (WAB), 81, 206, 233
World Boxing Association, 59
World Preservatist Movement (WPB), 233
World Trade Centre (Kempton Park), 266
World War II, 80

Xhosa language and peoples, 10, 26, 37, 61, 74,
    75, 103, 149–50, 181, 269

Yengeni, Tony, 102, 103, 133–34

Zagacki, Kenneth S., 162, 164
Zambia, 10, 17, 22, 23, 138, 190
Zazeraj, Victor, 67–68
Zimbabwe, 22, 64
    see also Rhodesia
Zimbabwe African People's Union (ZAPU),
    22
Zion Christian Church, 100
Zulu language and people, 40, 61, 196,
    249
Zuma, Jacob, 41, 231, 272
Zwide, 144

ABOUT THE AUTHOR

JUSTICE MALALA is one of South Africa's foremost political commentators and the author of the #1 bestseller *We Have Now Begun Our Descent: How to Stop South Africa Losing Its Way*. A longtime weekly columnist for *The Times* (South Africa), his work has also appeared in *The Washington Post, The Wall Street Journal, The Guardian,* and *Financial Times,* among other outlets. The former publisher of *The Sowetan* and *Sunday World,* he now lives in New York.